FORTUNES OF WAR

Ypres
Death of an Army

ANTHONY FARRAR–HOCKLEY

CERBERUS

First published in 1967

PUBLISHED IN THE UNITED KINGDOM BY;
Cerberus Publishing Limited
22A Osprey Court
Hawkfield Business Park
Bristol
BS14 0BB
UK
e-mail: cerberusbooks@aol.com
www.cerberus-publishing.com

© Cerberus Publishing Ltd 2004

British Library Cataloguing in Publication Data.
A catalogue record for this book is available from the British Library.

ISBN 1 84145 046 4

PRINTED AND BOUND IN ENGLAND.

CUMBRIA LIBRARY SERVICES

COUNTY COUNCIL

This book is due to be returned on or before the last date above. It may be renewed by personal application, post or telephone, if not in demand.

C.L.18

Titles in the 'Fortunes of War' series

ALERT IN THE WEST
A Luftwaffe Pilot on the Western Front

THE BATTLE OF THE ARDENNES

THE BATTLE OF THE ATLANTIC

BETRAYED IDEALS
Memoirs of a Luftwaffe Fighter Ace

BLACK SATURDAY
The Royal Oak Tragedy at Scapa Flow

CAMBRAI
The First Tank Battle

CONVOY COMMODORE

DEFEAT OF THE WOLF PACKS

ENEMY IN THE DARK
The Story of a Night–Fighter Pilot

FAITH, HOPE & CHARITY
The Defence of Malta

THE FIRST AND THE LAST
Germany's Fighter Force in WWII

FLY FOR YOUR LIFE
The Story of Bob Stanford Tuck

GALLIPOLI 1915

GINGER LACEY
Fighter Ace

THE GREAT INVASION
The Roman Conquest of Britain

HMS ILLUSTRIOUS
The Fight for Life

HMS WARSPITE
The Story of a Famous Battleship

THE LAST VOYAGE OF THE GRAF SPEE

LAUGHING COW
The Story of U69

LIGHTNING STRIKES
The Story of a B–17 Bomber

MANNOCK, VC
Ace With One Eye

MUSTANG ACE
The Story of Don S Gentile

THE MIGHTY HOOD
The Life & Death of the Royal Navy's Proudest Ship

ONE OF THE FEW
A Triumphant Story of Combat in the Battle of Britain

OPERATION BARBAROSSA

PHANTOM RAIDER
Nazi Germany's Most Successful Surface Raider

PRINZ EUGEN
The Graceful Predator

RELENTLESS PURSUIT
The Story of Captain F J Walker, CB, DSO★★★, RN

RICHTHOFEN
The Red Knight of the Air

THE SINKING OF THE BISMARCK
The Death of a Flagship

THE SINKING OF THE SCHARNHORST
The German Account

THE SOMME
Death of a Generation

SPITFIRE ATTACK

SPITFIRE COMMAND

STALINGRAD
Enemy at the Gates

TIRPITZ
Pride of the Kriegsmarine

TOBRUK
The Story of a Siege

U–BOAT 977
The U–Boat That Escaped to Argentina

U–BOAT ACES

U–BOAT COMMANDER
The Story of Günther Prien

YPRES
Death of an Army

Contents

List of Maps   *6*
Preface   *7*

PART I: THE PLAN   THE PLAN   11
                                            THE ARMY   15
                                            THE EVENT   21

PART II: A DIFFICULT SITUATION   NOTBEHELFE   30

PART III: THE GLORIOUS ENTERPRISE   ANOTHER PORTION
                                            OF THE BATTLEFIELD   41
                                            FIRST OUT; FIRST IN   45
                                            LILLE IN SIGHT   55
                                            FRENCH AND FOCH   66

PART IV: THE END OF OCTOBER   THE BEGINNING OF THE WEEK:
                                            18TH-20TH OCTOBER, 1914   70
                                            WEDNESDAY TO FRIDAY:
                                            21ST-23RD OCTOBER, 1914   80
                                            THE WEEKEND: SATURDAY, 24TH,
                                            SUNDAY, 25TH OCTOBER, 1914   97

PART V: A TIME OF CRISIS   VON FABECK'S PRELUDE:
                                            29TH OCTOBER, 1914   119
                                            OFFENCE RENEWED:
                                            30TH OCTOBER, 1914   126
                                            NIGHT WATCHES:
                                            30TH-31ST OCTOBER, 1914   131
                                            IN THE BALANCE:
                                            31ST OCTOBER, 1914   134

Bibliography   *161*

Index   *165*

Index of Military Formations and Units   *172*

List Of Maps

General: the Battleground in the West, 1914   10

Artois and Flanders   37

Ypres/La Bassée; Arrival of II Corps   47

Approach to La Bassée   49

Ypres/La Bassée: Advance of III Corps 57

The Approach of the 'New' Corps   74

Ypres/La Bassée: the Armies Clash   86

Bixschoote – Langemarck   91

Ypres/La Bassée: von Fabeck's Attack   106

The Yser Battle   108

Gheluvelt   123

Messines – Wyteschaete   137

Ypres/ La Bassée: von Linsingen's Attack   152

PREFACE

The periods of intense fighting in Flanders between 12th October and 11th November, 1914, have been classified by the official historians of the belligerents under a series of titles. They were known simply to the British soldiers who took part in them as 'First Ypres'.

The British contribution to the battle comprised one-hundred infantry battalions and about twenty-four regiments of cavalry, together with supporting batteries of artillery, engineer companies, administrative units and five squadrons of the Royal Flying Corps. Before the events of October-November, much of this army, the British Expeditionary Force, had experienced successive hazards beginning at Mons on 23rd August and continuing through Le Cateau in the retreat to the Marne, and in the subsequent defensive and counter-offensive there which led to the pursuit of the Germans to the Aisne. Throughout this time, the British were gradually acquiring – not always happily – a working understanding with their French allies and, later, the Belgians. The forces of these three nations were themselves learning by the rough methods of trial and error the measure of their German foe.

The documentary sources for the description of these background events, and for the accounts of the British Expeditionary Force, their allies and enemy during the battle are given at the end of the book. This has permitted me to exclude from the footnotes all references with the exception of certain sources of economics. The majority of the books and papers used have come from or through five libraries and I must acknowledge the great debt I owe to the librarians and their staffs: Mr D W King, OBE, FLA, and the War Office Library; Miss R E B Coombes of the Imperial War Museum; Lieutenant-Colonel Walter Young, MBE, and the Staff College, Camberley; Lieutenant-Colonel Alan Shepperd, MC, and the Royal Military Academy, Sandhurst; and Lieutenant-Colonel L H Yates, OBE, and the Prince Consort's Library, Aldershot. For other books and papers, I am similarly indebted to the interest of Brigadier John Stephenson, OBE, Director of The Royal United Services Institution and the library staff of the Institution. Lieutenant-Colonel E H Whitfield, MC, formerly librarian of the Joint Services Staff College took pains to find various books for me and to give me invaluable notes on the battlefield over which he fought.

Major-General R A Bramwell Davies, CB, DSO, and Major-General Henry Leask, CB, DSO, successive Colonels of the Royal Highland Fusiliers kindly permitted me to retain over a number of years private papers of the Royal Scots Fusiliers and the Highland Light Infantry; papers which Brigadier Charles Dunbar, MBE, was good enough to select. In Germany, I owe thanks to Dr A A Schmalz, Archivassesor and the staff of the Militerarchiv of the Federal German Bundesarchiv. Major G Holtorff, assistant military attache at the Federal German Embassy in London was good enough to undertake various enquiries amongst other sources in Germany. In France, the Commandant and staff of the Ecole Superieure Militaire Inter-Armes, St Cyr, took much trouble to obtain for me details con-cerning the French Army. Commandant J J de Grelle, MBE, military attache to the Belgian Embassy in London, kindly arranged for details to be sent to me concerning the Belgian railway system in the summer and autumn of 1914. I had the good fortune to learn from the late C T Atkinson, Esq., Fellow of Exeter College, Oxford, details of a considerable number of the official documents that came to him in the Historical Section in 1914.

A second source of factual information has been discussion with a number of survivors of the British Expeditionary Force. The late Colonel R M Grazebrook, OBE, MC. The Gloucestershire Regiment, gave me a good deal of his time to relate matters of regimental organization, training and administration prior to 1914 and of the adventures of the brigade in which he served in the early days of the British Expeditionary Force in

France and Belgium. Even as a young subaltern officer, he had the eye of an historian. I am most grateful to Brigadier-General B C Senhouse Clarke, DSO, MC, for relating to me details of the famous counter-attack on Gheluvelt in which he took part as one of the principals. He had much to contribute also on the events of First Ypres. Major-General B K Young, CBE, MC, most kindly provided me with personal papers describing the work of the Royal Engineers round Armentieres and Ypres during the battle and answered a great number of questions over a period of time. He is chairman of the Old Contemptibles, Aldershot Branch. His Branch Secretary and organizer-in-chief of many national meetings of the Old Contemptibles, Mr Paddy Smythe put me in touch with 'Chums' who fought with him at First Ypres. These were the men who showed that the German emperor was at least under a misapprehension when he described the BEF as a 'contemptible little army'.

I owe many thanks to Brigadier Peter Young, DSO, MC, MA Reader in Military History at the Royal Military Academy Sandhurst, for suggesting the subject of the book. As always I benefited much from discussion of the background and course of the British Expeditionary Force with him and his staff.

I have related all the many accounts, details and reflections written and spoken, to the battlefield by walking over the scene of every action described, guided by the maps in use at the time and aided by the fact that almost all the forests, woods, roads rail and water ways were restored to their original state – often to their exact lines and boundaries – after the war. Apart therefore, from a widening of the main roads, limited expansion round the towns, particularly along the coast, and a degree of industrial expansion, notable round Lille and La Bassée the battlefield remains much as the alliedand German forces found it

In preparing maps and sketches to illustrate these areas I have had much help from Mr J G Whitcombe of the Staff College, Camberley, Miss Victoria King, Corporal E P J Olive, Lance-Corporal M E Williams and my son Dair who also photographed a number of sections of the battlefield Mr J F Golding, Head of the Photographic Library, Imperial War Museum and his staff offered the most ready assistance as they always do and were particularly helpful in providing prints at very short notice.

My wife has undertaken much research, typing and correcting, often late into the night. She has my warmest thanks.

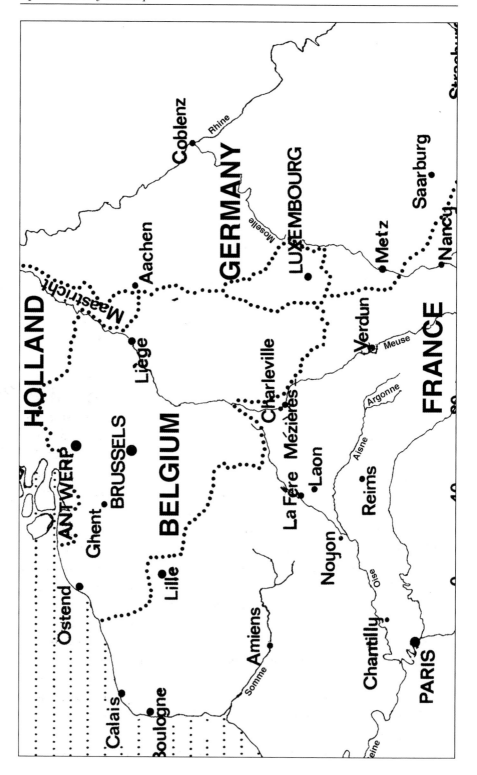

PART I

The Plan

'No plan survives the first contact of war.'
CLAUSEWITZ

THE PLAN

On the Christmas Eve of 1894, an orderly called at the flat of Major H. von Kuhl in Berlin to deliver a packet from Colonel-General Count von Schlieffen. It contained '...a great military situation designed by him as a specific problem to be worked out in the form of an operational plan. He would have been very surprised if the solution had not been in his hands by the evening of Christmas Day... Sundays and holidays were, in his view, intended for those profounder tasks requiring quiet and continuous work, undisturbed by day-to-day business.'

The intrusion into his festivities had been anticipated by von Kuhl. If he found these demands from his military chief disagreeable, he did not reveal it. In any case, he knew that his task master would himself be working on Christmas Eve and during most of Christmas Day.

Throughout his professional life, Schlieffen had a passion for duty and, following the early death of his beloved wife, he became wedded to it. It is true that he devoted a small but regular allocation of his time to his two daughters though, as they grew older, he derived some compensation from the practice by studying with them matters which widened his military knowledge. Thus he was to be found reading military history to them, sometimes until half past two in the morning. Despite such late hours, he rose always at 6 am. for exercise and work before breakfast. In the last years of his life, when he had become a field marshal and retired from the General Staff, all his energies were directed still towards military planning and studies. Indeed, it is said that when he died on 4th January, 1913, his last thoughts and words were concerned with Germany's war plan; and though this may be apocryphal, it is certain that he was working on a revised draft of the plan until he fell fatally ill. These papers were collected together by his son-in-law and passed personally to the chief of the General Staff.

Now, in most national armies, the professional opinions of retired senior officers are not apt to excite those still serving. It is therefore noteworthy that when the chief of the General Staff accepted von Schlieffen's final exercise, he not only read it with care but took the trouble to annotate it. He did so because it was the last of a series which had been begun when the author had himself been chief; a series in which the general concept remained unchanged. It enunciated the strategy that Germany would use in the event of war; the strategic plan from which sprang all mobilization and deployment orders, all tactical directives to army and subordinate commanders.

There had thus been considerable continuity in strategic policy between the time of Schlieffen's assumption of office as chief of the General Staff in 1891 and his death in 1913. However, he had not immediately conceived this strategy in its final form and he had certainly not inherited it from his predecessors, least of all from the most renowned of these. Field Marshal Count Helmuth von Moltke.

Moltke had no equal in all Europe – probably in the world – as a general in the second half of the nineteenth century. His genius for organization and training, his instinct for appreciating the probable reactions of enemy commanders to a given situation brought first the Prussian and then the German armies to victory through central Europe and finally over France. When the latter had been defeated, Moltke turned in 1871 to the problem of how Germany should defend itself in the future. France clearly remained the prime enemy; her aim would be revenge upon Germany and the recovery of her lost provinces. Moltke did not underrate the passionate strength of French patriotism. After quickly defeating the two armies of France decisively, he had been astounded to discover that the war was continued for three months by a loose organization of guerilla bands, ill-armed, ragged and half starving against his own well-found professional corps. That these irregulars were not instantly defeated was due to their willingness to march long distances for a brief encounter with a German detachment inferior in numbers and to march again to a remote place of safety to avoid the punitive action of a relief column. These marches, these battles were undertaken, moreover, during a European winter. The fortitude of the so-called 'People's Army' of France was the same which animated the citizens of Paris to endure a long siege, and both were engendered by the burning resentment of Frenchmen that Germans were trespassing on their soil.

Moltke was much impressed by this experience. France was clearly a resilient and hardy nation, not easily to be conquered and likely to seek early revenge. He pressed Bismarck, the German chancellor, to include the cession to Germany of Alsace and Lorraine in the final terms of peace in 1871 to provide a military buffer zone against a future French attack. But it was not only France whom he feared. Even at this stage, when Bismarck's prodigious talent in diplomacy safeguarded Germany's long land frontiers, he considered carefully and prophetically what he should do if Russia and France developed an alliance for the overthrow of the new German empire. In the following seventeen years, von Moltke gave much thought to the evolution of a defence against these two. Meantime, Bismarck's enemies multiplied until, with the accession of Wilhelm II to their number, the old chancellor was deposed, the possibility of a Franco-Russian alliance became a probability and, shortly after Moltke's death in 1891, a fact.

Schlieffen was now chief of the General Staff. He was of course familiar with the plans of his renowned predecessor[1] for the contingency of a war simultaneously against Russia and France. He knew that Moltke had considered and discarded an immediate offensive begun at the outset against both nations or against first one and then the other. Even with Austria-Hungary's active participation in the field, Russia was too spacious, too populous to be conquered: while France, though smaller, had prepared by 1878 a strong fortress system against Germany. Besides, for all his success in 1870, France had taught Moltke that he could not look for a swift or cheap victory on her territory.

Thus the plan which Schlieffen inherited left – by design – much to the initiative of Germany's enemies. In the west, the armies of France might hurl themselves against the defences of Alsace and Lorraine. If they penetrated them, it would be at great cost, but Moltke accepted the possibility and was prepared to withdraw as necessary to a line based on the obstacle of the Rhine and Main rivers. In gaining a portion of German soil by advancing to the river line, the French Army would lose immense numbers, while being drawn forward beyond its railway system as the Germans fell back on theirs. Eventually, when the moment was ripe, Germany would turn to the offensive against the weakened French forces

[1] The elder von Moltke was not his immediate predecessor; Count Waldersee held office from August 1888 until January 1891.

using the divisions behind the Rhine and Main, reinforced perhaps by others freed from the Russian front.

Russia required quite different measures. The frontier in the east was extensive: from the Baltic Sea to the southernmost point at Myslovitz, it was 800 miles. Looping east again, it ran for a further 650 miles between Russia and Austria-Hungary. Some tens of millions of soldiers would have been needed to defend such a frontier without counting the milliards of gold marks required to build and maintain defence works.

In these circumstances, Moltke determined to exploit his potential for rapid deployment. The German railway system was efficient and comprehensive: the Russians' scant, and imperfectly run. As the several Russian armies advanced, German striking forces would concentrate by rail first against one and then another to impose a series of separate local tactical defeats on the Russians. He could expect no greater victories but believed they would be enough to encourage the Tsar towards an armistice.

Almost immediately after taking office as chief, Schlieffen began to tinker with this plan. He did not at all like the notion of the campaign against Russia and saw no point in hanging back from the fight against France. Like Moltke, he had no high opinion of Austria-Hungary's soldiers and expected them to prove unreliable in the field. There were too many options open to the Russians to evade the thrusts against their advance in his view and, besides, it seemed wrong that they should be fighting Russia at all: Austria was to be blamed for dragging Germany into enmity with them. Germany's enemy in Europe was not Russia but France. He believed that France would attack Germany at the *moment juste* and in consequence German arms must be ready to attack and destroy France at the outset and march to Paris to dictate new and more effective terms for peace.

What Schlieffen believed and what influence he was able to extend into national policy were, however, quite different matters. Although the Army was an important and prestigious body in the state, it had a good deal less to do with the making of foreign policy than is sometimes supposed. In Bismarck's time, the Army's influence was, at most, occasional. After the great chancellor was deposed by the Kaiser in 1890, a number of generals were consulted by their sovereign intermittently while others conspired to certain ends with the Foreign Office. But the chief of the General Staff was not in a position to abrogate the Dual Alliance with Austria[2] and so, whether it suited him or not, Schlieffen had no option but to prepare for a war simultaneously on two fronts as his immediate predecessors had done.

---

[2] Subsequently, Italy joined Germany and Austria-Hungary to make it a triple alliance but withdrew rather than be dragged into war as their partner.

What follows is a tale of wilfulness. Schlieffen wanted to attack France, to be shot of Russia; he had to take on both. Little by little he found stronger and stronger reasons for abandoning the concept of tactical offensives against the Russian armies, better and better reasons for attacking France the moment war was declared. As he was officially unable to abandon the Russian front, he conducted successive staff studies of forms which the campaign might take there: but the most important of these envisaged the bulk of the German army being available. By 1899 at the latest, Schlieffen had reverted to the theory long discarded by Moltke as impracticable that Germany might safely first defeat France and then transport the bulk of the Army to the east to defeat Russia.

Seven years earlier, he had stated a strategy for defeating France quickly. Instead of launching the assault corps through Alsace and Lorraine on to the forts built by the French, a small German force should demonstrate there while the mass marched through Belgium round the flank of the fortress line. The fact that this involved the grossest abuse of a neutral in no way involved with the quarrels of France and Germany did not concern Schlieffen. He expected that the Belgians would eventually understand and forgive, particularly if they were fully compensated.

Thus the Schlieffen Plan grew. By the winter of 1905 it had become a most complete prescription for victory over France; not alone a deployment plan on which to base mobilization arrangements; not alone a plan for the first clash of arms. It embraced all these and, looking beyond to their fulfilment, ordered the gigantic wheel of the right wing armies through Belgium to envelop Paris and, at last, more than a month after starting, to take the French in front and rear to their destruction.

THE ARMY

As he worked on his plan over the years, two fears waxed in Schlieffen's mind: would the Army be strong enough when war came; and would the high command have sufficient nerve to mass divisions on the wheeling right at the expense of the centre and left facing France?

Ninety-four divisions were required for the execution of the Schlieffen Plan – disregarding any fragmentary numbers watching the Russians in the east. In 1905, Germany had scarcely sixty.

We have invented conscription and the People in Arms (Schlieffen wrote in his memorandum on the plan that year) and proved to other nations the necessity of introducing these institutions. But having brought our sworn enemies to the point of increasing their armies out of all measure, we have relaxed our own efforts. We continue to boast of the density of our population, of the great manpower at our disposal; but these masses are not trained or armed to the full number of able-bodied men they could yield. What irked Schlieffen was that France called-up the great majority of its young men for military service while Germany embodied, at the most, about two-thirds of those available each year.

The number of able-bodied (Germans) of military age exceeded increasingly the number of men called to the colours each year, and further the total strength of 'Germany's effective fighting forces lagged behind the strength of her probable enemies. France trained eighty-three per cent of the total able-bodied men of the 1910 class, whilst Germany called only about fifty-one per cent of that class to the colours, so that at the time the joint forces of France and Russia exceeded those of Germany and Austria-Hungary by about 1.5 million[3].

A superficial impression of Germany, held by many in Europe and beyond at that time, was of a bellicose nation bent relentlessly on aggrandizement: autocratic in rule, obedient in response; if not wholly a people in arms, at least ready to become so at a moment's command. The impression owed much to the ill-considered public statements of the emperor enhanced by his much-photographed frown, the sabre-rattling of the Pan-Germans – a vociferous minority – and the massive and closely reported annual manoeuvres of the Imperial Army. It is an impression that is with us still.

It is of course true that Germany was in a sense bent on aggrandizement: economic aggrandizement. It was achieving this. In the fifty years prior to 1914, Germany advanced from fourth place in the index of world industrial production to second, while Great Britain and France fell from first and second to third and fourth.[4] The now familiar pattern of domestic expansion was to be seen. Industrialists wished for tax concessions from government so as to develop their concerns: labour was drawn in from the country to tend the growing number of machines: the population was rapidly increasing but agricultural production was lagging behind. Foreign exchange was needed to pay for imported foodstuffs, the volume of which rose annually. In these circumstances, an Army which demands more men and more money is unlikely to obtain a sympathetic hearing from government or commerce.

Yet even if either or both of these had wished to provide what the Army requested, those who presumed to represent the industrial workers of Germany, the Social Democratic Party, would have objected. They had a

[3] *Reichsarchiv, Der Weltkrieg* 1914-18, Vol. I. *Kriegsrilstung und Kriegswirt-schafl* (Berlin, 1930), p. 481.
[4] Quarterly Report of the Institute for Economic Research, Sonderheft, No. 31, *Die Industriewirtschaft, Entwicklungstcndcnzen der deutschen und intemationalen Industrieproduktion 1860 bis 1932* (Berlin, 1933), p. 19.

strong following in the Reichstag. Though rule was autocratic to a degree in Germany, the people were by no means subservient. As it was, however, government and legislature alike showed no enthusiasm for Schlieffen's proposals towards total conscription. Whereas in 1899 he had obtained an increase in the military establishment of over 120,000 men, three corps, in 1905, the next year of expansion, the addition was 10,000, less than a division. Though he achieved a further limited expansion by reorganization of the reserve, he was still far from obtaining the strength offerees that he required. It was left to his successor to continue the struggle.

Schlieffen had been relieved by another von Moltke; the younger man being a nephew of the great field marshal and named after him, Helmuth. Like his uncle, he was an intelligent and intellectually honest man, but lacked the single-mindedness of the victor of 1870. He was more imaginative, less of a fighter. Thus he saw that another war against France would be a 'long arduous struggle with a country which will not admit defeat until the strength of the people is broken' and doubted that it was possible to direct effectively an army in the field numbering more than a million men. Concerned by the prospect of a war on two fronts, he believed that Schlieffen's plan offered the best chance of success but had two important reservations: in the east, the frontier with Russia could not be left unguarded; in the west, the violation of Belgium's territory must be accepted but the additional trespass on Holland[5] conceived by Schlieffen must be avoided at all costs. Despite these differences, however, the younger Moltke continued to read his predecessor's memoranda on his plan until death cut them off. Somewhat less actively, Moltke continued the struggle for a wider conscription of the nation's youth.

If it had been left to him alone, as chief, to continue the army's expansion, it is probable that he would have failed in view of the widespread opposition. Even the war minister was against it. But in charge of mobilization and deployment under Moltke was an officer of exceptional determination. Colonel Erich Ludendorff, who was dedicated to the Schlieffen Plan and hence convinced that Germany faced disaster unless a further nine corps were established. Yet the pace of expansion remained low. In 1911, additional manpower was authorized to form machine-gun companies but the other increases in the financial vote related to new weapons and the improvement of training facilities. Certain that time was against them, Ludendorff proposed that three new corps should be

---

[5] In order to make room for the numbers added to the right wing, Schlieffen believed it necessary for German troops to march through the 'Maastricht Appendix.'

authorized in each of the years 1912, 13 and 14. After an intense struggle, from which Moltke stood back as much as possible, Ludendorff succeeded in obtaining two and decided he would only get the remainder by extreme measures. He secretly briefed the Pan-Germans to agitate in the Reichstag and press. Though the Reichstag would not authorize an increase in corps, the pressure from the right wing was sufficient to permit a substantial increase in the units of the field force: the peace strength of the army was raised from 723,000 to 870,000, including an increase of 4,000 officers. But Ludendorff was to pay personally for the success of his campaign. The war minister posted him away from the General Staff to command an unfashionable regiment, the 39th Lower Rhineland Fusiliers at Dusseldorf.

Ludendorff left Berlin in the April, when the drafting of the Law of 1913 was complete. The Law itself, authorizing the induction of and funds for the additional numbers to the establishment was passed in June. It did not – could not, of course – provide an immediate reinforcement of trained officers and men to the Army. A period of training must elapse before the class of 1913 would be ready to take their place in the corps at active duty.

Most of the young men conscripted entered recruit service at twenty for two years, the exception being cavalry and horse artillery who had their soldiers for three. After this, each man was discharged to a reserve unit of the *Landwehr* where he would receive about 14 days training in camp for each of five years whilst in what was called the First Ban; He was now under earmark either to swell the ranks of the active units to war establishment on mobilization, or to form up with other reservists a unit in a reserve corps. Reaching his 30s, he remained on the reserve but without liability for further training, passing through the Second Ban of the *Landwehr* for six years and into the Second Ban of the *Landsturm*[6] until his 46th birthday. Cavalry and horse artillerymen had proportionately less time to serve in the *Landwehr* to compensate for the extra year of full-time service.

There were others in the ranks, a minority, serving under different terms. Sons of well-to-do fathers, educated at a high school and holding a certificate of graduation were usually enlisted as one-year-volunteers – *Einjährige* – who completed three months' recruit training before being posted to a regiment, but both there and in the depot they served less uncomfortably, supplying for example their own food. Many attended special courses from which they graduated to be officers or non-

[6] The First Ban of the *Landsturm* or Ersatz Reserve was for those men who, due to the excess of numbers, had not been called up by the age of twenty-three, for men who had been allowed to postpone their service, and for those with minor physical defects.

commissioned officers in the Reserve. The regular non-commissioned officers might enlist as volunteers at the age of seventeen, others came from special schools which they entered at fifteen. Like the officers, non-commissioned officers of the regular army enjoyed a position of favour in the state.

By the end of the nineteenth century, the admission of candidates from the middle-classes to the regular officer corps was commonplace; the nobility were unable to supply sufficient numbers to fill vacancies. Nonetheless, each regiment continued to vet closely the individual aspirant, and a vote was taken amongst the officers as to whether he should be accepted or not. About one-third of the young men came from the old-established cadet schools, which catered principally for the sons of officers or senior civil servants. The remainder came directly from high school – a few from university – after taking an entrance examination. Cadets and school entrants alike served a period in the ranks, the cadets becoming non-commissioned officers immediately, but all had to pass through a final training school before being commissioned. From school-leaving to commissioning, therefore, took two to three years; about the same time that it took to complete the training of the conscript private.

The number of months spent by a private soldier in recruit training – that is, at a depot where initial training was undertaken – varied between Arms: the artillery and engineers taking longer to train, for example, than the infantry. It also varied in time for all Arms during the fifty years prior to 1914, the tendency being for recruit training to last longer in the twentieth century. The essentials to be instilled into the newly-joined soldier were threefold: an understanding of the Army's duty to serve the emperor and to protect him and his people; an absolute, blind obedience to orders in pursuit of that duty; basic weapon skills and drill, the latter being entirely applicable to field manoeuvres except for a few special movements for ceremonial. Arms other than infantry also had an initiation into the particular work of their corps. But as in most armies of the day, the period of recruit training was mainly one of breaking-in the conscript to be ready for the more detailed instruction given by demonstration and practice in a field unit.

In the infantry and cavalry, there was a good deal of marching on foot or horse with full equipment, daily weapon handling – though without live ammunition; funds being inadequate for more than one range course to be shot each year – and drill, drill, drill. The mass formations for which drill was practised had not been devised, was not sustained for reasons long since defunct. It was clear to all officers who had been under fire that many men were frightened by bullets and shrapnel and some would always be prone to run away. In company formation this was impossible; the company sergeant-major was positioned left or right flank rear so that movement out of the ranks was instantly seen by him. It was recognized that a company, still more a battalion in close formation was a dense target, the more vulnerable to a single shrapnel burst than one dispersed but none had yet experienced the intense fire which became the rule in the twentieth century. Moreover, quite apart from the prevention of straggling or desertion under fire, the massing of troops had another major advantage which had proved itself throughout the wars of the nineteenth century: shock action. At a time when the machine-gun was hardly in service, the concentrated fire of the two hundred rifles in a German company was much more effective than the scattered fire of two hundred individuals. In the sum, men massed to move and fire collectively as one were a controlled weapon of war in the hand of the company commander.

As the infantry recruit grew more experienced, the more apt might find themselves attending the regimental non-commissioned officers' cadre from which the successful emerged as junior corporals. Others would be needed to join the signals sections, become clerks, orderlies, grooms, buglers, cooks. The newly-established regimental machine-gun companies absorbed the more intelligent men when the vacancies for signallers and clerks had been filled. The majority became riflemen.

Each year, the officers and men in the active corps would work through an annual programme moving progressively through platoon and company exercises to battalion, regiment, division, corps and finally the army manoeuvres held under the eye, though latterly not the effective direction of the emperor. These were autumn occasions, when the army assembled; the crops would be gathered in and farms, villages and even some towns became the battleground of opposing forces over wide areas. Though commanders and staffs were tested thoroughly in movement and supply, the application of major and minor tactics was often unrealistic. However, the enterprising squadron commander might bring himself to notice by the excellence of his scouting: a company commander would show that his troops were well enough disciplined to be allowed temporarily to disperse into a skirmishing line. Equally, colonels and upwards might make or break their reputations by opportune night marches to bring guns, cavalry and infantry out of the morning mist in flank or rear of an opponent. The concept of war, even in 1913, was still very much that of 1870 for the Germans. When a nation has once been wholly victorious, it is ever thus; the Army is content with its methods, and polishes but does not change them.

THE EVENT

For some years before the war of 1914, the great nations of Europe had been flinging politically combustible materials carelessly on to a common pyre. Though the greatest contribution was made by Austria-Hungary, the other Powers added in one degree or another. In June, 1914, the pyre was lit. By August it was ablaze.

At 5 o'clock on the evening of 1st August, the Emperor, Wilhelm II, signed the order for general mobilization of the German Army, believing that the anticipated war on two fronts was about to begin. Within an hour a telegram from his embassy in London led him – mistakenly – to believe that France and the United Kingdom might remain neutral. At once he ordered von Moltke to cease any preparations against France and to mobilize for a total effort against Russia.

Moltke was dismayed. 'It cannot be done, your Majesty,' he said. 'The deployment of millions cannot be improvised.'

He meant that, having accepted the Schlieffen Plan, Germany was trapped into its fulfilment; the military solution dictated the political course. There was no other option on mobilization.

Moltke did not mean to say that there were no other plans in existence; there were plans to mobilize against Russia alone and they were sufficiently up to date to take account of the most recent additions to the railway system. What he was saying was that they could not be implemented at this late hour without placing Germany in peril of early defeat.

To begin with, time was of the essence: the railways of Belgium and Luxembourg had to be seized before the enemy had completed mobilization – indeed, Belgium had had an ultimatum demanding free passage of German troops across her territory on 29th July as the emperor well knew; and troops of 16th Division were already *en route* to Luxembourg. If all this were cancelled, the security of the Schlieffen Plan was already in jeopardy.

To assist in the swift deployment into these territories and also to aid the prompt manning of the frontier against France, considerable quantities of ordnance stores and reserve rations had been located in western Germany. There were no major reserve depots in the east.

The movement of men, wagons, guns, stores from the country at large was already beginning and to stop it would cause confusion on a grand scale. For many of the mobilisation centres had been built and stocked to a plan whereby drafts reported, drew kit and formed-up, then moved on immediately to make way for others crowding in. Railway locomotives and rolling stock were concentrated on side lines, in spurs and sidings ready to feed on 2nd August the four trunk routes to the west: Green for Stettin-Berlin-Hanover-Aachen; Blue for Schneidemtthl-Berlin-Cassel-Cologne; Brown for Posen-Frankfurt and Main-Thionville; Red for Lissa-Dresden-Strasbourg. Day and night these trains were to run at 30 kilometres per hour, regulated at just such a speed so that none would hold up another: 11,000 trains – 180 for each corps – moving in an intricate pattern until active and reserve formations, *Landwehr* and *Landsturm* were delivered to the assembly areas from which they marched forward.

Even though it was only a matter of hours before the stream of movement swelled to a torrent, the Schlieffen Plan could have been cancelled and, eventually, its alternative put into effect; the communications were good enough to do it. But the delay that would be involved was incalculable. It was not possible on that evening of 1st August to say whether the millions of soldiers and the millions of tons of transport, stores, ammunition, guns needed to equip them for battle could be moved to the east in sufficient time to attack the Russians before the enemy had reached full strength. Supposing that they were able to do so, what would be the effect if France subsequently decided to go to war after all?

Fortunately, or so it seemed to Moltke at the time, the belief that Great Britain was willing and able to restrain France proved false. The *Aufmarsch* west continued as planned. It will be recalled that Schlieffen's Plan envisaged a holding operation from the Rhine to Metz inclusive while a massive force wheeled into France through the Ardennes and Belgium. Initially, Schlieffen thought that 'In a war against Germany, France will probably restrict herself to defence...' but later he discussed the case in which '...The French do not restrict themselves to the defence, as we said at the beginning, but instead take the offensive from the start... Such a French offensive would be most welcome to the Germans.'

Obligingly, the first echelon of the French Army sallied out from its line of fortresses to attack along almost the whole frontier line with Germany. An implicit, half mystical belief in the transcendent power of the assault, a recrudescent enthusiasm to regain the territories of Alsace and Lorraine, a misplaced confidence in weapons and leadership all contributed to the disasters of the *offensive a l'origine*. Much as the elder von Moltke had expected, apart from a brief initial success in Alsace, the French armies were routed from Saarburg to Morhange, from Morhange to the southern Ardennes by an enemy numerically weaker but better led, armed and trained. By 24th August, French losses on the frontiers and elsewhere were a quarter of a million men.

If these reverses were not enough, the French commander-in-chief had other grave news. He had heard previously that the Germans were attempting a turning movement through Belgium round his left flank. It now appeared that this was in greater strength than he had appreciated. Fortunately, the British ally had arrived in time to extend the flank as far as Mons. But their contribution was tiny: two corps and a cavalry division.

Without a reserve as such but believing that he was well placed to win the first encounter. Field Marshal Sir John French brought the British Expeditionary Force up to the Mons canal in a spirit of confident optimism. Fifty miles to his left lay the Channel. Between its shore and himself, the Flanders plain was held in token by scattered cavalry patrols and detachments of bewildered French Territorials. On the right of the British, connected by a French cavalry corps, was the Fifth Army of France under General Lanrezac.

On 22nd August, one of the German armies wheeling through Belgium – von Bülow's Second – struck the Fifth Army on the Sambre with great force and ferocity. By the evening of the 23rd, aware of French disasters in the Ardennes and shaken himself by the first experience of battle, Lanrezac gave the order to retire.

At Mons, the British had held their own that day in their first clash with German forces but, surprised and alarmed by Lanrezac's decision – made without any form of consultation – Sir John also ordered a withdrawal back into France.

In this area of south-west Belgium neither French nor Germans – still less the British – were clear as to what faced them. But the Germans had the advantage of working to a comprehensive plan which, to date, had progressed much as forecast. Squabbling between themselves, the German army commanders on the right kept up their advance, crossing now into France: von Kluck on the extreme right with First, then von Büllow with the Second, next again von Hausen with the Third (Saxon) Army. Often hindered, sometimes checked by French and British ambushes and delaying positions, by the first week in September they had nevertheless reached the line prescribed by Schlieffen ten years before.

So far so good.

Unfortunately for Germany, Schlieffen had conceived the war as being a repetition of 1870, the only changes being in the employment of greater numbers with weapons of enhanced power. Increasingly obsessed by the imagination and sweep of his central idea, he excluded from consideration the consequences of change when these were unfavourable to it. Though he amplified the home railway system to transport an army swollen to millions, and arranged for new weapons to support them, he did not create a headquarters adequate to control the force. Politically näive, he grew steadily more confident that the Belgians would surrender their territory and railways under the threat of subjugation. He appears to have discounted or ignored altogether the extensive development of the railway system in France after 1871.

In war, and in their planning for war, all commanders make mistakes. If the margin of error is small, the good commander is redeemed by luck. Where the error is profound, however strong the chiefs nerves, however quick his instinct, failure must ensue. Thanks to Schlieffen's initial capital errors, it ensued for Germany in that first week of September 1914.

The German Supreme Headquarters was established by 16th August at Coblenz on the Rhine. To the nearest point of contact on the frontier it was 137 miles by road – 206 miles to von Kluck's army on the right flank. As titular commander-in-chief, the Emperor was located here with Moltke and the bulk of the Great General Staff from Berlin, though the minister for war, Lieutenant-General Erich von Falkenhayn, remained with the other government offices in the capital.

It was a comfortable and well-equipped headquarters, the officers living in an hotel where they '...ate at small tables, simply but substantially'. Nearby, as Schlieffen had imagined:

> ...roomy offices where telegraph, telephone and wireless signalling apparatus are at hand, while a fleet of autos and motorcycles, ready to depart, wait for orders. Here in a comfortable chair by a large table the modern commander overlooks the whole battlefield on a map. From here he telephones inspiring words and here he receives the reports from army and corps commanders and from balloons and dirigibles which observe the enemy's movements.

There was a wireless service and it worked to an extent. But the equipment was rudimentary and all messages had to be deciphered by hand, sent by hand-operated morse key and deciphered again by an individual with a code book. It took many hours – days for a message of substance – to pass a text from writer to recipient. The signalling officers were not helped by the jamming operations of the French from the Eiffel Tower and, increasingly frustrated, took to sending portions of secret text in clear.

There were telephones and telegraphs but the former were not amplified so that there was endless shouting into microphones and straining of ears to catch a reply from places as distant as Luxembourg, as remote as East Prussia. The coding problems that inhibited wireless traffic were common to the telegraph. Both telephone and telegraph wires were prone to being cut by the Belgians and, later, the French. The carrier pigeon contributed but there was otherwise no regular aerial despatch service; 'balloons, dirigibles' and aircraft being engaged in looking for the enemy over the vast spread of land and water where the enemy might move. Despite all these marvels of communications science, the staff were concerned to discover day-by-day that they were unable to obtain timely intelligence from the battlefield or order events effectively upon it.

To improve control of the right wing, von Bülow had been ordered to co-ordinate the operations of both his own and von Kluck's army as they began the march through Belgium. It was not a happy decision. Bülow was inevitably preoccupied with his own affairs and, a deliberate man, bound to clash with the arrogant temeraire, von Kluck. After ten days of grizzling complaint and objection from First Army, this arrangement was cancelled on 27th August, but the problem of control on the right was not solved; an army group commander was needed and was to be needed yet more as the main armies closed. For the result of contact was that each army commander saw the opportunities offered on his own front and sought to exploit them. Thus, on the far left, with the Sixth Army, Crown Prince Rupprecht of Bavaria 'raised objections to continuing his retirement when everyone else was advancing. He, too, wanted to attack, and the Supreme Command allowed him to do so', placing the Seventh Army under his command. The German Crown Prince proposed to move forward prematurely his Fifth Army; Duke Albrecht of Württemberg the Fourth.

A little later, von Kluck asked permission to avoid the encirclement of Paris on the reasonable premise that, in extending westward round it, he would lose the opportunity to overcome the French forces forming-up to his front. Though he at first demurred and re-emphasized the general lines of the Schlieffen Plan on the 28th August, von Moltke relented next day and approved von Kluck's proposition. It was difficult for the chief of the General Staff to make a judgement and, uneasy and unwell, he tended to leave matters to the commanders in the field. He had besides, problems on the Russian front, to which he sent two corps[7] from France. For this and his weakness he has been much criticized but the criticism is overdone. If Moltke had insisted on exact conformity to Schlieffen it is arguable that the German armies in France would have sustained a crippling defeat. For the balance of advantage was rising in favour of the French. As matters stood, the railways of France permitted Joffre, the commander-in-chief, to redeploy his troops to any point on the arc of contact more swiftly than the Germans. It is said that the German rolling stock held in Lorraine was sufficient to transfer north much

[7] Originally three, the Guard Reserve, XI and X, only the first two were sent.

of the Sixth and Seventh Armies, were they not fruitlessly engaged in an assault on Nancy. But where would these wagons and carriages have been sent to, close to the front? The railway was clear from Lorraine through Luxembourg but not many miles beyond. Contrary to Schlieffen's expectation, the Belgian engineers had demolished bridges and culverts, cuttings and tunnels on a grand scale. Sixty per cent of the German railway construction and operating companies were at work on their repair and there was no traffic to France in August. And even if the men were marched forward with guns and limbers ready in support, how long would they be able to remain in action? Quite soon the armies in contact were feeling the effect of their intense expenditure of ammunition. The supply of shells, even of small arms ammunition was diminishing, partly because none of the European general staffs had anticipated such expenditure but also because in late August and early September the German supply railheads were falling too far in rear to permit the quick transfer of shell and cartridge by horse-drawn transport. It was not therefore a failure to stick to the Schlieffen Plan that led to Moltke's difficulties, or the absence of two corps sent to the east after 28th August; it was the weakness of the plan itself which had gambled on too many long shots and ignored obstinately the explicit strength of France's hand.

'There is no escaping the evidence of the facts,' said Joffre on the morning of 24th August. The French Plan XVII had failed on the frontiers and all the news was of encroachment by the Germans. Joffre, the immense, fat, engineer officer who had no depth of training or experience to fit him for the chief command, possessed the qualities which Moltke lacked: a steady nerve, an iron resolve and a ruthless hand with those whom he believed to have failed. No general in the French armies doubted who commanded in France. Despite protests, Joffre began to withdraw troops from the right to form a new army on the left under Maunoury. He sacked a number of commanders and senior staff officers and appointed in their place those whose mettle had been proved. The armies were reinforced, the immense casualties having emptied the ranks from general to private – indeed, the loss amongst officers of all ranks was the most serious blow to France's war potential. He alerted Adolphe Messimy, the minister of war,[8] that he would need speedily to expand armaments – particularly ammunition – production; and he warned the French Army as a whole to pull itself together.

Joffre's aim was to hold on the right and centre while opening a new offensive on the left. A more open-minded man might have asked himself whether or not this might have been a better gambit at the outset but Joffre

[8] Replaced on 27th August by Millerand.

had high confidence in his decisions, a characteristic that did not come amiss in this time of crisis, and it was his conclusion that the assault on the frontiers had failed simply because the army had fought inadequately. Hence his sharp message to all ranks. It is doubtful whether the words reached the majority of troops; they were preoccupied by fighting a hard-pressed withdrawal. But it is probable that, read at formation headquarters at all levels, it sharpened wits and spirits. What stiffened the tired men of the regiments, marching and fighting in the summer heat was the knowledge that they were fighting on and for the defence of their own land, field and village, town and city. When they left a position, they abandoned their own people and soil. Increasingly weary, progressively ragged in clothing and equipment, the French regiments began to bind spiritually once more as the moves ordered by their chief bound their numbers physically.

The Germans, too, some to the point of exhaustion. In First Army, it was Kluck's brutal leadership that invigorated his battalions but the army commander could do little to supply the needs of his men in shirts and boots. Packs, too, were often missing, lost in some sudden midnight move; blown to smithereens on a wagon by the burst of a French or British shell.

The problems of clothing supply were the least of those engaging Moltke and his staff, however. On 29th August, they had moved from Coblenz to Luxembourg, hoping thereby to increase control as they shortened communications. The position now was that the armies of the left – Sixth and Seventh under Crown Prince Rupprecht – were trying to break through the forts on the Grand Couronné. Not to be outdone. Fifth Army under the Crown Prince was attacking the Verdun position. The Fourth (Württemberg) and Third (Saxon) Armies were pushing on through the Argonne and across the Aisne, not without difficulty, while Bülow, mauled in the battle of Guise in August sought continually to keep his left flank up against the Saxon Army and urged von Kluck similarly to tuck in on Second Army's right.

Moltke's intention was that First and Second Armies should sweep across the British Expeditionary Force and the French Fifth Army obliquely from north west to south east. He reckoned these two armies to be nearly spent but he knew from covert intelligence sources that Maunoury's army was forming up quickly in strength east of Paris so that he ordered von Kluck to lie back in echelon behind von Bülow, maintaining direction towards the French and British forces ahead but, simultaneously, guarding the German flank against Maunoury. When this order arrived on 3rd September, however, von Kluck was already more than 12 miles in front, with his right-hand corps at Chantilly, less than

20 miles from the outskirts of Paris. Though he did not have such refined information concerning Maunoury's new army as von Moltke, von Kluck knew better than Supreme Headquarters that any delay in pressing the British and Fifth Armies would permit these bodies to redeploy in co-ordination with the forces adjacent to Paris. There would be no question of forcing the two armies south east away from the city. In this event, a turning movement would only be achieved by using Schlieffen's concept of an encirclement of Paris and, quite apart from needing an investing force that did not exist, this was beyond the marching powers of his corps without several days recuperation. So, disregarding his orders, he went on.

Next day, 4th September, with the nearest of Bülow's corps trailing 14 miles in rear, and reports from cavalry and the air warning him of large bodies of troops both to the south and south east (the BEF and Fifth Army) and on the west (Maunoury's Sixth Army) von Kluck began to feel very much alone. He signalled von Moltke for information.

The growing peril to the right flank was now plain to Supreme Headquarters in Luxembourg. That evening orders were sent by wireless to both First and Second armies to change their direction and face south west to guard against the anticipated attack on the right flank. But Moltke also knew well the obstinacy of the headstrong Kluck: he wanted no more 'mis-understanding' or disregard of orders. By car, he sent Lieutenant-Colonel Hentsch, head of his intelligence section, to pass to von Kluck the new instructions personally and to inform him of the overall position in France. The coded wireless message, sent at 7.45 pm on the 4th reached von Kluck and von Bülow about 6 am on the 5th. Hentsch arrived that evening and none too late. For Kluck's army had continued the march south east at 4 am and the message arriving at 6 pm had not inclined the army commander to restrain them. He had, however, maintained one corps to guard his open flank towards Paris.

When Hentsch arrived, von Kluck was less contumacious than he had been in the morning. For one thing his flank guard had had a sharp encounter with the foremost of Maunoury's divisions north west of Paris during the day; for another, Hentsch told him that none of the other armies showed signs of defeating the enemy as yet at any point. He promised to put the orders for the 5th into effect on the 6th. Hentsch assured him that the movement could be made at leisure; no special haste was necessary'.

No special haste was necessary because, in the view of Hentsch, his colleagues and his chief, they were not imperilled by their exhausted and dispirited enemy provided that sound dispositions were made to secure the

German right flank.

'Not a sign, not a word from prisoners, not a newspaper paragraph' gave warning of Joffre's return to the offensive on the morning of 6th August. He had finished regrouping: he had appointed the most ardent of his senior generals to command the assault forces; he had visited personally the British army commander and moved him to tears and acquiescence by his exhortation.

Facing east from Paris, the military governor, the veteran General Gallieni now launched in full Maunoury's Sixth Army, reinforcing its effort from the city's garrison, some 6,000 of these men being carried to the front in relays of taxi cabs. The Fifth Army – now under Franchet d'Esperey – and the Ninth under Foch attempted to bore in upon Bülow and Hausen. Reflecting the uncertainty of Sir John French and the timidity of his chief of staff, Murray, the BEF, starting late from a further withdrawal, moved slowly towards the gap between Kluck and Bülow, thinly held by a cavalry division and a light infantry brigade.

During the next three days action blazed between French and German soldiers along and about the streams Ourcq and Petit Morin. The assaults of the Fifth and Ninth Armies made painful progress limited to metres. Von Kluck's army, caught in the midst of changing direction recovered superbly and his troops responded to his ruthless hand, one corps marching 70 miles in forty hours from left to right behind the army front. A detachment of Maunoury's cavalry reached First Army headquarters and von Kluck manned the firing line in company with his staff in repulse. A brigade left by First Army to garrison Brussels railed and marched to his aid and by the 8th Maunoury was beaten.

Yet once more the First Army was isolated. Once more Hentsch appeared, sent by von Moltke to appraise the situation and holding powers to act as he thought fit. Swayed by the anxieties of Bülow concerning the gap between himself and von Kluck, impressed by the confusion in the area *en route* to First Army, Hentsch decided on retreat, 'basing my action on the full powers given to me, because it was only in this way one could bring (First Army) once more into co-operation with the Second Army'.

He was probably right. Whatever success Kluck might have had in following up the immediate victory over Maunoury, his left flank and the lightly held gap between it and Bülow was already undermounting pressure from the British Expeditionary Force. Refusing to see him, even to admit to knowing of Hentsch's presence, Kluck left the visitor to his chief of staff.

In the rainfall marking the end of the long, hot summer, withdrawal began that night, 9th September.

PART II

A DIFFICULT SITUATION

*'The general situation of the Central Powers had become
extremely difficult by the middle of September 1914.'*

FALKENHAYN

NOTBEHELFE

On the day that he moved from Coblenz to Luxembourg, 29th August, there was good news for Moltke from the east. The German army in East Prussia had defeated decisively one of the enemy's and was now preparing to tackle a second. This happy outcome of the first complete clash with the Russian forces was due not at all to the two corps despatched from the west which arrived too late to participate – but to a change of commander and chief of staff sent on 22nd August to replace the dispirited incumbents. Though the tale of success continued from East Prussia – and von Moltke the elder was as much vindicated there as Schlieffen continued to be discredited – the pleasant reading of these reports did not sustain the ailing mind or body of the younger von Moltke. On 7th September, his daily letter to his wife included these words '...Terror often overcomes me when I think about this (blood spilled), and the feeling I have is as if I must answer for this horror...', and on the 8th'... The suspense, with the absence of news from the far distant armies, almost goes beyond what human strength can stand, when one knows the issues involved'.

The suspense, at least, was not protracted. Soon Hentsch returned to tell his chief what he had done in his name.

They knew then the worst at Supreme Headquarters. The Schlieffen concept of encirclement and destruction of the French had been abandoned but the marching right wing had been recovered, more or less intact, and could fight again. Already the regiments were marching back out of contact, all footsore, some puzzled, a few bitter that their endeavours had not secured the expected victory. Soon, in commanding positions on the north bank of the Aisne, Kluck's army was joined to Bülow's, Bülow's to Hausen's and so on through the Army of Witrttemberg to where the Crown Prince's Fifth Army had desisted at last in its attempts to break through at Verdun, and Crown Prince Rupprecht of Bavaria had come to realize that Nancy was not to be his.

Yet with all these movements accomplished safely, there was no lightening of spirits at Supreme Headquarters. In the professional lifetime of most of its officers, it had been an accepted fact that France must and should be defeated quickly – in the first forty days indeed – so as to permit the concentration of the army thereafter against Russia.

The recovery of the right wing was of course welcomed but the event simply endorsed the total failure of Germany's strategy. They were now faced with the dreaded war on two fronts. In the east, there were certainly insufficient German forces to bring matters to a conclusion. It was cold comfort to learn that the Austrians had proved as ineffective as predicted. They had already been thrown back by Serbia and shortly, on 14th September, were to be worsted in a gigantic battle between the Vistula and Dneister rivers. Supreme Headquarters began to form a second German army in the east, principally at the expense of the victorious forces in East Prussia, whose front was now quiet.

On the western front, the immediate need was to prevent the allies from holding the German forces on the Aisne by frontal attack while enveloping their open right flank. One corps had just completed a crippling forced march from Mauberge and two more were on their way from Antwerp, withdrawn from the siege force masking the great seaport. Others were moving from as near as the Argonne, from as far as the Vosges. They would probably be sufficient in numbers to stabilize the line and extend the flank but would they be in time? None of the railways were open along the direct routes of these reinforcements. All would be obliged to march considerable distances in consequence.

Fearing a defeat on the Aisne or envelopment along the Oise, Supreme Headquarters gave permission to the three right wing armies to fall back to the line Rheims-Laon-La Fere at their discretion.

These orders, made mostly at the instigation of subordinate members of the staff, were the last to be over-seen by von Moltke. On the evening of 14th September, Lieutenant-General Erich von Falkenhayn, the minister of war, was received by the emperor in Luxembourg and told at once that he was to be chief of the General Staff. For reasons of public morale, it was decided that the change of appointment should not immediately be released; Moltke was obliged to sit on as a puppet in Supreme Headquarters. For reasons of personal expediency, Falkenhayn retained his post as minister. His acute perception sharpened by the wide powers and responsibilities now in his hands, the new chief surveyed the scene.

'The general situation of the Central Powers had become extremely difficult...'

The Central Powers – then, Germany and Austria-Hungary[1] – were an active partnership politically but not militarily. Austria-Hungary's difficulties were all in the east with her principal foe, Russia; Germany's in the west with France and Britain. There was as yet no co-ordinated military command in the east, though on the day of Falkenhayn's appointment a step was taken towards this necessary end. Meantime, as the Russians encroached progressively on Galicia, the northern province of Austria-Hungary, the German countryside of Upper Silesia was imminently threatened. Yet Falkenhayn could only endorse Moltke's policy in this region. The German army grouping in the area must cope alone, gaining what aid it could from the Austrians when their wholesale withdrawal was at an end and they had reformed.

In the west, action was needed in two stages in time. Immediately, the drift into further withdrawals, perhaps into whole-sale retreat, had to be stopped. The permission given to fall back as necessary to a line in rear of the Aisne was cancelled. To gain time for the corps moving from left to right, all armies were to mount local attacks to prevent the French command itself from transferring troops freely to the north. Falkenhayn knew well that the men in the line were bone weary, their ranks depleted, the deficiencies in their arms and equipment now even worse than in the final stages of the advance. As minister for war, he had been aware for some days that the shortage of ammunition was serious. But he insisted on attack, while promising to remedy the most immediate needs in the forward areas. In sum, all units must accept a policy of *notbeheife*, makeshift. The dead and wounded, they were reminded, were a perpetual source of ordnance supply, the areas of France which they had crossed so swiftly in advance still held an abundance of food.

With Falkenhayn's arrival, the atmosphere of indecision at Supreme Headquarters disappeared. The staff were clear as to what was required of them; the army commanders knew better than to disregard orders, even if

---

[1] Turkey joined them on 1st November 1914.

they continued to protest at many of them. So soon as he had made known his immediate requirements, Falkenhayn began to plan for the future; to search for a new strategy.

> 'It still seemed possible, if the present German front held, to bring the northern coast of France, and therefore the control of the English Channel into German hands. It was all the more inadvisable to abandon this possibility, since the chief of the General Staff clung to the object which was at the root of the original plan of campaign – first of all to seek the decision in the west...'

These words, written by Falkenhayn after the war, reflected the spirit and intention of the hour.

His problems were twofold: men and material. To solve them, he needed a dimension beyond his control: time.

The armies in the line urgently needed reinforcement to make good the losses of battle casualties. The reinforcement camps could provide about two-thirds of the private soldiers needed but less than a quarter of the officers and NCOs. It was true that there were other sources of replacement. He could take instructors from the training units in Germany but if he did that the enormous reserve of untrained manpower left over from conscription in peace would be lost to him for ever. There were, however, two bonuses. The first was that the forces remaining in Belgium – chiefly those disposed to take Antwerp – were strong in infantry, even if not of the first rank, and heavy artillery. If Antwerp could be captured quickly, they were well-positioned to move on to the Channel coast to the west. Second, as minister for war, Falkenhayn had begun to form up six new corps and a further division on 16th August. Styled 'reserve' corps and divisions, they were far from the quality of the reserve formation which had taken the field at the beginning of the month, bodies of young men who had all served with the colours in recent years. Seventy-five per cent of the new corps were drawn from the many young men who had not been called up with their age group; the military depots had been inundated by their demands to be taken for service once war had been declared. A degree of experience was instilled in their ranks by the inclusion of older men from the Second Bande of the *Landwehr* and even some from the *Landsturm*. There were few regular officers below the majors commanding battalions, though some of the adjutants were also regular officers. Company, battery and squadron commanders were either regular officers recalled from retirement or reserve officers, many from the *Landwehr*, while the platoons and troops were commanded by cadets awaiting commissions –

offizierstellvertreter – or selected NCOs. The NCOs themselves were entirely from one or other of the reserve echelons, a high proportion of them being elementary schoolmasters. On the day of Falkenhayn's appointment, they had been training together for just a month.

In the matter of industrial support, Falkenhayn had been insistent in the week before the war that industrial reorganization was necessary if the needs of the army were to be provided. There had been a degree of apathy to overcome; even in late July, the finance minister had been unwilling to provide credits for the purchase of grain reserves in the belief that war was improbable.[2] After the outbreak, the concept of 1870 militated against the expansion of the munitions industry until the early returns of ammunition expenditure from the front were circulated. Thereafter, attitudes changed quickly and by 15th September the production of pig-iron and steel had risen, whereas that of the allies had dropped. Germany's fortune lay here in the mass of men still available on the land and in industry whereas France and, shortly, Britain were to exhaust their male labour force by indiscriminate conscription and recruitment. In fact, in Germany, there were considerable numbers of unemployed workers due to the closure of such factories as those producing textiles. It was precisely because he wanted to maintain his voice in the organization of manpower and industry that Falkenhayn remained, at his own request, minister of war.

Naturally, in this anxious autumn there was no question of the minister making his base in Berlin. His place was dictated by his work as chief and in order to do this work better he decided to move Supreme Headquarters into France, selecting Charleville and Mézières, twin towns on the Meuse, as its site. It was clear that the zone of the future action would be in Belgium and northern France. Like Joffre, Falkenhayn began to develop his resources towards it.

It was not unreasonable for Joffre to feel a degree of triumph as the German armies drew back from the Marne. However many officers were subsequently to claim a share of the credit – and the numbers of claimants multiplied as the years passed – Joffre had a major share in and total responsibility for the event. As his own tired divisions pushed north towards the Aisne, their British allies on the flank, he planned to develop the pursuit into a grand movement to complete victory, the next phase being the destruction of the German right wing. On the 11th September, he outlined his concept of operations to army commanders. Next day, he sent particular orders to General Sarrail opposite the centre to pursue

---

[2] *Die Wirtschaftliche Mobflmachung in Deutschland, 1914, von Delbruck,* ed. (Verlag für Kulturpolitik), pp. 101-2.

closely the Crown Prince around Verdun so as to prevent the thinning out of enemy forces from that zone for the reinforcement of the north. On the same day, Maunoury was instructed to be ready to march up the right bank of the Oise if von Kluck made a stand on the Aisne.

'I am obliged to say that the execution of these instructions did not respond to my intentions.'

Joffre was understandably disappointed that his orders were not energetically pursued; he could see the opportunities for victory passing for want of exploitation. But although the want of response owed something to the characters of Sarrail and Maunoury individually, the prime reason was that, like the German armies, his own were temporarily spent. The tempo of their operations was slow and shortly it became slower as Falkenhayn's orders reached regimental level and the Germans began their own local counter-attacks. Neither side succeeded in doing anything other than to prevent the advance of its adversary. Only the British seemed to have the spirit to break into the enemy's new positions, but they had had less fighting to do than the great armies of either side. They were led forward too slowly, however, and von Kluck's reinforcements from Belgium beat them to the post.

Denied the immediate successes he had looked for, Joffre hoped still to accomplish his strategy. From the Oise to the Channel coast 170 miles to the north was a military vacuum. The Germans had not garrisoned the area because it lay outside their line of communication as they marched confidently south; the French had never positioned troops there apart from the scattered detachments of veteran reservists and Territorials who remained, left in suspense by events. French divisions, withdrawn from the central and southern sectors before the German counter-attacks began, were now coming to hand and, under de Castelnau, should deploy beyond the Oise and march round the enemy's open flank. There was one inhibiting factor, though, which occupied Joffre increasingly through September. He was growing ever shorter of artillery ammunition.

On 21st September, Millerand, the minister of war, responded from Paris:

My Dear General,

The manufacture of 75-mm ammunition is the source of no less intense preoccupation to me than you. Before receiving your letter (of 20th September) I had come to the same conclusion as you, namely that we must produce 50,000 rounds a day. But this is impossible under conditions as they now stand.

I therefore brought together yesterday representatives of the War and Naval Ministries and of private industry in order to see how we should reach this figure ...However, I do not despair of reaching 30,000 rounds in three weeks: at the most, in four... I urgently request you, on your side, to take every possible measure to prevent waste where it can be avoided. Please see that fatigue parties gather up the cartridge cases left on the battlefields, or else offer to pay the inhabitants for all they bring in...

M Millerand was the devoted supporter of the commander-in-chief. With the need to expand production urgently appreciated in Paris and a firm promise of improvement, Joffre had no other course but to collect stocks held in garrisons and forts – Paris, for example and, surprisingly, Dunkirk – to create a temporary reserve supply to Castelnau, whose Second Army had been assembling in Picardy behind a screen of French Territorial divisions. By the 20th, it had begun its advance. Next day, the corps north west of Lassigny seemed on the point of marching round the German flank when a German corps appeared to oppose this move. Soon, de Maud'huy had been placed beyond Castelnau and a mass of cavalry north again. Yet as quickly as they arrived, the Germans arrived too. A fierce battle flared up around Arras. Falkenhayn and Joffre were engaged in a race to outflank each other but seemed unable to achieve more than a dead heat as they closed mutually and progressively the gap open between flank and sea.

So September passed. In October, as the uncontested ground between the embattled armies and the Channel rapidly diminished, the plans of Falkenhayn began to mature.

Opposite Antwerp, after a very slow start, the German forces hived off to effect its capture were about to complete their task. The commander was General von Beseler whose tardy movement was due less to extremes of prudence than a digression in tasks. In his own time on the staff, the Schlieffen Plan had provided five reserve corps for the reduction of Antwerp, a number of other reserve formations to the total of a division at least and a considerable number of siege artillery and engineer units. In the September of the war, he had only a total of six divisions – of which two alone were properly established as reserve formations – and had besides to cover Brussels against a sortie by the Belgian Army or its allies, and to guard every metre of the vital and vulnerable section of the railway between Liège and Brussels, which absorbed the effort of four battalions.

In order to carry out these tasks of protecting this flank and line-of-communication, von Beseler's forces had of necessity deployed immediately to the north of Brussels, Louvain and Tirlemont; that is, on an alignment

Artois and Flanders showing main railways

roughly due south of Antwerp. The original plan had arranged that the attack on the great city port should be made from the east because there was no water obstacle on that side but any attempt to move thence would uncover Brussels and the railway. Thus a new plan had been required, not only to break through the rings of forts, outer and inner, surrounding Antwerp, but also to cross the river Nethe, covered by a number of guns of the Belgian fortress artillery. Planning, reallocating troops to tasks, redeployment including the movement of the heavy and super heavy guns, howitzers and mortars had taken time. By 29th September, all was ready and the results justified the forethought of von Beseler and his staff.

For when it came to it, the operation was a walkover. There were casualties but they were light on either side because the Germans, using their immensely powerful siege artillery directed by observers in 'sausage' balloons, concentrated on smashing the protective forts and their guns. These gone, the Belgian defenders were obliged to withdraw into the city. The garrison troops were, in any case, of poor quality and would probably have withdrawn at the first advance but for the presence of the Belgian field army, pushed into the Antwerp area by the German right wing in August. A small British contingent arrived to assist but if it raised the morale of the besieged, it brought little weight to the defence. A so-called naval and marine division, the majority of the men were civilians who had only recently put on uniform for the first time in their lives and, apart from small arms, they lacked weapons and equipment of every sort. More encouragingly, the British 7th (Infantry) and 3rd Cavalry Divisions were embarked for Antwerp on 5th October. Under pressure from London, Joffre agreed to contribute a Territorial division, a regiment of Zouaves and a naval brigade under Admiral Ronarc'h to hold Antwerp with his allies until operations north of the Oise could take effect.

These were the allies' hopes.

By 30th September, de Castelnau's attempts at envelopment had been defeated in Picardy; on 7th October, it was clear that de Maud'huy would find no open enemy flank round Arras; during the morning of 9th October, General von Beseler sent a *parlementaire* into Antwerp to demand the surrender of a city now completely at his mercy – at much the same time as the military governor decided that he must ask for terms. Once more the shell had proved superior to the fort.

Von Beseler's reports to Falkenhayn had indicated daily, as was customary, his expectations for the morrow; and day by day these expectations were exceeded as the force broke through the southern forts towards the city port. When, on 8th October, the siege artillery was skilfully moved across the river

Nethe without loss, it was clear that the fall of Antwerp was imminent. Falkenhayn had now to make an important decision.

The fall of Antwerp would release a force of some power – not only in infantry but weight of artillery – for other operations. It would be inexpedient to move them south into France when rolling stock was needed for more pressing tasks elsewhere. Von Beseler's troops should therefore exploit westward towards the Flemish coast, pinching out any remnant of Belgian military opposition as they did so. This left open the main question as to where the *ersatz* reserve corps, formed on 16th August, should be committed.

By now, ten German corps and more had been withdrawn from Alsace, Lorraine and the Champagne. North of the Oise, the newly arrived formations were commanded by Crown Prince Rupprecht of Bavaria who had moved up with his Sixth Army headquarters. As Joffre showed no signs of abating his own flow of forces northward, one concept was to bring in the new corps to the Aisne and the Vesle to relieve the veterans in the line for an offensive round Rheims. The same might be done in Picardy round Bapaume, or in Artois to strike at Arras. In all these sectors, the Germans held the advantage of ground. The railway had been open for a month to Noyon and was now working through Cambrai to Bapaume. A break-out near Arras would permit a drive to the Channel and the mouth of the Somme, isolating the remainder of Belgium and northern France. Noyon was only 60 miles from Paris. But the prospects of any of these, though bright, were not so dazzling as to obscure an inescapable fact; it would take time to effect reliefs and during this time the Franco-British forces would concentrate in Flanders where von Beseler's forces alone would be too weak to hold them. This left Hobson's choice. The new corps, the 'schoolboy corps' from Germany must be committed to Flanders; and since there were no veterans there to form the assault forces, they must undertake this work themselves.

On 9th October, orders were sent to move forward four of the six corps under training.[3] Duke Albrecht of Württemberg and Fourth Army headquarters were brought from the centre of the line to command in Flanders, and von Beseler was instructed to disengage as quickly as possible from the walls of Antwerp. By the morning of the 10th, as the raw, eager young soldiers in Germany packed their kit for the front, it became apparent to Falkenhayn that the Belgian field army had not been trapped inside the besieged city; almost all had succeeded in escaping to the west – though the advance of a Bavarian *Landwehr* brigade on the 10th came close to cutting off the British sailors and marines covering the Belgian withdrawal. Von Beseler

[3] Of the two remaining corps, one was sent to the eastern front, one to Metz on the western front. There was in addition the 6th Bavarian Reserve Division, formed up on the same basis at the same time. It came forward to join the battle in Flanders on 26th October, 1914.

was to move as quickly as possible via Ghent and Bruges towards the coast – both in pursuit and as a right flank guard for the corps *en route* from Germany. The 14th saw his troops in both these ancient towns with advanced detachments closing fast towards Routers, Thourout and, on the coast, Ostend. Anxious to avoid a premature disclosure of his intentions, Falkenhayn ordered von Beseler not to move beyond this line for a few days and sent similar orders to Crown Prince Rupprecht, whose northern-most corps had come into the line opposite Annentières. Between this body and Roulers was a screen of German cavalry through which the four fresh corps of Fourth Army were to be launched against the allies while they were preoccupied with the business of concentrating and reorganizing.

The aim of this operation was to seize one splendid consolation prize in 1914: Calais.

PART III

THE GLORIOUS ENTERPRISE

'United thoughts and counsels, equal hope,
And hazard in the glorious enterprise.'
PARADISE LOST

ANOTHER PORTION OF THE BATTLEFIELD

Sitting in a field near the river Aisne on 17th October, Lieutenant J G W Hyndson of 1st Battalion, The Loyal North Lancashire Regiment, wrote up his diary for the preceding day.

16th October,

We are to be relieved by the French, and are to proceed to another portion of the battlefield, the exact location of which is kept secret, and accordingly plans are made to leave the Aisne that night. The relieving troops turn out to be French Territorials, and everything went off like clockwork with the exception of one mishap, for by real bad luck one of the periodical salvoes let off by the Germans struck the head of the French column as it was coining up the road, with the result that some fifty officers and men were killed or maimed.

Before the relief operations commence, a dense fog descends, and this possibly helps to deceive the Germans as to what is happening on our side. At midnight the relief is completed, and without the loss of a single man we tramp away from the area we have fought so hard to retain... By this time the fog is so thick that it is impossible to see any distance from the road and we tramp steadily across the Aisne at Bourg, by a temporary bridge constructed by our engineers. After going another two miles we bivouac in a field; although we have come only a short distance we are so out of training owing to our inactive life (in the trenches) that we are tired out and are glad to be able to rest for the remainder of the night.

Until the 20th, Lieutenant Hyndson was unable to add more; but then he added the next instalment.

17th October,

After resting far into the afternoon of the 17th, we once more get on the move and take the high road to Fismes, where we are to entrain. Off we go light-heartedly, through country almost devoid of any sign of war, where the French peasants are filling the fields. The men are in exceptionally good spirits, singing practically all the way, and on reaching Fismes we find a train drawn up and ready to take half the battalion. In a very short time Headquarters, A and C Companies are aboard, and the train groans out of the station to be followed later by another train with the remaining half battalion. During the day Captain E C Miller from the Special Reserve[1] arrives from England, and takes over the command of my company... We are now at full strength once more, having received a continual stream of reinforcements in officers and men to replace the casualties sustained on the Aisne, both in the battle and during the subsequent trench fighting...

For two whole days we jerked and rattled along, passing through Paris (St Denis), Amiens, Abbeville, and Boulogne where we stop for some hours. During the journey we do not excite the same interest on the part of the inhabitants as we did when we first landed; the French have got used to the sight of British soldiers and take our presence as a matter of course. At Boulogne some of us manage to get a few hours' leave, and we sally forth to the nearest eating house where I order the largest omelette I could get to eat. The intense joy at once more being able to feed on eggs, butter and cream cannot be described in words, and I shall always remember this meal as one of the most enjoyable I have ever eaten. We then hurry back to the train, which shortly afterwards moves off again, and crawling through Calais, we finally reach Cassel in the early morning of 19th October, where we detrain and march away to billets in the surrounding farms. With the exception of the officers, who sleep in the farmhouse, the whole of my company pass the night in a large barn. We remain here resting and waiting for our orders to move to Ypres, which we are informed is our

---

[1] The Special Reserve was largely constituted of officers and other ranks who had served for a time with the colours but had no obligatory liability in the reserve.

destination...

He was right.

A month previously the commander-in-chief of the British Expeditionary Force had decided that he must move his army once more to the extreme left of the allied line. On the Aisne, his three corps were hemmed in and he could not use his cavalry – a circumstance the more irksome because he was before all else a cavalry officer. The Indian corps were due to join him as soon as they had disembarked at Marseilles, and the 7th and 8th Divisions were shortly to join him from home with a third cavalry division. Besides he did not like being so far from the coast and his direct line of communication to the British ports. Sir John French was not a man capable of mulling long over his thoughts without utterance and when Mr Winston Churchill, First Lord of the Admiralty, visited him on 26th September, he raised the matter to get a government view. Encouraged, he wrote to Joffre to propose the move on the 29th, receiving a reply of oracular courtesy which said, in effect: yes, but slowly.

Like a horse behind the starter's tapes, the British field marshal was, however, anxious to be off. He agreed to achieve his aim by a process of thinning-out but accelerated the relief beyond what Joffre considered prudent. The cavalry going ahead by march route, II Corps entrained on 4th October, III on the 7th and I, after repeated personal requests by the field-marshal, on the 17th. There is a tone of morose satisfaction in Joffre's memoirs when he points out that, after this haste, the weak French force substituting on the Aisne heights for the departing British were shortly hurled into the river by a local German attack, while the 'rich region centering on Lille' was lost because, with the British on all the available trains, French divisions were unable to secure the city.[2]

These are matters of opinion rather than fact. Yet whatever the reason, the loss of Lille was a serious matter compared to the surrender of a few acres of the Aisne heights. A centre of the coal, iron and engineering industry of northern France, the city was also a junction for five main railway lines. Joffre and French had agreed that the BEF should concentrate south west of Lille to turn or break through the enemy line before it reached the outskirts. The news that the city had been taken by a German corps on the night 11th/12th October meant that the same British movement must now be made to the north. Though Antwerp had fallen and the Germans seemed able to deploy northwards as quickly as the allies, Joffre still did not despair of finding an open enemy flank before the line reached the sea. After a period of anxiety as the Germans counter-attacked

---

[2] But see *Memoirs*, Joffre, i, pp. 292-3.

de Castelnau and de Maud'huy, the prolonged French line seemed stable. De Maud'huy now commanded the left flank army of France, the Tenth, whose left-hand unit held Vermelles, 4 miles south of the canal between Bethune and La Bassée. To the north of the canal lay Hazebrouck and Armentières, Poperinghe and Ypres, within whose compass two French cavalry divisions played hide-and-seek with three of the Germans'. Shortly, the British cavalry began to arrive from the Aisne to join the skirmishing. North of Ypres lay Dixmude, Nieuport and Ostend, as yet bare of developed defences and uncontested. But a stream of disconsolate soldiers were now moving thence from Bruges: the Belgian Field Army, experienced in nothing but defeat were reaching the end of their withdrawal from Antwerp. On the left the British 3rd Cavalry Division and part of the 7th Division covered the Belgians as they marched west, while the remainder of the 7th Division and the French naval brigade under Admiral Ronarc'h secured the exit from Ghent. Though von Beseler was not slow in pursuit, all these forces retired safely so that, by 14th October, the Belgians were in position behind the Yser and the canal leading south from Dixmude towards Ypres. Dixmude itself was held by Ronarc'h's brigade and the 7th Division and 3rd Cavalry Division were covering Ypres from the east and south.

These two British divisions, intended originally for Antwerp, had been passed to Sir John French's command on 9th October when, under Lieutenant-General Sir Henry Rawlinson, they had formed into IV Corps. With their arrival at Ypres, not only was a defended line established by the allies to the sea but, a matter of great satisfaction to Sir John, the British Expeditionary Force was concentrating fast under his hand for a second excursion into Belgium. But this time he was far stronger than he had been when he had taken them forward to Mons. The Germans, he believed, were weaker; perhaps close to the end of their resources.

On the 10th, he had consulted with General Foch, commander of the French northern army group and, to the degree that national pride permitted, coordinator of the operations of British and Belgians as well. Foch, too, was optimistic – he was by nature a super optimist – and advised that France and her allies were never more strongly placed than now. They should unite in 'this glorious enterprise'. Thus the orders for the BEF issued on the evening of the 10th stated that 'It is the intention of the Commander-in-Chief to advance to meet the enemy, prolonging the French left.' They should advance to meet their foe and, in encounter, win and advance again, taking the opportunities of the day as they came.

It was a simple policy and if the German forces were reduced indeed in this region to a cloud of cavalry, as they believed, it might have proved an effective one. Regrettably, it took too little account of von Beseler's group, of which there was some intelligence, and none of Duke Albrecht's army of the new corps, of which the Allies had not heard.

FIRST OUT; FIRST IN

Apart from the Cavalry, the British II Corps had been the first to leave the Aisne. They were thus the first to be committed to operations in the new sector.

Sir Horace Smith-Dorrien, their commander, was an officer who had been promoted on his merits as a simple, frank soldier with a high sense of duty and a very real affection for those who served under him. His earlier commands had been successful principally because his subordinates, liking and trusting him, did their best in any test of war or peace to which they were put. As a general, his faults were that he was too kind and, primarily, that his comprehension of tactics scarcely rose above regimental level.

The regiment was the strength of the British Army but in a sense its weakness. Unique amongst the armies of the Powers of Europe, the British was a wholly professional body; all its officers and men were long-service volunteers as distinct from conscripts. The result was a high standard of training in weapons, field-craft and map-reading and an exemplary discipline; the standards being enhanced by service in a series of minor colonial wars. Close bonds of friendship bound officers and soldiers due to their long association together in and out of the firing line. A company commander in an infantry battalion would find as his company sergeant-major a man with whom he had soldiered intermittently for 20 years. He would know every man in the battalion as a whole by name and many by number. But whereas the warrant officer, non-commissioned officer or private had few outlets beyond the battalion, the officers had several, the staff being the principal means by which ambitious officers might accelerate their promotion. Yet few took this opportunity. On joining, it was made clear to the cavalry or infantry subaltern that the Regiment was the prime interest in his life which no other professional duty could supplant. In consequence, though some colonels became more indulgent in releasing officers for the staff college after the turn of century, and one or two regiments encouraged it due to an excess of numbers, the quality of officers entering the staff colleges at Camberley or Quetta was not high and, since the instructors were originally from the same system, the quality of the syllabus and methods was equally mediocre. An officer did not have to be brilliant to shine in this circle. A degree of higher intelligence, determination or other dynamic trait was sufficient to secure a key post. So, too, was the advantage of a keen eye in polo, football or cricket, even in an inarticulate officer. With exceptions, the best of the infantry and cavalry officers were to be found at regimental duty and for this determined self-sufficiency the regiments were to pay in blood.

Because they were scattered throughout the Empire, the British officers were less acquainted with those outside their regiment than in the great continental armies – even some of the general officers were on little more than nodding terms. Sir John French and Sir Horace Smith-Dorrien had been old friends and comrades-in-arms, however, though much or all of this amity was at an end by the time of their association in France.[3] The fault lay with Sir John. In 1907, Smith-Dorrien had relieved him in the Aldershot Command where, subsequently, he had changed certain of Sir John's tactical doctrines, including certain concepts concerning the use of cavalry. Offended, Sir John grew steadily cooler towards his former friend and came in time to think of him as an obstinate meddler. During the retreat from Mons, II Corps had made a stand at Le Cateau against the field marshal's instructions – Smith-Dorrien had in fact had no alternative – but this event was taken as a deliberate disregard of orders. From this time on, every mistake by II Corps, however trivial, was noted and often magnified by Sir John. Thus, though there was civility, there were no warm words exchanged when the commander-in-chief and II Corps commander parted after a meeting on the afternoon of 11th October.

II Corps was now concentrated round Bethune with 3rd Division on the left and the 5th on the right. Next morning, the 12th, they were to relieve the French holding the line ahead of them and, moving generally north east, advance about a mile or so beyond to the La Bassée road between Lorgies and Estaires. Contact with the French unit at Vermelles was to be maintained.

Doubtless, seen as a map operation, this task appeared simple; particularly in view of the belief that the enemy ahead were detachments of cavalry. Operations devised solely by use of a map are to be regarded with suspicion, however, especially when they have been conceived against a background of faulty intelligence. Even if he did not recognize this principle, Smith-Dorrien's apprehensions should have been roused by a number of other warnings.

On the 11th, a German wireless message concerning an attack from Lille

---

[3] First choice for the command of II Corps on mobilization had been Lt-General Sir James Grierson. However, he had died while travelling to the concentration area in France in August. Kitchener had selected Smith-Dorrien as his successor.

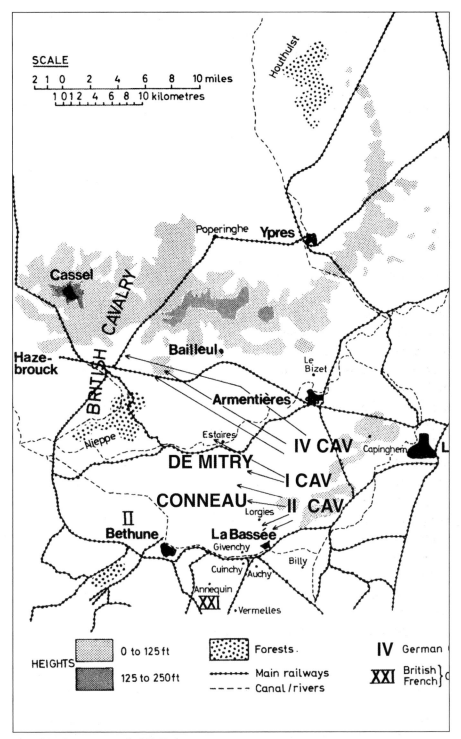

Ypres/La Bassée: arrival of II Corps

towards the Bethune area was intercepted. During that day, the French cavalry screening his advance reported an increase in German fire during the morning and that afternoon they were suddenly pushed back south of the La Bassèe canal. The posts of the French XXI Corps extended only to Vermelles village, and that night they lost Vermelles in a sharp attack. Smith-Dorrien knew all this. To protect the sensitive junction point with the French, he sent a battalion – 1st Norfolks – to dig in at Auchy, immediately south of the canal on the 11th and, later, his corps reserve, 13th Brigade, were positioned in the same area. During the night 11th/12th, a liaison officer brought news of a further loss by the cavalry but, in spite of the warnings, the advance next morning continued to take the form of a long extended line, somewhat like a beat of the enemy area: the only concession being that the direction was changed from north-east to east so as not to draw apart the forces on the critical right flank of the Corps.

The morning of 12th October was freezing and darkened by thick fog. As the British soldiers began their march, an added vexation was the need to search for the French to be relieved, who were rarely to be found at the rendezvous agreed the previous afternoon. Thankfully, the fog began to lift at 9am. The searching officers of the infantry and gunners were soon discovering the true positions of their allies, though here and there shots were exchanged between them as one or the other thought they had met the enemy. There was little stealth; most of the French soldiers were standing about in farmyards, talking and calling out to one another from around the blazing fires while a few sentries, pushed forward amongst the hedgerows, watched for signs of approach from the German lines. A proportion of the units relieved were French Territorial, infantry but the majority were cavalry and the British soldiers were intrigued to find them wearing multi-coloured jackets, sweeping cloaks, plumed helmets and, here and there, steel cuirasses. The popgun appearance of the cavalry carbines heightened an impression of comic opera.

The weather cleared completely about 11 o'clock. As the last wraiths of mist dispersed, the men of II Corps found themselves in a flat countryside of small enclosed fields amongst which wound muddy lanes connecting old, primitive farmsteads and huddled villages. Between pasture, orchard, spinney, the rich earth was intersected by numerous streams and drainage ditches. The water-table was at most two feet below the surface except where, rarely, a low ridge rose a few metres above the confined landscape. Much of the thick foliage of the summer months remained along the banks and hedgerows. Amongst the banks, behind the hedges, elevated in the lofts of the farms, the towers of churches, a mixed force of German jäger –

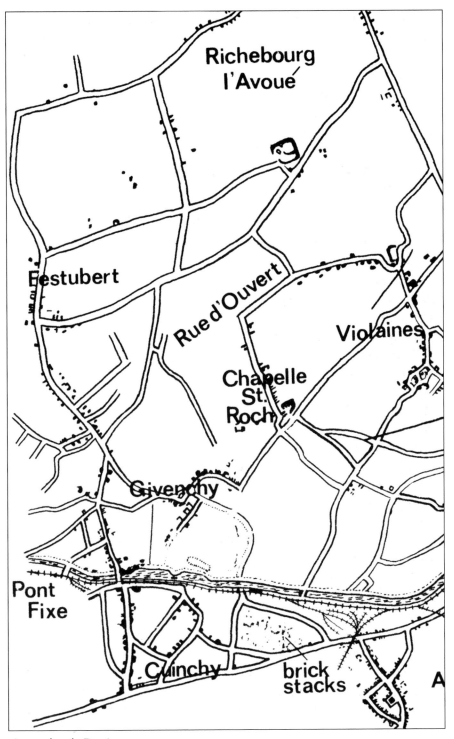

Approach to la Bassée

light infantry – and dismounted cavalry, backed by horse artillery waited for the British to advance.

> It is the C-in-C's intention to follow the enemy tomorrow (12th October) with a view to bringing him to action... The II Corps will advance to the line Estaires-Lorgies...

Sir Horace Smith-Dorrien's long thin line of infantry, connected here and there by divisional cavalry squadrons, advanced by fits and starts. By the evening of the 12th, the road between Estaires and Lorgies had not been reached – indeed, in many places, there had been no advance beyond the points taken over from the French – yet the casualty tally was surprisingly high. German snipers had been active throughout the day and the German horse artillery and medium howitzers in rear had repeatedly shelled the static positions of the British, many of whom were lying about in fields or along roads waiting to advance. There was no sense of urgency at the corps headquarters, none at either of the two divisional headquarters – 3rd and 5th – or at the five brigade headquarters along the line. The sixth, 13th Brigade, sent to the south of the La Bassèe canal to connect with the French, was committed equally to attack but did nothing, the brigade commander waiting to see what others were doing alongside before ordering forward his battalions. To the south, the French were similarly inactive but they had at least had a struggle for the possession of Vermelles village during the night. Immediately to the north, 1st Dorsets, attempting to make some sort of an advance in response to the general notification to attack during the afternoon, managed to stop the Germans from infiltrating along the canal.

The battalion had relieved French Territorials in the hamlet of Pont Fixe on the north side of the canal bank before the fog cleared. A Company was slipped south across the bridge and D kept on the near side. Both companies were to advance in parallel. This movement had actually begun when a message came from Brigade Headquarters – the battalion was in 15th Brigade – to say that an attack would be mounted along the entire line in concert with the French at 3pm that afternoon. At half past two there was no sign of any movement forward by 13th Brigade south of the canal and reports from the battalion observations posts told of small cumulative parties of German riflemen stealing forward. Several prisoners were taken.

The commanding officer, Lieutenant-Colonel L J Bols, decided that it would be wrong to wait for further orders. There was no danger that he would upset arrangements made in rear to support him and the units on either flank – not a scrap of artillery fire had been planned and he had no guns or gunner officers to shoot for him. He ordered D and A companies to advance.

Covered by a medium machine gun high up in the roof of a partly built factory, the advance continued. From time to time the machine-gunners fired at targets some way ahead, as they had been doing for several hours. They had an excellent view straight down the canal and along the railway track on its southern bank. Two thousand yards to the east, several railway lines joined forming a triangle whose western side – that is, nearest the Dorsets – was partially screened by a mass of stacked bricks, some of which had been scattered into broken heaps.

It was from amongst these that the German troops were clearly seen moving forward. The Maxim fired about 8,000 rounds in burst over a period of time. There was no blazing away; they were picking targets, tapping left and right on to others and changing elevation as they switched to the railway triangle from the brickstacks and back to the canal bank.

Unfortunately, the canal turned north east to La Bassée by the far side of the triangle and though they could see something of La Bassée town through field glasses they had neither the range nor sufficiently distinct targets to engage in that area.

After passing out of Pont Fixe and clearing half a dozen enemy outposts from scattered buildings on either side of the bank, the two rifle companies came out into open ground: D into a root field, A into stubble. At once they were heavily engaged by rifle fire from Cuinchy and machine-guns from the brickstacks. Some of the soldiers believed that they saw flashes from positions dug into the canal bank 800 yards ahead. No one stopped to argue; all dropped for cover, of which there was little, the wounded having to be dragged prone. The battalion second-in-command. Major R T Roper, was close by D Company and he hurried forward to see what was happening – only to be killed. The company commanders rallied their scattered platoons, some reaching a bank forward, some a culvert or a stone wall a little in rear. It was now evident to Colonel Bols that the French were not counter-attacking Vermelles, 13th Brigade had not advanced and the 1st Bedfordshire and Hertfordshire, immediately to the north, were still deploying in and around Givenchy which the French had held that morning. He had not seen his brigade commander, Brigadier-General Count Gleichen, whose headquarters was at Festubert, only 2½ miles distant along a good and covered road. It was dusk. Colonel Bols organized a defence to cover Pont Fixe. For an advance of 250 yards towards the enemy he had paid with eleven killed, two missing and thirty wounded.

At 7.30 pm that night, Sir John French's orders were issued for the 13th October, beginning with a paragraph of certifiable inaccuracy:

1. The French today were driven out of Vermelles (*it was the previous day*). The II Corps is attacking the enemy on the French left flank (*13th Brigade had remained on the defensive*).
2. It is the Commander-in-Chief's intention to continue the advance, passing the army to the north of Lille and driving the enemy before it.
3. Objective of II Corps will be the line Le Bizet (inclusive) Capinghem.

This order, again simple and straightforward, may not seem unreasonable. A glance at the map will show that it involved an advance of about 12 miles on a front of about seven, the incidental capture of the town of Annentières and, by implication, the masking of the corps' right flank towards La Bassée. Sir John did not think it too much to ask because he believed that the enemy ahead were scattered and withdrawing and because he was unaware that the advance ordered for the 12th had not been accomplished. He urged Smith-Dorrien to press on next day to take advantage of his ostensible superiority in numbers.

At 9.30 pm, Smith-Dorrien gave his orders for the 13th to his divisional commanders, Hubert Hamilton and Charles Fergusson. The long line should move on as before; the absence of a reserve of any weight being accepted. These orders filtered down through division to brigade to battalion level. The company commanders were awakened about 3 o'clock in the morning to hear their tasks while the cooks were roused to prepare breakfast before dawn.

In many of the battalions there was a feeling of frustration. They had come forward expecting to advance but nothing had happened. In eight of the battalions, the commanding officers decided individually that they must obtain details of the enemy against whom they expected to move on the 13th and thus a series of patrols went out between the evening meal and midnight on the 12th. All of these made contacts; the enemy reaction was violent at several points revealing occupation of particular buildings or areas. But some drew a useful blank, discovering empty key points. One of these was the Chapelle Saint Roch, a farm with many outbuildings (see map 4, page 49), a position of tactical importance on the front of 1st Cheshire, anticipating an advance through Rue d'Ouvert, immediately to the north. Major Vandcleur, commanding the Cheshires,[4] decided to put a half company into Chapelle Saint Roch under his second-in-command and he joined them forward in No-Man's-Land to reconnoitre the area over which he shortly expected to move. It was a bold policy whose only failing was that it was implemented too weakly; but this was as much a

[4] An officer of the Cameronians who had only just taken over command.

matter of misfortune as misjudgement. The Germans had also realized the importance of Chapelle Saint Roch and intended to occupy the area before dawn. While it was still night, they sent two companies to occupy not only the farm but many of the houses along the Rue d'Ouvert. When Vandeleur, Young and the half company arrived they were fired upon but managed to rush the farm, which was thinly held. As soon as the Cheshire platoons had taken up defensive positions, Vandeleur attempted to return to his headquarters only to discover they were surrounded. At first this did not seem too serious; B Company had been brought forward to support the occupation of the farm and were no

more than 400 yards away. They would surely either intervene or report back the news of the attack. In any case, a general advance was to be expected at dawn, when the brigade would be moving forward on either side of Saint Roch. Aware that their position was attracting increasing numbers of the enemy, Vandeleur and his party settled down to keeping them off until help came from outside.

None was coming.

Once again the battalions were ordered to advance in thin, extended lines against an enemy in strong defences and in process of being reinforced. There were no arrangements to concentrate artillery fire on any particular sector or enemy position and the British batteries, though eager to help the infantry, found few observation posts from which to support such a wide front of operations.

Disturbed by the movement towards La Bassée, the Germans had been reinforcing their positions on either side of the canal since the previous day – though the activities of 1st Dorsets had held them back for the most part. Their units in the line here came from the Guards Cavalry Division reinforced by a composite formation of cavalry, infantry and guns under Major-General Trotha. At half past six on the morning of the 13th, a German heavy howitzer battery in Billy, south of the canal, began to drop a mixture of 6-in shrapnel and high explosive into the area of 15th Brigade.

As instructed. Colonel Bols had begun to advance at 5.30, taking advantage of the mist. This temporary cover soon lifted but there was no sign of the sun; the sky was obscured by endless grey clouds. The Dorsets were now more than a mile beyond Pont Fixe with an expanse of open plough ahead. Although the Maxim – now in a house by the bridge – was once again supporting the advance and the battalion had a section of two 18-pounder field guns under command, the enemy's small arms and artillery fire was intensifying, there was again no sign of any advance by 13th brigade south of the canal and no sign of an advance on the Dorset's left, where the 1st Bedfords were holding Givenchy. But the lack of movement in the Bedford's area was not so surprising: a considerable number of enemy guns were concentrating on the village and the Dorsets could see and hear the flash and crackle of rifle fire amongst shell smoke and the clouds of dust from the shattered houses.

Just after 12 noon, it began to rain. The foremost of the Dorset's posts was 2,300 yards beyond Pont Fixe, and they had killed or captured more than eighty of the enemy. A German battery of 4-inch field howitzers, located in Auchy, appeared to have no target other than the Dorsets and Colonel Bols heard from all sides that enemy riflemen were continuing to reinforce Cuinchy and the canal bank from the brick stacks despite the fire of his two 18-pounders and machine-gun. At 1.30, there were signs of a great number of Germans moving forward into the east end of Givenchy village. In Givenchy, the Bedfords had had an unnerving morning. Numbers of men had been killed and wounded by walls and rooftops falling upon them as the high explosive of the heavy howitzers exploded. Despite this, they had fought off two attacks without falling back. Between 1pm and a quarter to 2pm, the shelling became heavier and at 2pm they were assaulted by two of General Trotha's battalions plus a number of dismounted cavalry squadrons. Two platoons at the eastern end of the village were completely overwhelmed while the remainder got back as best they could, carrying their weapons and ammunition but leaving most of their kit, including a large batch of mail from home. Covered in dust and plaster, they fell back to the road junction immediately to the west.

This withdrawal, though understandable, isolated the Dorsets more than ever. The Maxim had just been knocked out in an assault mounted from Cuinchy when the forward companies, B and C, saw a mass of enemy, some carrying lances, debouching from the east of Givenchy and as fire orders were given to the riflemen about 300 German infantry, at first thought to be French, advanced from the west end – that is, from the left rear of the Dorsets. Colonel Bols sent back word for A Company to take up a stop line at Pont Fixe while he attempted to extricate those in front. He shouted to the few officers and sergeants still unwounded and several of the sections began to move back, but they had barely reached the nearest buildings when the enemy were in amongst the Dorset's line. The commanding officer and his adjutant, both wounded, joined in the last desperate minutes of fire with rifles but were overwhelmed. Behind them, the artillery subaltern and the gunners of his section worked the 18-pounders until all were casualties.

At Chapelle Saint Roch, the beleaguered party of 1st Cheshire, of whom almost two-thirds were killed or wounded, surrendered at 9 p.m. when the farm began to catch fire.

'Altogether,' the brigade commander, Count Gleichen recollected, 'it was a damnable day, and we on the staff were pretty well exhausted by the amount of staff work and telegrams and messages going through all day.'

1st Cheshire had lost sixty-three, 1st Bedfords 117, and the Dorsets 399 of whom 148 were killed. Half a dozen of the Dorsets isolated and wounded managed to crawl painfully back one by one during the night, amongst them Colonel Bols.

LILLE IN SIGHT

It should not be thought that the formation commanders and staffs of II Corps were alone in their ineptitude. Those in or approaching the Flanders battle line in III, the Cavalry, IV or I Corps were lacking no less in professional expertise. The fact was that none had had adequate training for their duties in war and while many had a degree of experience of active service they either lacked the imagination or the confidence to draw upon it.[5]

For their experience was related solely to imperial campaigns in distant theatres against lesser foes. Over many decades, the British Army had fought these using the old formal manoeuvres of position warfare; and whilst the dressed lines of assault or squares of defence had occasionally triumphed, they had proved progressively to be unsuitable. The early events of the second Boer War led finally to their abandonment. When Roberts, a shrewd veteran of the Frontier, became commander-in-chief in South Africa he insisted on the tactics of open, mobile warfare. The new methods, which began to make use at last of the potential of the modern weapons and equipment in his force, enhanced the quiet confidence of the infantry, artillery and engineers. Yet when the war was over, numbers of senior commanders and staff officers expressed doubts as to whether broken formations, quick fire and movement would be effective against the precisely defined massed formations of a first rate force such as the German Army. In South Africa, the British had been fighting what was, largely, a guerilla war in open veldt, amongst bare mountains where they were quickly able to control the greater part of the communications. However deadly at times, it had been a minor campaign. War in Europe meant involvement in the major league. Neither the general officers commanding nor the general staff were warmongers in the first years of the twentieth century but they saw the prospect of war and could not but be impressed by the millions of men, and thousands of guns to be seen annually at the manoeuvres of the Continental Powers. Whilst those who wholeheartedly admired the German

[5] See, for example, *The Commander*, Gen. Sir Ian Hamilton, Hollis & Carter, 1957, pp. 46-7.

or French Armies were in a minority, there were numbers who tended to feel that their experience on the Frontier, the Nile or in South Africa counted for nothing in comparison with those of their contemporaries in France and Germany. Lamentably, they overlooked the fact that neither the French nor the German Army had any experience of war since 1870-71. The British had been fighting in one part of the world or another ever since that time in conditions where they had learned cumulatively that personal leadership by the commander was a prerequisite of success. Roberts had set an unforgettable example by commanding from the saddle in his major battles, seeing the ground personally whenever possible before his operations and using his presence to inspire the faint-hearted or check the foolhardy when the fighting had begun. Overawed by the magnitude of the forces and the arrogant confidence of the European general staffs, many of Roberts' pupils abandoned their priceless understanding of leadership in war to take up the very methods which were to lead France and Germany into a series of defeats. It was for this reason that the British Expeditionary Force had adverted, from the moment of its arrival in France, to a form of position of warfare, a retrograde step aggravated by a tendency of commanders to stay perpetually with their staffs.

Thus we see III Corps approaching the battle line from Hazebrouck. Its commander, Lieutenant-General W P Pulteney, had been instructed to move forward on 13th October to secure the Ypres-Annentières road between the villages of Wytschaete and Le Bizet. He was to do so in conjunction with Smith-Dorrien's corps, who were expected to take Annentières and Capinghem to the south, and the Cavalry Corps who were to complete the line northward between Pulteney and Rawlinson's corps forward of Ypres.

These orders were issued on the 12th, the day on which II Corps had sought to relieve the French in the morning fog. But the late morning and afternoon had been clear and had General Pulteney come forward to take advantage of the visibility he would have found two useful points of vantage in the villages of Pradelles and Strazeele from which to see in detail the country held by the enemy as far as Bailleul and, less distinctly but usefully, the panorama of high ground beyond. He would have found elements of 2nd Cavalry Brigade in the area and from the church tower of either village, he could have seen the 9th Lancers, supported by two 13-pounders of H Battery, driving German cavalry and light infantry out of Merris, the village lying in the low ground immediately to the east. Discussion with the cavalry would have revealed that elements of the Bavarian cavalry division had dug in immediately to the east of Merris behind the bank of the Meterenbecque, a thin stream running across the

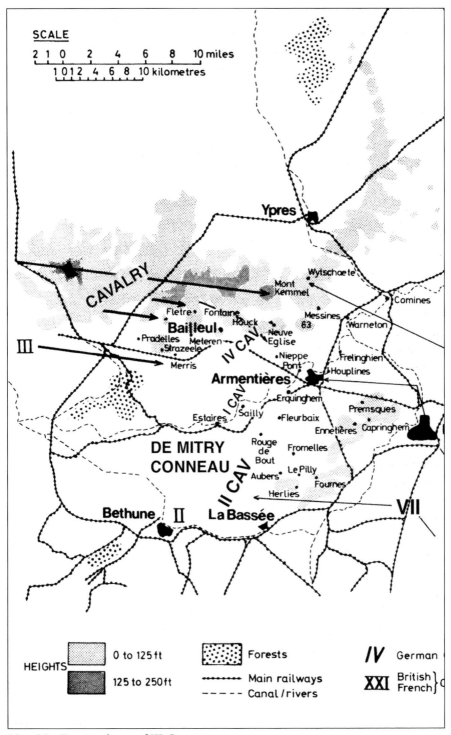

SCALE

2 1 0   2   4   6   8   10 miles

1 0 1 2   4   6   8   10 kilometres

Ypres

Wytschaete

Comines

CAVALRY

Mont Kemmel

Fletre• Fontaine

Houck

Messines

Warneton

Bailleul•

63

•Pradelles Meteren

Neuve

Frelinghien

•Strazeele

Eglise

IV CAV

Merris

•Nieppe
Pont

Houplines

Armentières

III

Erquinghem

I CAV

Premsques

Estaires Sailly

•Fleurbaix

DE MITRY

Rouge
de
Bout

Fromelles

Ennetières Capringhem

CONNEAU

Aubers

Le Pilly

II CAV

Fournes

Herlies

VII

Bethune

II

La Bassée

HEIGHTS ▢ 0 to 125 ft   ▩ Forests   *IV* German

▦ 125 to 250 ft   •••••• Main railways   **XXI** British }
French }

– – – – Canal/rivers

Ypres/ La Bassée: advance of III Corps

front. In this low ground the squadrons had found it impossible to get forward – mounted or dismounted – even when the guns came up to fire over open sights. But a glance to the north-east would have shown that the nearby spurs of the Mont des Cats offered prospects of outflanking the Meterenbecque by an attack from Flêtre to Fontaine Houck and Meteren.

Unfortunately, although he had eighteen hours in hand before the arrival of his corps, General Pulteney did not go forward in his motor-car the 20 miles to Strazeete or Pradelles. He was busily occupied much of the time in making arrangements for the move forward of his troops to Hazebrouck by bus, a task one might think better left to his staff, particularly as there was a tedious muddle resulting in a number of battalions waiting some 12 hours at Saint Omer railway station while their transport went elsewhere. He did not go forward and was obliged therefore to make a plan from his map. It was not a novel plan. He ordered his two divisions – 4th left, 6th right – each to put out a brigade as advanced guard which, without regard for contour or enemy positions, should extend into a long line to sweep the Bavarian cavalry and light infantry away.

The 6th Division were the first to advance. They were soon learning what the 9th Lancers could have related on the previous afternoon: the Meterenbecque was strongly held. The divisional artillery could not give assistance because it was again a foggy morning; a circumstance which might have helped the infantry in attack but for the obstacle of the stream which was marked to a metre by the enemy's rifles and machine-guns. On the left, 10th Brigade were the advanced guard for 4th Division. The brigade commander had only two of his four battalions at 7 am, the hour at which he had been ordered to move; the missing element being amongst those whose transport had gone astray. At 9.45, he decided that he could wait no longer and set off as he was, soon coming up to the village of Flêtre, held by the cavalry, chafing to be relieved to join the remainder of the Cavalry Corps advancing immediately to the north. Brigadier-General Haldane of 10th Brigade had been given no information about the enemy up to that point but he now learnt that there were Germans in Meteren village, whose church tower could be seen from time to time through the mist, and on the intermediate spur between Meteren and Flêtre. 1st Royal Warwicks shook out quickly and began to push forward with a smart combination of fire and fieldcraft.

It was now about 11.50. A light rain was falling: the mist hung in the still air with the smell of damp pave and wet earth. The continuous crack and thump of the bullets was muffled only by the rush and explosion of German shells. General Haldane had ordered his artillery – 88th Battery – to come into action at Fletre when Major-General de Lisle, commander of the 1st

Cavalry Division, drove up in a motor-car. He had come to tell Haldane that one of his brigades was about to attack Fontaine Houck, an arrangement which suited 10th Brigade commander very well. Haldane promised that he would press on to Meteren. By 1 o'clock, the Warwicks had cleared the intermediate spur, captured a Bavarian *jäger*, and were sitting comfortably in farm buildings at the head of the Meterenbecque. Two companies were now working forward on either side of the road into the western end of Meteren, despite the enemy machine-guns sited in the lofts of several houses. At this point, the commander of the 4th Division appeared.

It appeared that the corps commander was worried by an aeroplane report that 500 enemy had moved into Meteren from Bailleul at 9 a.m. that morning. Combined with the news that 6th Division were held up on the Meterenbecque, he was convinced that the Germans were in such strength that he must mount a corps attack. None of Haldane's information concerning the success of the Warwicks could dissuade the divisional commander from halting and withdrawing that battalion, pushing 10th Brigade to the left to attack Fontaine Houck, where the cavalry were in difficulty, and replacing Haldane's brigade opposite Meteren with the 12th.

The high hopes and spirits of the morning evaporated. Haldane walked forward to the Warwicks' headquarters, and the battalion's adjutant was sent forward from there to stop the troops who were already entering Meteren. On the point of evacuation, the Germans quickly discovered that they were no longer under pressure and began to reoccupy their positions, from which they fired heavily at the withdrawing Warwicks' companies. Casualties, of which there had been only eleven during the swift movement of infiltration, had reached 246 by the time the battalion had withdrawn to hand over to another from 12th Brigade. The attack, which the corps commander had hoped might begin at 1 pm., and the divisional staffs had put back to 1.30, was postponed until 2 pm, but did not in fact go in until 3.15 pm. The battalions could not move as quickly as the staff could write orders. It was dark and raining heavily before Meteren was taken – the Germans had abandoned it some time before – and the capture of Fontaine Houck was similarly delayed when the 2nd Royal Dublin Fusiliers were diverted on a wild goose chase by a message of alarm from the cavalry. One of the soldiers in 10th Brigade remarked that the 13th, as a day of ill-omen, had shed its full load of bad luck on them.

If the 13th had been a bad day for II and III Corps, it had not been wholly so for the Cavalry. Major-General Hubert Cough's 2nd Cavalry Division had been encroaching fast in a series of lively operations along the high ground running into Belgium. The task was well-suited to Cough's quick brain and bold heart. Five of his regiments were hardly out of the saddle all day except for dismounted attacks amongst houses. The light guns of his horse artillery batteries were dragged up and down the slopes of the main ridge and spurs round Mont Noir, whose central height was secured by dusk. In the wet, dark night Cough sent patrols on to Mont Kemmel and, skirting Bailleul on the north, two troops of de Lisle's division reconnoitred the long spur of Neuve Eglise. It was this action, more than anything else, that caused the commander of the German IV Cavalry Corps, Lieutenant-General von Hollen, to withdraw hurriedly from Bailleul; and he was wise to do so. The main road back to Annentières was in danger of being cut by the energetic thrusts of the British Cavalry. Carrying over 500 wounded in carts or the saddle, the German 3rd Cavalry Division and several units of Bavarian infantry inarched east in the rain, leaving eighty-five of their comrades too seriously hurt to be moved in the care of two medical officers and a few orderlies. This little group waited apprehensively for the dawn and the arrival of the British.

They over-estimated General Pulteney. Not even the most ardent of his admirers could fairly describe him as a bold commander. When the dawn light showed another day of heavy grey clouds, his battalions and batteries were ready to march. No order came. During the night, Sir John had had a request for help from Smith-Dorrien to recover from the loss of Givenchy and counter the rising pressure from La Bassée. He asked specifically for a division from III Corps. Sensibly, Pulteney pointed out that he was more likely to relieve II Corps' difficulties by continuing on his present line of advance – that is, round to the north of Lille – than by committing a division to an unfamiliar area. But these representations and their consideration were made slowly. Though the delay was in part due to the inhibiting influence of the cautious Murray, Sir John's chief of staff, Pulteney might have resolved the matter in an hour by jumping into a motor car and driving to Saint Omer. Since jumping into motor cars was not in his nature, however, it was well into the afternoon before a soldier of III Corps set off on the two miles from Meteren to Bailleul and almost dark when 4th Division linked up with the cavalry north east of the town, half way along the Neuve Eglise spur.

In fact, the Cavalry Corps were considerably further forward than this. During the day, they had cleared through Mont Kemmel to establish a firm link with the right flank of IV Corps in Wytschaete. Neuve Eglise was occupied by the 11th and 18th Hussars and C Squadron of the latter, under Captain Thackwell, had ridden on to Hill 63 and Ploegsteert. That night, while the commanding officers of III Corps were ordered to improve their defences in preference to patrolling, the cavalry were active once more. Lieutenant Gore-Langton of the 18th Hussars rode south with half a troop to Nieppe, mid-way between Bailleul and Armentières. It was empty. About a mile towards Armentières moving lights were seen and they rode on to Pont de Nieppe, where the road bridge crosses the river Lys. There were flares everywhere, illuminating the lines of marching troops coming in from the north and turning east to Armentières. Halting, Gore-Langton sent one of his troopers to see which unit was passing.

'Are you infantry?' asked the soldier, approaching a man watching from beside a street barricade of earth and stones.

'Eh?' The man turned and peered at him in the gloom. Then, '*Englander!*' he shouted. Each recognised the other's mistake simultaneously but the British soldier was quicker to act. He thrust his rifle forward as he pushed off the safety catch, fired and ran for his horse. Pursued by bullets and then an enemy detachment, the cavalry patrol galloped back through Nieppe at full tilt and two miles on towards Bailleul until they reached the byroad north to Neuve Eglise. Quite apart from this being the sort of adventure of which cavalry subalterns dream, th substance of their report was that the road to and through Nieppe was empty and the Germans were withdrawing across the Pont de Nieppe into Armentières. With the cavalry at Wytschaete and on Hill 63 by Ploegsteert, it seemed that the enemy were again pulling back to avoid being cut off by a turning movement coming in from the north.

Next day was 15th October. Notwithstanding the report by Gore–Langton and an aeroplane reconnaissance at 9.30 am, which saw a huge column withdrawing from Armentières towards Lille, the troops of III Corps stood fast once more. Allenby had orders for the Cavalry Corps to reconnoitre the river Lys ahead from Menin to Estaires, an instruction which caused this vigorous general to raise his eyebrows; for the Lys runs for about 60 miles between the points given. Though his squadrons were for the most part stronger than those of the French cavalry – who were hard put to it to muster fifty men each – very few had more than seventy-eighty officers and other ranks. They were better equipped than the French, having the short magazine Lee-Enfield used by the infantry as distinct from the ineffectual carbine carried by French and German troopers alike, but as with all cavalry, his support consisted of light horse artillery. The 13-pounder had only shrapnel to fire when what he needed was weight of high explosive. Sending a liaison officer to the French cavalry corps commander, Conneau, to ask what he would undertake by way of reconnaissance to the Lys forward of Estaires, Allenby made arrangements to operate initially between Menin and

Armentières so as to have sufficient troops to search out the close country thoroughly and to keep a reserve to seize important ground on an opportunity basis. His methods were shrewdly professional.

The leading squadrons began to ride down from the ridge through Messines in a drizzling rain about 7 am. It was an odd morning, foggy as usual on the low ground, with little definable opposition but marked by the mortal aggravation of irregular periods of sniping, bullets flying suddenly in between patches of mist to strike down one or another of the horsemen.

To the south, Conneau was already in Estaires and had sent a regiment north to secure the bridge at Sailly-sur-la-Lys. But the regiment, 190 strong, meet a hail of fire from German Chevautegers in occupation and retired somewhat uncertainly. This was regrettable because the Chevaulegers were almost without ammunition and for this reason they abandoned the bridge at noon and withdrew 12 kilometres. This was the limit of Conneau's activity during the day and so the dispersed enemy detachments along the river line between Armentières and Estaires had a morning and afternoon without incident, which they appreciated as they were making ready for the most part to withdraw.

At midday, Sir John French met Pulteney and Allenby at III Corps headquarters. Allenby made it clear that he could not undertake the reconnaissance of the Lys from Menin to Estaires simultaneously. He had not had a reply to his message to Conneau – and none had heard of the abortive attack on the Chevaulegers at Sailly – but his own information from such patrols as that of Gore-Langton's and the information from the Royal Flying Corps suggested that the enemy were withdrawing, if they had not already gone, from the Lys above Armentières. Disappointed by the slow rate of progress towards Lille and ever ready to be fired by a strong speaker. Sir John at once modified his plan for the Cavalry Corps and indeed the British Expeditionary Force as a whole as will be seen from the text of the written confirmatory order issued by Murray at 1.40pm that afternoon.

OA 500

1. It is the intention of the C-in-C to advance eastwards, attacking the enemy wherever met.

2. The Cavalry Corps will establish itself on the right bank of the river Lys between Menin and Armentières and then move in an easterly direction, eventually covering the left flank of the advance. The in Corps will closely support the movement, its right moving through Sailly on Fleurbaix, the general direction after crossing the Lys being astride that river and downstream.

The II Corps will push forward drawing towards the in Corps as opportunity offers. If the II Corps draws to the N E the French will extend their left flank to keep in touch. The IV Corps, covered by its 3rd Cavalry Division on its left flank, will move between Courtrai (6 miles E N E of Menin) and Routers, the cavalry being north of Roulers. This corps will not move much in advance of the left of in Corps and it will also observe towards the N E for the advance of the enemy against the Belgian Army.

3. Reports to Saint Omer.

The grand turning movement north of Lille was about to begin. III Corps should clear their own way to and across the Lys south of Armentieres while the Cavalry Corps cleared the ground north of it. These preliminaries would permit III Corps to commence a right wheel abreast of Armentières for a direct advance eastward, leaving Lille on their right. IV and the Cavalry Corps should act as the left flank guard white n Corps fought their way forward to act in the same capacity on the right. It is possible that Sir John hoped that an opportunity would arise for Allenby to break out between Menin and Turcoing. He had certainly had high hopes in his conversation with Foch a few days recently, after which the latter had written to Joffre, 'The marshal (Sir John) wishes at all costs to go to Brussels. I shall not hold him back. I shall help him to the best of my powers.'

The letter referred to the plan jointly agreed between Foch and Sir John that was issued on the 12th. It provided for a major attack by de Maud'huy's Tenth Army so as to free, *inter alia*, Smith-Dorrien's corps from the pressure round La Bassée. It did not succeed in doing this, hence the reverses on either side of the canal. Yet on the 15th, without the division asked for from III Corps, Smith-Dorrien's battalions returned to the assault, mostly with plans of their own devising; their comrades of the field artillery now up amongst them in the foremost line, when they fired the guns over open sights into the German strong points. These tactics led to the recapture of Givenchy and a subsequent advance to the edge of La Bassee and on to the ridge overlooking Lille.

III Corps issued orders at 2.45pm that afternoon to 4th and 6th Divisions to secure four bridges over the Lys: Pont de Nieppe and the bridge at Erquinghem to be taken by the 4th; Bac Saint Maur and, hard by, the bridge at Sailly by the 6th. 1st Hampshires were detailed for Pont de Nieppe but inevitably the orders had taken some time to pass through division and brigade. They were briefed at 6 pm and set off in darkness. Nieppe was of course empty but when B Company closed up towards the bridge through the scattered houses of Pont de Nieppe, an unseen machine-gun fired at them, causing a dozen casualties; and though the leading platoon commander was not hit, he had the mortifying experience of diving into a cesspit to take cover. He crawled out and forward to discover that the bridge was barricaded and shortly four machine-guns were identified in enfilade from the far bank. While the Hampshires were considering how to tackle this target, they were surprised to receive a message from brigade headquarters to stand fast and make no attempt to cross.

The reason for this order was the weather. It was again foggy with occasional rain. General Pulteney had decided that the weather was unfavourable for a night advance and given orders to postpone attempts to cross. But he was too late to hold back his ardent soldiers who had been chafing to move throughout the afternoon. 1st Somerset Light Infantry had received their orders to capture the Erquinghem bridge when they were in the act of marching back to Bailleul at dusk to billets. At 11 pm they set off supported by 1st Battalion the Rifle Brigade and 7th Field Company, Royal Engineers. At 2 am they reached the bridge and made a reconnaissance. It was abandoned, though surrounded by trenches with overhead cover. Just as the battalion prepared to cross, a staff officer from 11th Brigade brought the corps order and they were withdrawn 600 yards. The brigade staffs in the 6th Division were not quite so quick: at Bac Saint Maur the swing bridge was open but intact and held by forty German cavalrymen. While the British infantry kept them under deliberate fire, sappers of 12th Field Company made a raft, floated across the river and swung the bridge into place. Within minutes the village was occupied. At Sailly, a mile upstream, the vanguard of 18th Brigade found the bridge timbers damaged and a chain of empty enemy defences illuminated by the blazing houses, fired by the Germans in the moment of departure. Here, too, the infantry crossed before they could be stopped and 38th Field Company set to work in repair.

As if regretting his temerity in encroaching on the enemy, Pulteney kept much of his corps static during the next two days, 16th and 17th October. He did not exploit his two bridgeheads across the Lys until ordered to do so by GHQ, when an advance of 3,000 yards was made without encountering any resistance. On the initiative of Brigadier-General Hunter-Weston, the local brigade commander, 1st Somerset Light Infantry were permitted to cross at Erquinghem at midday the same empty bridge that had awaited them the previous night. At Pont de Nieppe that afternoon, Hunter-Weston brought up an 18-pounder to help the Hampshires and, the first round striking the barricade, the defenders fled.

But A and D Companies in pursuit were stopped on the western edge of Armentières. Despite the manifest absence of an enemy to impede him, Pulteney had decided that the 4th Division should not cross the Lys until the 6th had cleared the far bank.

On the 17th, no possible excuse could delay further the occupation of Armentières; the populace sent messengers out to say that the Germans had gone. As it happened, there were still one or two small parties to offer resistance – a dozen men in all who had become lost during relief – but these did not mar an entry which was '...in the nature of a triumphal procession and we were loaded up with gifts of eats and smokes by the excited populace.' One battalion of the 4th Division was still acknowledging the cheers of welcome as far as Houplines in the north of the town before a volley of rifle shots from Frélinghien caused military and civil to take cover, but immediately south and south west the only contact during the entire day was with two patrols of Germans, sent forward from the low ridge which covered the approach to Lille. From Armentières to Bois Grenier, Pulteney's line ran to Rouge de Bout, occupied by him on the previous day. 5,000 yards south-east, Conneau's cavalry were attacking Fromelles with the 2nd Royal Irish Regiment on the extreme left of II Corps. This operation – and indeed the operations of all the 3rd Division on Smith-Dorrien's left -must have been facilitated if Pulteney had brought the right of his own 6th Division up into line with them. If his riflemen had protected their flank; if his gunners, who had no targets, had been brought up to support II Corps, the situation must have been improved. For even without this aid, Fromelles was taken with fifty prisoners and eleven dead in the village.

Whatever Pulteney had felt about the ridge during the day of the 17th, the news he received that evening made him aware of its importance. The German stragglers who had been rounded up in Armentières had confessed to belonging to the XIII and XIX Corps of Crown Prince Rupprecht's Sixth Army. Their units had been relieving the cavalry in the town when evacuation had been ordered and they had been left behind. The men from XIX Corps believed that the main body were occupying the ridge west of Lille, where trenches were to be dug. These stories were confirmed by much of what the prisoners taken at Fromelles recounted except that they were all from VII Corps; and the reconnaissances of the Royal Flying Corps made during the few hours of clear weather in the early afternoon noted the movement forward of infantry towards La Bassée and Fournes, and from Lille towards Armentières.

In these circumstances, Pulteney realized that he could not consider a movement down the bank of the Lys with 6th Division; he would be passing his right flank straight across the front of an enemy on higher ground. They would have a grand view and a grand shoot. Telling the 4th Division to force the crossing at Frélinghien he instructed the 6th to capture[6] the northern end of the ridge, that is, the high ground on either side of the road from Armentières to Lille. He made no attempt to co-ordinate his operations with Smith-Dorrien, and the left-hand battalions of II Corps were unaware that the right of III was, at 9.15 that morning, less than a mile from them at Bacquart.

At 10 am, the 2nd Leinsters fought their way into the village of Premesques and saw the great spread of the city of Lille 6,000 yards to the east. Singly and in pairs, the remaining six assault battalions pushed their way forward through fortified villages between noon and nightfall with a mixture of shell and rifle and machine-gun fire, of stealth and cunning and audacity, until all had got a hold in some degree on the western slope. They were now in contact with Conneau's cavalry and the line of trenches they dug was thus an extension of those held by II Corps. Though unable to communicate with one another, the commanding officers of the battalions on the ridge in both corps were aware that they had reached an enemy line more closely packed with troops, and troops who were better armed than those they had fought hitherto.

The 18th was, therefore, a disquieting day. From the canal bridge by the brickstacks and the railway triangle to the trenches on Aubers Ridge the units of II Corps felt instinctively that resistance was hardening; and the same impression continued through II Corps and found no dissent in the Cavalry beyond. Outside Ypres, facing down the road to Menin, Rawlinson's corps was aware of a new liveliness amongst the enemy on the right of the road, and heard from the French on their left that the Belgian line, which ran to the sea, was under heavy bombardment.

FRENCH AND FOCH

Alone of the senior British commanders. Sir John French remained optimistic on the evening of the 18th; and this is remarkable since his spirits tended to fall quickly with the receipt of bad news. That night, his headquarters staff were aware that the Cavalry Corps had not progressed during the day; that III and II Corps had similarly come up against strong infantry defences; and that in addition to the identification of von Beseler's corps between the coast and Routers, and the three of Sixth Army discovered between Menin and La Bassée – XIII, XIX and VII – the Royal

---

[6] Originally conditional, this order was confirmed before noon. See III Corps G.229 of 17th October.

Flying Corps had seen other large columns approaching the line towards Thourout and Roulers from the east and south-east.

Sir John dismissed these tidings as insignificant. Both II and III Corps' commanders had told him on previous occasions that they were held up by 'stiff opposition', only to advance again within a day or so. They had, after all, made a lodgement on the ridge overlooking Lille and thereby procured a considerable tactical advantage. The French XXI Corps had at last succeeded in fulfilling its promise to put a battalion north of the La Bassée canal and five more were earmarked to join it. Smith-Dorrien should be able to close up to Pulteney's right flank and permit the withdrawal of Conneau's weak cavalry force altogether. The news that Allenby's corps was still in the trenches scrapped the previous day did not surprise Sir John; the lightness of their armament was well known to him but he anticipated an easement of their difficulties on the Lys once Rawlinson pushed the 7th Division into Menin.

> ...IV Corps will move on Menin covered on its left by the cavalry division of that corps.
>
> Four French cavalry divisions (under de Mitry) have been ordered to move from Ypres on Roulers and will keep in touch with the cavalry division of IV Corps...

Rawlinson had obediently moved his 7th Division towards Menin, advancing it 4,000 yards during the early morning against the token resistance of several enemy standing patrols which withdrew before they had fired a dozen rounds. A few minutes before midday, a liaison officer arrived at Rawlinson's headquarters from GHQ to see what progress had been made, and when he heard that 7th Division had completed their advance for the day and were now digging trenches, he expressed astonishment. General Rawlinson was told that the commander-in-chief expected him to occupy Menin. An argument began in the operations office of the headquarters at Poperinghe which transferred itself through to the chief of staff and then to Rawlinson himself. It was pointed out to the liaison officer – and subsequently to GHQ – that the wording of the instruction was 'move on Menin' in an order containing the explicit term 'attack' to describe the requirement of II Corps. The riposte of GHQ was that they had ordered IV Corps to 'move on Ypres' on the 14th and he had obediently occupied the town on the same day. But while the argument was continuing and expanding, Murray sent a second and unmistakable order at 1.45 pm that IV Corps should advance into Menin at once.

By the time this arrived and had been decoded, it was well on into an autumn afternoon. Rawlinson demurred that it was too late to do anything that day but promised to send 7th Division off early next morning.

It was Sir John's impression that Rawlinson was overawed by the reports of German reinforcements which had been passed freely by airmen and refugees. It was his positive suspicion that Rawlinson's failure to order 7th Division into Menin was a matter of equivocation, and this suspicion was heightened when IV Corps' evening summary of operations admitted that the infantry had hardly been challenged that day, while the account from 3rd Cavalry Division told of the enemy 'melting away to the north' after earlier clashes with Uhlans.[7]

Aside therefore from the approaching enemy columns, whose size and portent he discounted. Sir John felt that the strategy he had agreed with Foch on 10th October was progressing, even if the pace was slower than he had expected. The withdrawal to the north of the enemy opposite 3rd Cavalry Division and de Mitry's cavalry corps – identified through prisoners they had captured as units of von Beseler's – meant that the main flank of the German Army was somewhere between Menin and Comines. If Menin was seized, the flank would be masked, the British Expeditionary Force might at last march for Courtrai and open country. His bargain with Foch would be kept.

Sir John was happily unaware that he was to an extent a tool of Foch's. Expressed thus, there is an imputation of cynical deceit to the French northern army group commander which should at once be disregarded. The truth is that Foch was obliged to use indirect methods because he lacked the authority to do otherwise.

His function as a commander extended only to French forces, of which the number in Flanders at that time was small. Yet Joffre expected and he himself wished to see the British and Belgian forces incorporated in a single strategy. The Belgian commanders, particularly the King, needed no urging to co-operate, at least in so far as the organization of defence was concerned. They needed no reminding that they held the last fragment of their soil. If that was abandoned, it might be forever.

Securing the co-operation of the British posed a different problem. The British soldiers were not fighting in their own land; they insisted on maintaining their independence. Their commander-in-chief was personally a brave man and often a generous one but limited in intelligence and excitable in temperament. He agreed frequently to participate in French plans because Foch brought a lively, bustling optimism into Sir John's headquarters. He reassured Sir John. He spoke and wrote to him with a tact whose subtlety was refined by the tips concerning Sir John's state of mind passed to him by

[7] German light cavalry, used mainly as scouts or skirmishers.

Henry Wilson, the francophile deputy chief of staff at GHQ.

Whether Foch cared for using this method is uncertain. Whether he liked it or not, he was prepared to make any sacrifice to defeat Germany. A man of passionate and profound courage, he believed that the allies' only hope of victory lay in fighting, fighting, fighting their dangerous, aggressive foe. It was said of Foch that he knew only one phase of war: attack. Whilst this was true of the earlier period of his professional life his experiences on the frontiers in August and along the marshes of Saint Gond during September had taught him other lessons. He had gone to war for the first time as a corps commander and had expected his colleagues to command in the same determined, offensive spirit that he used himself. To his astonishment and disappointment, he had discovered within the first week of war that many of them lacked the mettle to pursue the theories they had so often discussed in mutual sympathy as students and teachers at L'Ecote de Guerre. Corps were routed, their divisions streamed to the rear. By the first week in September, Foch was learning under fire as an army commander that difficult operation of war, holding a defence line with men exhausted by terror and fatigue. He had begun to see that attack was not the only option in battle, though he remained convinced that it was the only one which counted. He learned therefore to speak often of attack, to remind subordinates and colleagues that the enemy were as tired as they and perhaps weaker; and he meant what he said. But his new experience prompted him to make ready for defence when this was the only means remaining to fight the enemy. As the German opposition grew stronger on 14th and 15th October against his XXI Corps and on Smith-Dorrien's front, he wrote to advise a downcast Sir John to site a defence line immediately in rear. Fresh from advising the Belgians that they should be ready as soon as possible to join an allied attack, he wrote on 16th October to Admiral Ronarc'h at Dixmude:

> Under the present circumstances, any idea of manoeuvring [your brigade] is out of the question and your tactics must be confined purely and simply to resisting on your actual position... Your mission is to stop the enemy in his tracks... Nothing short of a formal order from your superiors or the capture of the whole of your position by the enemy will justify you in evacuating your position...

He was willing to back any movement of offence to the limit but had learned, too, the wisdom of laying off.

CHAPTER FOUR

The End of October

The skies they were ashy and sober ...
The leaves they were withering and sere;
It was night in the lonesome October
Of my most immemorial year.'

ULALUME, E A POE

THE BEGINNING OF THE WEEK:
18TH-20TH OCTOBER

It would be interesting to know what thoughts of the Flanders battle were in Falkenhayn's mind as he shaved on the morning of Monday, 19th October. Since the fall of Antwerp ten days before, much had been accomplished in preparation for the thrust to secure Calais.

The new Sixth Army under Crown Prince Rupprecht of Bavaria had begun to relieve the cavalry on 13th October. VII Corps had come from the Aisne heights where, in September, it had opposed the British Expeditionary Force as it opposed Smith-Dorrien and Pulteney now between the La Bassée canal and Armentières. XIX Corps had come from the Champagne, arriving opportunely to capture Lille before marching to the banks of the Lys between Armentières and Warneton. Its battalions prevented Allenby from crossing the river. XIII Corps[1] had marched north east from the Argonne to railway stations along the Meuse. A mixture of passenger coaches and goods wagons – French, Belgian and German – had carried them north through the Ardennes to Flanders. Its two divisions extended the line through Comines towards Menin.

[1] Composed originally of the 26th and 27th Divisions, the latter was left in the Argonne and replaced in the corps by 25th Reserve Division.

Von Beseter meantime had swept across northern Belgium, firing villages suspected of harbouring spies, driving before him a growing host of refugees.

Old men and women ran breathless; children trotted by their mothers' sides; some had all their possessions in carts drawn by ponies or dogs; others were pushing wheelbarrows loaded with all the goods they could carry away. All had a look of terror in their eyes...

Too late to capture the Belgian Army, the task of the three German divisions[2] released from Antwerp was to screen the advance of the unfledged corps arriving from the Reich and to seize bridges to convey them across the river Yser when the offensive began. But aircraft reports sent in on the afternoon of the 14th showed that British and Belgian troops were massed round all the crossing places and lines of trenches had been identified along the western bank.

While agreeing that von Beseler should test out the strength of the French marine brigade in Dixmude on the 16th, Falkenhayn gave orders that his entire line in Flanders should remain defensive from 15th October, preserving above all its integrity as a screen. Already, by that date, the four new corps[3] – XXII, XXIII, XXVI and XXVII – had arrived at Brussels by rail. Passing through the city, they alighted at a number of country stations immediately to the west, from which the infantry at once set out along the excellent main roads, followed soon by guns and wagons when these had been unloaded with the draught horses from the sidings.

By the 18th, all four were forward of the main road from Courtrai to Bruges, one corps having reached Thourout. Von Beseler's screen was drawn in to the north – the British 3rd Cavalry Division had correctly reported them to be 'melting away' in that direction – and the last adjustments were made before the offensive began. Of these, the most important was the return of much of the cavalry to the line. Falkenhayn was assured that the Lys between Warneton and Menin was threatened only by British cavalry – Allenby's Corps – and he agreed with Crown Prince Rupprecht that their own would oppose it adequately. This permitted the withdrawal of XIII Corps from that area and their reallocation to a sensitive sector already under some pressure: the low ridge overlooking Lille. In pouring rain, on the night of the 18th, in darkness lit only by the flash of gun or burst of shell, the two divisions of XIII Corps

2 5th Reserve, 6th Reserve and 4th *Ersatz* Divisions. The Marine Division was placed on coast defence duty.
3 XXTV and XXV Reserve Corps were not sent forward to join Fourth Army. XXIV Reserve was committed to the Metz sector but lost one of its divisions, 48th Reserve, to Flanders in late October. XXV Reserve was sent to the Eastern Front against Russia. The 6th Bavarian Reserve Division, formed in September, remained in Bavaria until 21st October, when it was sent forward to Lille for the Ypres battle.

marched back from the Lys along roads crowded with the supply wagons of the cavalry. Tired and wet, they reached their billets in Lille in the early hours of the morning and were soon asleep.

On the Monday morning. Fourth Army began to close up in readiness for the opening of the offensive.

On the Channel coast, von Beseler had already committed 4th Ersatz Division to seizing the Belgians' posts immediately east of the Yser and the giant siege guns brought from Antwerp had assisted this work. Throughout Monday, the monstrous shells from these crashed into the tiles and brick of the hamlets in which the Belgian battalions were concealed and by the afternoon the whole of III Corps and XXII Corps were fighting for their possession. The French sailors in Dixmude made a sortie, supported by a Belgian regiment, to recapture two of the foremost strong points but there were fears that they would be isolated. At nightfall they withdrew, leaving only two positions east of the river: the outskirts of Nieuport and the town of Dixmude. At once the siege artillery began to pound the defences on the far bank and the routes leading forward to them. During the night, heavy mortars were brought up to add to the work of destruction. The Belgian army could not doubt that they were about to be heavily attacked.

Further south, the process of closing up had been less completely accomplished: a day of skirmishing for the most part which intensified towards the evening. This was due to the fact that Rawlinson's divisions and the French cavalry on their left had only general information as to the movements of the columns approaching their front, while Duke Albrecht was misted into believing that an order captured from a prisoner gave him the detailed dispositions facing him – they had, in fact, changed as the British IV Corps deployed to advance. The contacts made, the clashes of increasing violence were not therefore those between Rawlinson's infantry advancing to capture Menin and the German cavalry holding it but between Rawlinson's and de Mitry's cavalry and the German infantry of the new corps.

Early on the Monday morning, six divisions were advancing across the Menin-Thourout road towards the British and French. Each division marched as a column, regiments in formation one behind another on the roads, carrying full packs, ammunition, water, a midday meal of a quarter of a loaf of bread and a piece of cheese or sausage besides rifle and bayonet. The divisional artillery, drawn by horses, marched behind the leading brigade. Ahead, the corps cavalry detachments advanced in small parties on a wider front, galloping forward across open ground to the shelter of hamlet or wood which was at once searched. Immediately behind the cavalry marched companies of jäger, stripped of their packs and ready to give quick support to the horsemen in their reconnaissance.

The 45th Reserve Division had spent the night in billets at Lichtervelde, the 46th at Ardoye. These two were therefore closest to the road between Routers and Thourout and within 30 minutes the columns of the 46th had stopped as word came back from a cavalry scout that there were enemy ahead. About 10 minutes later the 45th stopped similarly, the scouts' news being amplified by shells from French 75s landing near the leading battalion. At once, in both divisions there was a bustle. This was the first action for the ardent young men in the ranks. The elderly senior regimental officers, warrant officers and sergeants were anxious to set an example of soldierly skill and calm in this testing moment. All troops were moved off the road into whatever cover could be found, reconnaissance parties were sent forward from the leading regiment and the divisional artillery dispersed by batteries into firing positions.

Waiting ensued. The alertness of all, born of expectation of an immediate clash with the enemy, began to deteriorate. Within an hour, men were chatting naturally again in low tones, though conversation was apt to die away when rifle and machine-gun shots were heard ahead. Sometimes shells burst at a distance but none came so close as those at the beginning of the halt. Two hours were spent in this way and then, abruptly, orders were given to resume the march.

There were several halts of this sort. It became known that the cavalry and jäger were opposed by French troops but none of these had been seen by the infantry regiments or indeed any of the divisional columns. Bread and cheese and sausage were eaten during an enforced halt at noon. Those men who were distant from barns or houses were wet and cold in the gusting wind and occasional showers. But exercise was soon to warm them. The company commanders came hastening back from a conference, orders were given to move off to the right or left of the road in column of companies; and the guns began to range over the low horizon. At 1pm, two regiments of the 45th Reserve Division began to attack Cortemarck as two brigades of the 46th advanced on the low ridge of Hooghe[4] and the village of Hooghlede above.

The companies of 46th Division advanced in line over stubble and thin grass. The men were densely packed in the ranks. There were constant cries from the officers and senior non-commissioned officers to check the dressing; but dressing was difficult to keep when there were successive

[4] Not to be confused with Hooge, immediately nest of Ypres.

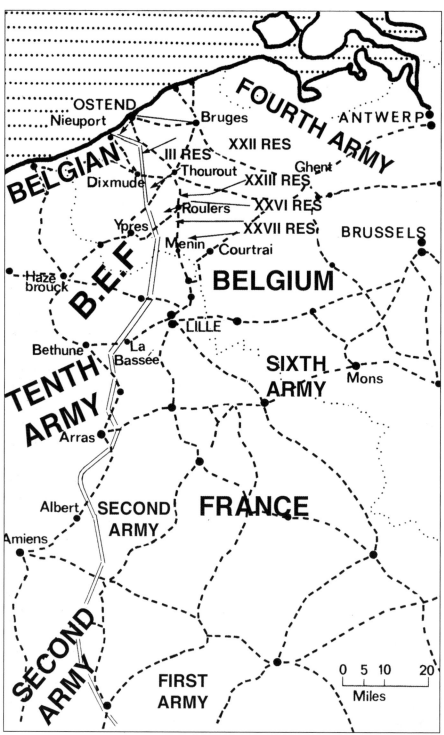

The approach of the 'new' Corps.

ditches and streams to cross. The red-brick houses of Hooghlede and the windmill on the crest of Hooghe were clearly in sight when the fighting novices heard the curious echoing thump of rifles discharged directly at them and the sizzling crack of machine-gun bullets. Shells flew overhead to burst amongst the support and reserve companies behind. The ranks were closed up as men began to fall dead or wounded on to the wet ground. By 2 pm, the two battalions in the centre were somewhat ahead of the others, who had lost formation negotiating wire fences, farmyards and a broad dike. The foremost companies were checked by an earth bank, about five feet high, which gave excellent shelter until men began to clamber across to the far side. Heavily laden, the German soldiers found it a cumbersome business, the more oppressive because they were only 180 yards from the firing positions of the French dragoons under the crest. This was well within the range of the little French carbines, whose fire became devastating.

The two battalions ahead stopped; the others came up into rough alignment on either side but it was impossible for them to move forward. Messages were sent back to the artillery, whose observation posts were in Gits 400 metres behind, to shell the crest but it was difficult to identify the scattered fire positions of the dismounted French troopers. Shells were still falling along the crest line when the light began to fail. Gradually it became apparent that the enemy were no longer firing at the 46th Division and when patrols went forward they found Hooghlede smoking, silent and empty save for a few terrified civilians crouching in cellars. The ridge had been abandoned.

The French dragoons had been forced to retire by the action of the 51st and 52nd Divisions of XXVI Reserve Corps. Although these two had had further to march to the Menin-Thourout road from their night leaguers of the 18th/19th October, they had met no opposition east of Roulers and had thus made better time in reaching it. The 51st Reserve Division reached the town after a brief skirmish with the outposts of one of de Mitry's divisions, a contact too slight to cause a moment's delay to the marching troops. They entered the enclosed streets at about the same moment as a regiment of French cavalry was trotting out eastward to join the outpost line. The two bodies clashed headlong. As rifle and carbine opened fire, civilians in the streets fled for shelter.

For a little while, de Mitry's cavalrymen were at an advantage; another regiment was immediately at hand to reinforce the town and the local householders were ready to help with directions, point out sniping posts, aid the wounded. Lacking assistance amongst the maze of buildings, alleys and backyards, and as yet untrained to react quickly under fire, the Germans were unable to make use of their greater numbers and heavier weapons. It was an hour before control was re-established among the battalions and companies broken up in the first scamper into cover. Even then, the excitement and eagerness of the young soldiers maintained a level of confusion: sections and platoons would dash off prematurely or in the wrong direction. Orders were given and countermanded almost in the same breath. The middle-aged company commanders, themselves inexperienced in this type of fighting, were hard put to it to collect and keep their platoons let alone to launch them in a concerted assault. To add to their difficulties, two armoured cars appeared and opened fire at both French and Germans, wherever troops were detected, but left before they could be identified.[5] A Taube aeroplane flew over, scouting, as the battle began and noted the disorder in the town before it was chased away by two British Be.2Cs.

Time gave the advantage to numbers. The French cavalry occupied a broken line running north-east to south-west, hastily chosen and thinly held. Inevitably, there were gaps between squadrons. Both flanks on the outskirts of the town north and south were open. Gradually, these weaknesses were exploited: in the centre of the town a battalion passed through the cavalry line; to the south a regiment enveloped it. By the end of the afternoon, the last French troop had hastened back across rooftops and through dark passages to its horses, mounted and departed, leaving the town, the dead and the prisoners to the 51st Reserve Division. South of the town, the 52nd Reserve pushed a British cavalry brigade back to Moorslede before nightfall. These were the advances which had compelled the abandonment of the Hooghe ridge by the French dragoons.

The effect was much the same towards Menin, though enhanced here by Rawlinson's precipitate and hasty withdrawal of his infantry. The foremost brigade of the 3rd Cavalry Division was fighting to the east of the Roulers-Menin road when it discovered that a cyclist battalion of 52nd Reserve was moving past its left flank. On the right the British infantry were abandoning ground on Rawlinson's order. Thus isolated, the cavalry had to conform. They rode 10,000 yards back to the new line of defence. It was a consolation to the men and a relief to the horses to be given a night's rest in billets behind de Mitry's outpost line.

While these events of the Monday satisfied most of Duke Albrecht's hopes, the position on Crown Prince Rupprecht's front was not quite so satisfactory. From Allenby's sector, his forward positions had received a

5 Both sides attributed these to the other. It is just possible that they were British – and lost!

good deal of light shrapnel, delaying and preventing reconnaissance and preparation of the Lys crossing places. It seemed likely that the British aircraft, flying whenever there were periods of clear weather, had spotted the two cavalry divisions moving forward to reinforce the four already in position for the next day's assault. Immediately more serious was the news that the British had advanced from Herlies to capture the hamlet of Le Pilly, while the French simultaneously attacked Fournes (see Map 7, p. 86). If they were not to wrest this whole area of high ground from him in a strong offensive, the effect of his own assaults must be diminished. His chief of staff was reassured by VII Corps that the losses would be recovered at once. It was more comforting to hear later by telephone that Fournes had never in fact been taken: Coneau's dismounted cavalry had proved too weak to enter the village. Le Pilly was therefore isolated; a desirable and obvious prey. But it was covered by machine-guns in Herlies, 800 yards distant and would not be easy to attack by day. It was therefore decided to take it before dawn.

Long before dawn on the 20th October, the lines of the Sixth and Fourth Armies were crowded and active. The offensive was about to begin from Arras to the sea.

The distant growl, the nearer bark of guns and howitzers were heard by the waiting troops; but these indications that other men were active in other places did not relieve the sense of isolation amongst detachments. The mist lay thickly almost everywhere, dividing them.

Among the first to move forward were two Westphalian battalions who followed guides along the road to Le Pilly. After two or three hundred metres they stopped to form up on either side of it, each with two companies in front. This took some time in the darkness and it seems probable that a number of men became lost. Slowly then, feeling their way deliberately along the edge of the road, the two battalions moved towards Le Pilly while their guns fired into it. The days had not yet come of drumfire, the rain of shells of all calibres, delivered hour after hour for many days, but the weight of shells falling on and around Le Pilly was devastating. Roofs were blown in, walls smashed, roads blocked. Fortunately for the defence, 2nd Royal Irish Regiment, their commanding officer, Major E H E Daniell, had placed the majority along the edges of gardens and fields outside the hamlet. When the Westphalians came at them out of the half light of the new day, an intense fire was opened from the British rifles. Soon the British artillery joined the battle, firing on the half circle of Westphalians east and south of Le Pilly attempting to gain by local rushes what they had sought by joint assault. At mid-morning, a

German company appeared from the south-west, crossing in front of the British battalion at Herlies,[6] but it too was held off. In the early afternoon a third battalion arrived and a new assult was made. To the relief of the Germans, the defenders' fire slackened; their ammunition was exhausted, their numbers depleted. At 3 pm Major Daniell ordered the survivors to fix bayonets and the few whole men were joined by as many of the wounded as could walk and hold a weapon. In this counter-attack, Daniell was killed and his battalion destroyed. In two days of fighting, a unit of seventeen officers and 561 soldiers had lost 257 killed, 290 captured, of whom about 240 were wounded thirty survivors returned to their own lines.

Le Pilly had attracted troops and artillery support which were needed elsewhere. VII Corps had few other successes that day except to drive Conneau's squadrons back to the hill of Fromelles. But XIII Corps, fresh from a night's rest in Lille, attacked vigorously the three brigades of Pulteney's corps which had pushed forward on to the ridge overlooking Lille. It was open country here. Then, as now, there were few hedges or banks between fields and the only wood of consequence lay inside German lines. From 7 to 8 am, as the mist was succeeded by drizzling rain, the British trenches and villages were shelled while eighteen battalions of German infantry came forward in extended order.

The British soldiers were armed with the short Lee Enfield, whose magazine held 10 rounds in comparison with the 5 of the French and Germans. The British were accustomed regularly to firing at 800 yards with this weapon and many could hit a man approaching at 1,000. It is doubtful if they had sufficient visibility on Tuesday, 20th October in Premesques, Ennetières and Radinghem; 700 was a likely limit. But whatever the range when they opened fire it was with the same deadly effect as at Le Pilly.

By the early afternoon, the enthusiasm of III Corps for assault had waned. The wind had dropped and the falling grey rain clouds hung low over the landscape. The Hessian and Württemberg soldiers pressing the British were spread along 7 miles of front, some in the shelter of the Chateau de Flandres, the villages of Escobeques, Englos and Capinghem, some in the old French fortifications guarding Lille, others less lucky in hollows and shallow re-entrants, in roadside ditches and under stream banks with the clinging smell of the wet earth in their nostrils. Between the lines of opposing riflemen – 500-800 yards – lay the wounded, and amongst them the dead.

---

[6] It is almost certain that this was a company of one of the assault battalions which had become lost during the approach march.

At 3 o'clock, as at Le Pilly, a final attempt was made to assault the salient of Ennetières held by the 2nd Sherwood Foresters. But the salient was not as exposed as Major Daniell's, as isolated from support and supply. Ammunition was available in quantity. Holding the rifles firmly, taking a first sight, squeezing the trigger, turning the rifle slightly outwards with the left wrist as they flicked the bolt open and shut with a perfectly co-ordinated movement of the right, the men in the British rifle companies shot and shot again through the afternoon as through the morning until the obscured sun fell early away once more and the night shades and the night mists began to gather.

The reports of their actions by the two divisions of XIII Corps did not please their commander, General von Fabeck. His orders from Crown Prince Rupprecht had been to break through the enemy line to capture Estaires on the river Lys eight miles distant, and by the afternoon of the first day bombardment and assault had gained no ground at all. Though aware that an assault was planned for 3 pm by the 26th Division, he ordered a night attack to capture Ennetières, and La Vallée and Le Touquet, hamlets immediately in rear and to the north. After the failure of the afternoon attack, the corps' artillery was turned on to the two hamlets, the divisional field batteries and some of the howitzers firing in enfilade from positions behind Erquinghem and Lomme. As the mists rose in the early dusk, two companies of 122 Regiment discovered by chance a gap between platoons of the Sherwood Foresters through which they slipped in and, following the railway line towards Armentières, found themselves unopposed immediately in rear of La Vallée. Before they could capture the hamlet, their own battalion appeared with another from the regiment, having broken through the Foresters' line. La Vallée, held by half a company, was taken by surprise. But there were more terrible surprises in store for the Foresters. At 6 pm three battalions of 25th Reserve Division held back from the assaults of the day, attacked Ennetières. They had been brought forward to Englos village and the old French fort d'Englos from whose shelter they suddenly rose up to double forward across the 800 metres separating them from the defences of Ennetières. The light was now too poor to shoot at long range: the Foresters could not fire rapidly enough to cut down the assaulting Germans before they reached their trenches and the houses. In this moment of crisis, the three forward companies were told to get out of the village as quickly as they could and rally on the gun position by the windmill to the north of La Vallée. Without packs, many without caps and greatcoats, but carrying rifles and ammunition, about half the battalion managed to disengage themselves from the confused close fighting in the darkness to hurry back along the road towards La Vallee. At the western end of Ennetières, the roads cross for Le Touquet and La Vallée and here, for a moment, officers and NCOs attempted to reorganize the breathless remnant of the Foresters amidst the last of the deserted, broken houses whose masonry strewed across the pavé. Immediately to the east, the sound of rifle shots continued as detachments of the battalion, cut off, continued to resist. From the cross-roads, to the relief of many, a voice called,' 'Reinforcements coming up, sir' and all at once marching feet were heard and a host of dark figures appeared from La Vallée. Then, a shriek, 'It's Jerries!' and the survivors were plunged once more into a mêlée from which, this time, there was no escape. Between fifty and sixty men under two officers fought their way into the houses and kept the Germans out until 5.15 next morning, when they expended the last of their ammunition. At this time, on 21st October, 2nd Sherwood Foresters ceased, as a regular battalion, to exist.

WEDNESDAY TO FRIDAY:
21ST-23RD OCTOBER 1914

Sir John's optimism lasted through much of 20th October, enabling him to order Lieutenant-General Sir Douglas Haig to take his I Corps, now arrived from the Aisne, north east from Ypres to break out towards Bruges. He left it to the corps commander to decide whether, having reached Thourout, he should strike north for the coast to cut off von Beseler's corps attacking the Yser line, or to move northeast 'to turn the Germans' northern flank'. These instructions, given personally and issued later in the Army operation order for the 21st, were substantially the same as those passed to Haig on the evening of the 19th. So the events of the 20th, so far as he knew them, had proved insufficient to make Sir John reappraise his immediate battle policy, though they had forced concessions from him: II III, the Cavalry Corps and 7th Division of IV Corps were to 'strongly entrench and maintain themselves on the line indicated...', and his one reserve, 19th Infantry Brigade, was committed to Pulteney for the gap between III and Smith-Dorrien's corps. He conceded too that where he had spoken on the 19th of 'one (enemy) corps between Ostend and Merlin, not more', there might now prove to be as well 'several *Landwehr* or similar divisions – nothing of any quantity or consequence'.

Next morning, the 21st, he was down in the dumps.

What changed his spirits? Murray had signed the operation order at 9.30 pm on the evening of the 20th; an order which had opened with the sentence: '1. The enemy has today made determined attacks on the II, III and IV Corps which have been successfully repulsed.' The news of Le Pilly's loss had not yet reached GHQ – it did not get to corps headquarters until after midnight. The loss of Ennetières and La Vallée and its consequence, withdrawal of the entire 6th Division to the western side of the ridge, would not become clear until the morning of the 21st. But certain reports were in the hands of Sir John's intelligence staff which may have been digested by him during the night hours: the Belgians and French marine brigade had clearly identified from prisoners the presence of both III and XXII Reserve Corps opposite the Yser; prisoners taken by the French cavalry had admitted to being in the XXIII Reserve Corps and spoke of the XXVI and XXVII. The French and Royal Flying Corps had identified large columns in the sector between Roulers and Menin.

Whatever depressed Sir John, he was in a mood of uneasy apprehension when General Joffre called to see him at St Omer on the 21st. The French commander-in-chief brought the welcome news that he was transferring his IX Corps to Flanders where it would become part of the Army detachment currently forming under General d'Urbal. Present at the meeting. Henry Wilson, the deputy chief of staff, wrote in his diary:

> ... All went satisfactorily until Sir John asked for facilities to make a great entrenched camp at Boulogne to take the whole Expeditionary) F(orce). Joffre's face instantly became quite square and he replied that such a thing could hot be allowed for a moment. He would make some works to guard against a *coup-de-main*, but an entrenched camp he would not allow...

A week or so before, when he was in low spirits after Smith-Dorrien's early reversal at Givenchy, Sir John had mentioned to Foch that an entrenched camp should be prepared at Boulogne for the BEF to fall back on if they should again be defeated in Belgium. Foch had tactfully replied that it might well be a good idea, but as an immediate measure, it might be better to construct a comprehensive reserve defence line along the St Omer-Aire-Bethune canal. Now, with the enemy's pressure mounting and the surprising strength of his assault forces revealed, the British commander-in-chief recalled his abortive advance to Mons in August and the long, exhausting retreat that followed. He wanted to have ready what he had yearned for then: a defensible haven on the Channel coast into which he could withdraw if necessary, with the Royal Navy at his back to guarantee the journey home.

This climate of defeatism in the British high command invoked no less for Joffre memories of August and the first half of September, and the difficulties he had had in persuading Sir John and his chief of staff to co-operate in the Marne strategy. He concealed to a degree his anger at their want of confidence – he was to pour it out privately later – and reminded all those present that the allied armies were under attack from Nieuport to Arras. He reassured them that France would not favour her own part of the line before theirs. Certain prudent preparations had been made; the sea dykes had been opened to flood the approaches to Dunkirk; the second line of defence had been sited and partially prepared. But most important of all, they should fight and defeat the Germans where they stood.

With formal expressions of goodwill, Joffre departed for Furnes, headquarters of the Belgian Army and its royal commander-in-chief, the King. He recounts that his own spirits were lifted to see arriving in the town the leading battalion of the French 42nd Division, the 16th Chasseurs.

> I immediately gave orders for them to pass in review before His Majesty. The march past of this splendid battalion, hardened by months of strenuous campaigning, was a magnificent sight, and I had the feeling that those Chasseurs, divining my intention, were determined to give the King of the Belgians an evidence of that unconquerable determination which animated the whole of France.
>
> Belgians are rarely demonstrative, but their enthusiasm now broke out in shouts of applause; and the King looked as though he had been suddenly warmed by the spectacle. As for me, the emotion I felt still stirs me as I look back upon that moment.

Joffre's pride in the presence of Grossetti's famous division is natural. He knew Grossetti to be a hard practical soldier and it was a comfort to him and to Foch to have such a man and his command in Flanders to stiffen allies whose chiefs appeared to be stricken by forebodings. The situation gives point yet again to a serious weakness in the allied camp: the command was not united. In the light of our present knowledge it may be argued that, as it turned out, this was fortuitous. But the events of October and November, 1914, in Flanders demonstrate in favour of the opposite view. Time and resources were continually wasted when both were at a premium.

French and British artillery fired side by side. When it became obvious that the batteries of one nation might fire with advantage on the front of the other, or where one was critically pressed and needed the help of the other, local contacts were exploited[7] and local agreements made. But this took time while the enemy targets were passing or allied soldiers were

[7] In particular on the extreme right of the British line, British guns and howitzers supported the French XXI Corps against Cuinchy, Auchy and Vermelles, while the French supported operations of the British Division on the right of II Corps.

falling for want of support. A unified command at the top would have permitted a sector command of all artillery, irrespective of national origin.

When Haig's corps began to advance on the morning of 21st October, he discovered that, due to individual fears and misunderstandings, the British and French cavalry had fallen back behind Westroosebeke and Passchendaele and, worse, de Mitry had abandoned the Forest of Houthulst without firing a shot. Then,

> ...about 2 o'clock in the afternoon, without any warning whatsoever, the French Cavalry Corps on our left (de Mitry's) received orders to retire west of the canal. The reason for this withdrawal was stated to be that the enemy was advancing in strength of about a division from the direction of Clercken. The GOC of the French Cavalry Division on the immediate left of our 1st Division (of Haig's corps) fully realized the effect of his withdrawal and declined absolutely to obey this order until it was repeated. He refused to uncover our flank without 'une ordre formelle.'[8]

The local French commander was acting arbitrarily to protect the interests of his national contingent, which included French Territorial infantry[9] immediately in rear of the British. The British acted just as arbitrarily with Conneau and his depleted cavalry corps between II and III corps on the 20th and 21st October. Writing off the loss of ground and life due to these divided interests, there was a happier outcome to the series of incidents. Little by little, attitudes began to change: French and British commanders began to be more considerate of one another, to prepare contingency plans for mutual assistance, and even to pass units to one another's command. But the change was slow and waited often on the spur of common crisis.

Other changes were manifest as the opponents clashed.

On the German side, the harsh campaigning experience of the summer and autumn was leading regimental officers and men to cast aside the rigid tactics taught to them on the manoeuvre grounds in peace. These lessons were not suddenly abandoned. The change was in part delayed by the attitude of formation commanders and staff officers for whom the problem of survival was less acute. Thus the veterans in VII, XIII and XIX Corps continued to form up for assault that autumn in close ranks, dressed by flank or centre to begin their advance in the regulation formation. But as

---

[8] Extract from Haig's diary, 21st October 1914.

[9] French Territorials were not volunteers but men who had passed through the active army and reserve over a period of 11 years. Service in the Territorial army and reserve continued immediately thereafter for a further period of 14 years. The Territorials included also a number of men unfit for full conscription.

the range shortened and the enemy's fire grew more intense, they no longer persisted en masse as men were struck down by shell or bullet. Ranks broke for cover. At once, the officers and non-commissioned officers began to form *ad hoc* assault groups to stalk the enemy trenches. Lacking communication between one another, other than by voice, the storming power of the group was rarely effective. Yet its presence, fleeting, close to the enemy's line denied at least to the defence a chance to rest. Sometimes more was achieved: sniping or the fortuitous discovery of a gap through which to infiltrate. The German infantry were coming to see that, in contrast to the time-honoured mass assault, the operation of numerous small groups of aggressive, determined men achieved often significant results at a low cost in casualties. It was an art at which the Germans were to become accomplished.

In the morning mist of 21st October, eleven battalions of VII Corps attacked four of the British 3rd Division on the high ground between Herlies and Ilies, continuing the operation begun at Le Pilly to sweep the enemy back from the high ground overlooking Lille as a preliminary to breaking through to Estaires. XIII Corps attacked Conneau's positions on either side of Le Maisnil at 7 am. The wraiths of mist screened the approaching Germans in both sectors so that they remained *en masse* until 200 yards from the defending trenches. Even as close as this, they were beaten off by the British, chiefly by rifle and machine gun fire. Now the ranks scattered and withdrew into the mist. At 7.30, a swarm of small groups came forward, surprising one of the British battalions and finding a gap between two others. They were not ejected until the afternoon, and in the close fighting 1st Duke of Cornwall's Light Infantry lost the eight officers remaining with the battalion. Round le Maisnil, the French were subjected to the same penetration tactics and were unable to hold their ground. From Le Maisnil south through the 3rd Division, the last of the allied trenches on the ridges were abandoned during the night.

XIX Corps had launched its assault earlier than its compatriots, eight battalions of infantry forming-up and attacking in the early morning of the 21st. Crossing the Lys in darkness and fog there was every reason to keep the ranks closed up; often in single file, five battalions crossed water and marsh by a foot-bridge repaired by the engineers, the other three by pontoons in position beside the main road. Le Gheer was taken and Ploegsteert Wood entered before a brigade, sent in reinforcement by Pulteney, forced back the Saxons. Immediately to the north, the two divisions of British cavalry fought five of the Germans', the German cavalry being strengthened by its cyclist infantry and two battalions of jäger.

Allenby was uncomfortably aware that his corps was holding one of the most important pieces of ground on the British front; the Messines ridge. Yet his numbers were fewer, his artillery support lighter than in the other corps. One of his regiments had now under 180 effectives. Another, having drawn in almost every individual from its administrative echelon, numbered 181 in the trenches. Like the other corps – apart from Haig's – his regiments had been fighting for over a week with progressively less rest; with only 180 officers and men to hold a regimental front on the Lys, to find night patrols and sentries, a commanding officer could not permit more than 2-3 hours sleep each day. Even where regiments numbered 200-300, the prolonged shelling along the Lys line interfered extensively with rest. It was clear to Allenby and his staff that the ability to think and act quickly was deteriorating. Ambiguous orders were given; clear messages misunderstood. Hollebeke and its chateau were abandoned on the 21st because of muddled and misread instructions and in conformity the whole of Gough's division began to retire. Gough himself came forward to see his brigadiers and to ensure that each regiment returned to its line. He was relieved to discover that there had been no panic and all but the Hollebeke chateau[10] had been reoccupied before he left the line. The enemy had not taken the ground abandoned.

The fact remained, however, that the German cavalry and jager were across the Lys in strength: four divisions attacking between Le Gheer and the Ypres canal; the Bavarian division attacking two regiments of British cavalry to the east of it; and a sixth division attempting strongly to penetrate the right flank of Rawlinson's corps. This point, like the whole of IV Corps' front under attack by XXVI and XXVII Reserve Corps, was badly sited. Rawlinson's half-hearted feinting at Menin had led in the end to the worst of all options. He had neither struck the enemy at a distance nor taken time to select close in the best ground for defence. The abandonment of Passchendaele had given the German field artillery and machine-gunners commanding positions in enfilade. Voluntary withdrawal from the Becelaere feature made a present to the attacking troops of a gateway on to the remainder of the ridge. The corps staff had drawn a line on the map for 7th Division to hold without regard to contours and, unhappily. General Capper, the divisional commander had accepted it. His infantry were therefore dug in on forward slopes in full view of Passchendaele, Becelaere and the mount of Terband. From these posts of observation, the artillery officers of the two reserve corps and cavalry division directed a slow steady bombardment, continuing by night

---

[10] It was recaptured later.

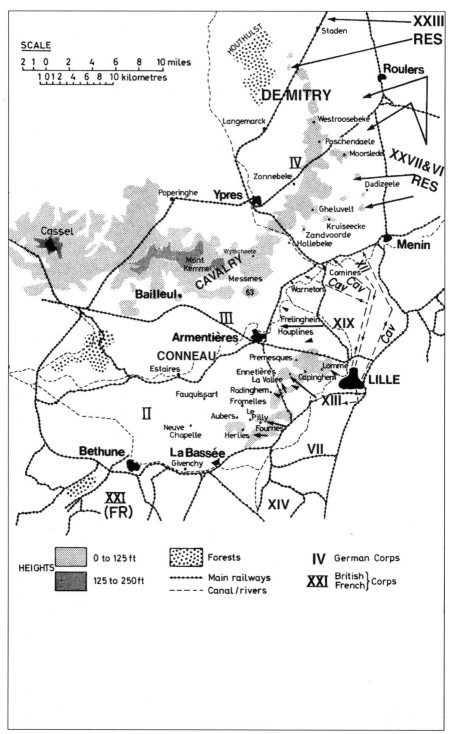

Ypres/La Bassée: the armies clash.

to shell the targets they had registered at leisure during the day.

The brightest element of the 21st was the weather; by noon the mist had cleared in a light wind which blew away also the grey clouds. The sun shone continuously until half past four or five o'clock. The aviators flew eagerly; French, British, German and even a few Belgians scouted along the front of the offensive. Above the Forest of Houthulst, an observer of the Royal Flying Corps recorded '...Dixmude can hardly be seen for a mass of shells. French sailors having hellish time – much smoke rising from area of Nieuport – difficult to see enemy movement nearer than Clercken but close to 3,000 troops moving forward on road that area'. A French Morane swooped down above the trees of the forest in an attempt to peer through the canopy. It was shot at and the observer wounded. Although they could see little through the clusters of decaying leaves, the pilot noted beyond them the same flow of marching German soldiers from Qercken and observed two concentration areas immediately behind the road to Dixmude.

Receiving these reports that evening. General d'Urbal, commander of the French in Belgium, decided that he would attack from the flank, moving from south to north across the western end of the forest. A hazardous, if attractive venture, it might have proved successful if the IX only force available was a brigade of French Territorials – six battalions – supported by a division of de Mitry's cavalry and three batteries of 75s. Obediently at 6 am, on the morning of the 22nd, they emerged from behind the Ypres canal to advance through the left of Haig's corps.

The British soldiers watched them curiously. There was a natural comparison in their minds with the British Territorial Army, whose units were beginning to land in France. But these trudging, heavily-laden figures in their blue great-coats were neither young men nor volunteers but men too old for service in regular corps or too unfit. They disappeared across a ridge and were lost to view. Soon the 75s were heard supporting them and there were rifles and machine-guns firing. Between 11 and 2.30 in the afternoon, about half came back in disorder, blocking the roads to the rear at a time when the British 1st Division were fighting a local action. Some retired, explaining that the Germans were firing at us but we could not see them'. Others rallied to return to the defence of Bixschoote which they held until 5.30 pm supported by French and British batteries. This was the limit of the sweep.

The French Territorials had been fighting six battalions of the 45th Division from XXIII Reserve Corps. The other six attacked Haig's left flank with 46th Reserve while XXVI and XXVII strove to break Rawlinson's line. During the morning and afternoon, at one point or another along this front, the bombardment would intensify then slacken as the spiked helmets and field grey of the new corps came into view, the young battalions advanced in waves of massed ranks. The one or two machine-guns[11] with each British battalion boiled in their water jackets, the riflemen could not touch their barrels as they fired at these extensive targets, opening at about 900 yards and firing still as the diminished frontages reached 200, seeing clearly the individual survivors closing up shoulder to shoulder as their comrades fell. Some units shouted patriotic songs as they advanced; amongst others the colours flew. Bullets took the leading companies, the field gun and howitzer shells those following behind. It was a day of fantastic courage, of defiant slaughter.

The only British losses of note were at either end of their line. On the right, towards the La Bassée, three battalions of VII Corps came swiftly out of the early morning darkness to surprise the 1st Cheshires digging trenches in the open. 382 officers and men remaining with the battalion were reduced to 153. The fragment of the Dorsets on whom they fell back lost their front trenches but held those in rear. The total of the battalion alive and unwounded was thirty-four, apart from the administrative platoon with the quartermaster. Smith-Dorrien resolved to withdraw to the reserve line which he had been constructing and was relieved to know that a brigade of the Indian corps was on its way from a railhead to join him.

On the left, close to the Forest of Houthulst, four battalions of the 45th Reserve Division at last succeeded in reaching Haig's flank, aided by the dusk and rising evening mist. By luck several companies passed through gaps on either side of the 1st Cameron Highlanders at the hamlet of Kortekeer Cabaret, and soon the Camerons were being fired at from all sides. In the darkness the highlanders withdrew, leaving a number dead and fifty-four captured. The battalion reformed behind the road under Lieutenant-Colonel D L MacEwen, their commanding officer. He was found here a little later by Lieutenant-Colonel E Osborne-Smith of 1st Northamptons, who had been sent forward from divisional reserve to mount a counter-attack, an operation which was swiftly prepared with the help of the Camerons. But the leading company had only just moved off into the darkness when the attack was cancelled; the brigade commander sent a staff officer to say that as it was dark and as the ground was unknown to Colonel Osborne-Smith and his men the affair was too risky.

This event illustrates again the curious reluctance of British formation commanders to use the night for operations. It contrasts with the readiness

[11] The establishment of machine-guns to each battalion was two – Maxim or Vickers. By this time only about half the battalions had more than one each in action due to shortage of spare parts. There were no light machine-guns in use at this time.

Major-General von Delmensingen, Chief-of-Staff, Sixth Army.

Duke Albrecht of Württemberg Commander of the Fourth Army (centre, front row) with Major-General Ilse on his left.

General Joffre, French Commander-in-Chief, Lieutenant-General Sir Douglas Haig, Commander I Corps, and General Foch. Commander of the French northern army group.

Lieutenant-General Sir Horace Smith-Dorrien, Commander II Corps.

Crown Prince Rupprecht of Bavaria, Commander Sixth Army, with his son.

(right) Lieutenant-General Sir Edmund Allenby, Commander, Cavalry Corps.

French 75-mm gun in action.

Lieutenant-General Pulteney. Commander III Corps (second from left, standing).

(left) General Erich von Falkenhayn.

Lieutenant-General Sir Henry Rawlinson, Commander IV Corps.

A Captured German machine-gun post.

British and German wounded.

The ruins of Ypres Cathedral, 1915.

The White Chateau, HQ of the I Corps.

The ruins of Ypres as seen from the air.

Maurice Farman aircraft in service with the Royal Flying Corps in Flanders, 1914.

French Morane-Saulnier showing fixed machine-gun firing through the propeller. This device was only in the inceptive stage in 1914.

German scout aircraft, the Rumpler Taube.

German 250-mm mortar-type used in breaking fortifications and the defences at Dixmude.

The wrecked annexe of Hooge Chateau after being struck by German shell fire during the conference of divisional commanders.

German cavalry enter Sailly.

The Ypres-Comines canal (taken in early 1915 but virtually unchanged from November 1914).

A typical trench under construction at Zandvoorde in October, 1914. many trenches were still only at this stage when the major assaults began.

A company of 2nd Scots Guards moving from Zandvoorde (in background) towards Gheluvelt. Though posed the picture is not faked, being taken during the movement by an NCO, Sergeant Pilkington, attached to the unit.

British troops in the snow just outside Ypres, winter 1915.

German prisoners marching along the Menin road after the first battle of Ypres, October 1914.

Trench 47, Ypres, 1915. This trench was situated to the north east of the Zillebeke-Zwarteleen road.

11th Hussars in the trenches, cleaning a machine-gun. This shows a more developed trench with a degree of overhead cover using logs.

of the regimental officers to do so and the continual movement and assault under cover of darkness urged on regiments by German divisional and corps commanders. After three days of daylight assaults, von Beseler had failed to cross the Yser but he had done so on the night 21st/22nd October by stealth. On the night that the Northamptons were being pulled back, he was extending his bridgehead to divisional strength in darkness. The best that could be done opposite Kortekeer Cabaret was to prepare and form-up during the night for a brigade attack next morning.

Meantime, the French were thinking of a counter-attack on a wider basis.

Since the 19th, Foch had been chafing at the inactivity of the allied line. He believed that the three armies in Flanders were inviting defeat by spreading themselves in a long defensive line; a policy which permitted the Germans to concentrate numbers against them at selected points of assault. He waited a little to see whether Haig's movement on Roulers would be successful, and when it was not, delivered instructions to d'Urbal to press forward with the troops 'under your immediate command'. He sought to persuade the King of the Belgians and Sir John to do the same with their own contingents.

D'Urbal's first venture with the brigade of Territorials was by way of being an overture. On the 22nd, reminded by Foch that von Beseler had won a bridgehead over the Yser, he ordered a major counter-attack. Grossetti was to strike out from Nieuport along the Bruges road with the 42nd Division.[12] Admiral Ronarc'h was to thrust towards Thourout. The 17th Division – the leading formation of JX Corps – was to attack in the direction of Roulers, assisted by two of de Mitry's divisions. The Belgians were asked 'to associate yourselves in these offensive movements to the limits of your resources'. Sir John French was told that 'It is greatly to be desired that the whole British Army should support the French attack by acting offensively along its whole front, the left wing moving on Courtrai'.

These were staggering demands yet not so exorbitant as they seemed to the British and Belgian commanders who had convinced themselves that their only course was to hold on. Falkenhayn's offensive had now reached the limit of its immediate strength. In the Sixth Army, Crown Prince Rupprecht had started with a superiority of between 2 and 3 to 1 in numbers and a considerable superiority in medium and heavy artillery. His advantage in strength had certainly been amplified by concentrating regiments at sensitive points but the massed assaults had proved costly and the prospect of penetrating the French or British lines between Arras and

---

[12] The Royal Navy were asked to assist this movement with naval gunfire. British ships had been firing continuously in support of the Belgian defence since 17th October and continued to do so.

Menin was waning. The Fourth Army had begun with an immense superiority in numbers, every unit at full establishment with first line reinforcements immediately to hand in each corps zone. But their casualties over the four days 19th-22nd October had been high; and they were feeling particularly the rising losses amongst the cadre of experienced leaders. A major counter-attack by the allies, mounted between Nieuport and La Bassée at half a dozen points might have unbalanced them, sufficiently at least to force them to withdraw some distance.

Unfortunately, all the circumstances of the moment were against it. Foch had no power to command the Belgian and British armies, no authority to make a plan and insist upon it. He was in any case so precipitate that it was physically impossible to meet his wishes. The 17th Division was not sufficiently near the battle line to fight on the morning of the 23rd. General d'Urbal's orders did not reach GHQ or I Corps Headquarters until almost 2 am and they requested that Haig and Rawlinson should join and support the 17th Division at 9 to recapture Passchendaele, Zonnebeke and Becelaere, the French axis of advance running between the British corps. The British would need to adjust their boundaries to let the French come in, to agree objectives and to plan their fire support with the utmost precision, not only for the security of their infantry but because artillery ammunition stocks were dwindling. Haig protested that they must postpone matters to the 24th. But Sir John could no more order d'Urbal to stop than Foch could order a British attack. Since it was too late to arrange a postponement, Wilson suggested at GHQ that they should assist the French to pass through I Corps and that Haig and Rawlinson should support the flanks of the 17th Division as far as possible.

While these high matters were under excited consideration, a sapper officer, Major H L Pritchard, had reached Langemarck with 26th Field Company, Royal Engineers. He had been ordered to strengthen the defences of the town, particularly towards Koekuit on the north side. For some little time, he searched for the infantry, but they had gone. The Germans' capture of Kortekeer Cabaret had caused the 1st Coldstream Guards to draw in its companies and a gap of 400 yards was opened between the Guards Brigade on the left and 3rd Brigade on the right. Major Pritchard put out a platoon to watch the road to Koekuit, set his sappers to work digging a trench and sent a pair of runners off to 3rd Brigade Headquarters for an infantry detachment to take over the gap.

An hour and a half later, two platoons of the 1st Glosters were roused and inarched to Langemarck in response, amongst them Private J S Barton who recorded the event.

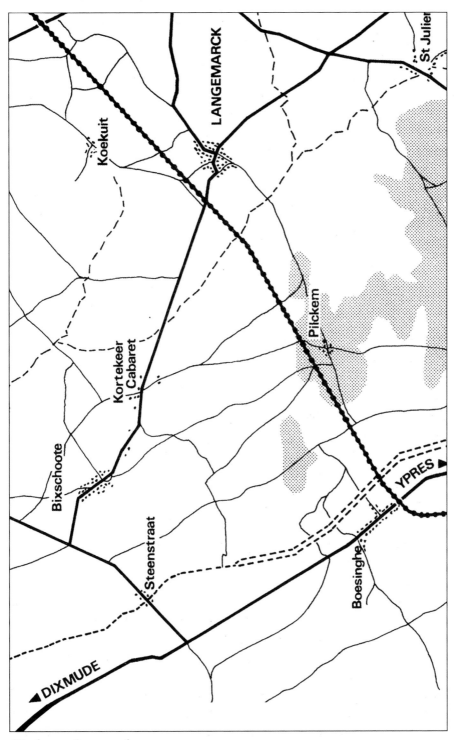

Bixschoote – Langemarck

We passed through (Langemarck) and at a point fifty yards beyond the village on the Koekuit road we stopped. Three sappers were with us and sited a trench which the platoon dug. The work was finished about 6 am. The trench was on the left of the road, the right edge being at the side of the road. It ran back towards the village at an angle of 45 degrees from the road. No. 3 platoon (Lt D Baxter) was on the right of the road but not in sight owing to the camber of the road. There were no troops or trenches visible on our left which seemed to be in the air.

The inhabitants had only left on the two preceding days. Cattle were grazing in the fields and pigs were wandering about. There was no sign of the enemy.

Shortly after 9 am German cavalry were seen coming towards us down the Koekuit road, which ran in a straight line for about a mile. At a point about 350 yards from us they turned to their right down a lane to a farm some 325 yards from our position. They were going at full gallop and although we fired on them I did not observe any casualties. They remained at the farm and fired it. A large body of enemy infantry was then seen to be coming down the Koekuit road led by mounted officers. About 800 yards from our position they deployed and advanced. They got into dead ground and reached the farm lane before we were able to fire on them. Fire was not opened on them at the point of deployment as, owing to our position, there seemed little chance of getting more ammunition.

The enemy then opened fire on our trench, to which we replied, but as their road was sunken we could not see the effect of the fire. The enemy fire increased in intensity and we began to suffer casualties.

It was then observed that cattle were moving down a ditch on the left of our trench at a distance of about 125 yards. They were moving quicker than cattle usually do. Closer observation showed that the Germans were coming down the ditch on the far side of the cattle. The men in the two traverses on the left were ordered to open fire on the ditch. This was done and the advance down the ditch was stopped. The enemy fire from the farm, which was for the purpose of masking the advance down the ditch, became very heavy and the whole platoon replied to it. Shortly after this the smoke from the burning farm was seen to be increasing in density and was blowing down the ditch. The enemy were then seen advancing up the ditch amidst the smoke. The fire of the whole platoon was turned on the ditch. Our fire was very effective and the movement dwindled away. The line at the farm road then commenced to attack and at the same time the movement down the ditch recommenced. The men in the two traverses on the left of our trench were ordered to fire at the ditch and the remainder dealt with the attack from the farm. The latter was pinned down about 200 yards from our trench. We were then able to give more attention to the ditch on our left and again stopped the movement. The Germans then formed a strong firing line in the ditch and under cover of this a party with a machine-gun was seen going along. The whole platoon concentrated on it and the gun remained there out of action for the rest of the fight.

About this time (somewhere about 10.30 am), Lieutenant Hippisley, the platoon commander, was hit. The bullet struck in the middle of the forehead. He was attended by his servant, Private Brown, who was under the impression that if he kept the brain from oozing out of the hole he would be all right. After a time he was convinced that the wound was fatal and that his master had no chance. He then divided his time between the parapet, where he would fire a few rounds and then return to Lieutenant Hippisley. Between his concern for his master and his desire for revenge on the Germans he seemed to have gone crazy.

Sergeant Eddy was now in command of the platoon.

The enemy from the line attacking from the farm road then began to push their attack under cover of heavy fire from the ditch. The wounded who could by any means work a rifle were brought into action again. Two were wounded a second time. Private King who 'was shot through the left shoulder propped himself up in a corner of the traverse and worked his rifle with one hand.

The gallantly of Private Cratchley is worthy of record. At this time he was hit in the left jaw by a bullet which passed out of the right side of the neck. Blood was pouring from the wound and he fell to the floor of the trench. The wounded in the trench put a field dressing on his wound as best they could. He then crawled to the corner of the traverse, got on his feet and continued firing at the enemy. A lull in the firing took place and he had to be forcibly removed from the parapet and his wound again dressed. The attack recommenced and Private Cratchley appealed in a most piteous way to be lifted up to the parapet. He eventually burst into tears of rage at his helplessness and shortly after lapsed into unconsciousness.

Our casualties were mounting rapidly. In the left traverse of the trench only one man was left out of seven and in my traverse, the second from the left, only two out of six.

Ammunition was becoming scarce. All the wounded and killed were searched for ammunition. The attack from the farm direction was again pushed and reached a point 75 yards from us where it was pinned down. The fire from the ditch was so intense that many of our bayonets were broken by bullets. When hit they snapped like glass and the flying fragments were responsible for seven head and neck wounds, two of which were very serious.

By some means mangolds had been built in the parapet and the air was full of particles as the bullets hit the parapet. The pieces showered in and around the trench.

Shortly after 1 pm the enemy fire died down from the ditch and quietened from the front. Some men ran from the village and Sergeant Wilson of D Company brought more ammunition. The Germans were then seen to be trickling in small parties down the ditch in retirement. The platoon now respectable in numbers kept up a continuous fire on them and caused great numbers of casualties. Strangely enough we were not again fired on. This continued for an hour or so and the line in front which had attacked from the farm road were seen to be making movement. They arose in groups of five or six and as we were at point blank range and waiting for each party, they were mown down immediately after rising. No man reached the shelter of the road.

Shortly after 6 pm the action ceased. One wounded German on our front was seen to be making attempts to rise. On his third effort he got to his knees, pointed his rifle in the direction of our trench, pulled the trigger and collapsed.

There had been no artillery fire directed on the trench. When the retirement commenced the enemy shelled the village very heavily and fired the church. About 4 pm, our artillery opened on the line of dead and wounded from the farm road attack, apparently under the impression that they were still attacking. The bodies were being blown in the air.

During the day, I fired about 600 rounds of ammunition.[13]

Close by, Brigadier-General E S Bulfin had been preparing deliberately but methodically a counter-attack on Kortekeer Cabaret with two battalions, 1st Loyals and 1st Queens.[14]

At 10 am, the commanding officer of the Loyals issued his orders.

'We are to attack and recapture the lost (Camerons') trench, and will be supported by the 2nd Staffords ... A, B, and C Companies are to lead, and D Company is to be in reserve under my direct orders. The machine-guns will support the attack from the best position possible.

[13] The British soldier carried 120 rounds with him.

[14] He had a total of five battalions under command for this attack.

Any questions, gentlemen? No. Then off you go; the attack will begin in half an hour from now.'

At 1045 (wrote Lieutenant Hyndson in his diary) having explained all we know to the men we deploy and advance. My company is on the right and we almost immediately come under long distance rifle fire, so I order the men in my platoon to open out to four paces interval... Soon we work up to within 250 yards of the enemy trenches, where we find the survivors of the Cameron Highlanders... We are now close to the 'Boche' trenches, and must pause to wear down his nerves until he dare not show a hair, before we can complete the attack. We commence to fire for all we are worth at selected portions of their position... About this time Miller made a gallant attempt to gain ground, but unfortunately both he and the men who followed him were shot down, and the command of the company descends to me again. I noticed the Germans dodging past a gap in the hedge some 250 yards to my front, and order a section to fire at them as they slip past. Remembering their snap shooting in peace-time on the range, the men enter into this task with zest, and many of the flitting figures are seen to fall. We afterwards found twenty or thirty dead Germans in this area. A red house in front also gives us considerable trouble... And so the fight goes on until about 1 o'clock, when the firing from the enemy trenches almost dies down. The time has now come to put the finishing touches to the battle, and we work forward in small groups...

The 1st Queens had also reached the point of assault and together the two battalions ran in upon the German trenches and occupied houses firing their rifles from the hip. Coming towards the reserve trenches. Lieutenant Hyndson expected to meet with a stout resistance, but the Germans have had enough, and suddenly the glorious sight of masses of grey-coated men standing up to surrender meets our gaze... Isolated bodies of Germans still continue to resist and must be rounded up; one particularly brave man established on the top of a windmill continues to fire, and refuses to surrender, so we have to set fire to the building; but in spite of this he goes on firing until the building collapses and its brave defender perishes in the flames. I go on past a house... when suddenly... from the rear a screaming noise, followed in rapid succession by others with resounding crashes, as one after another shells land amongst us ... Our guns have mistaken us for retreating Germans, as we are now well ahead of the remainder of the battalion... I shout to the men to get back to a house flying the Red Cross flag. Back we run, with the exception of a few unfortunate men who are knocked out, and we get out of the danger zone. On reaching the house, what a sight meets my gaze! The whole place is crammed with German dead, dying and wounded, all lying together on the floor, packed as tightly as sardines.

It was a glorious success. The two battalions had killed 490 of the enemy and captured 791 including 352 unwounded.[15] Luck had been with them: the German positions were over-crowded and the defence confused because they had been joined during the night by the battalions which had captured Bixschoote that previous evening from the French Territorials. Sometime after the battle for the village had been won, their commander had mistaken the meaning of an order and withdrawn his force to join those on the Cabaret. Amongst these many prisoners were fifty-four of the Camerons, captured the previous evening but now released, shaking hands and banging everyone on the back. Like a party, everyone was laughing and talking. Some of the men were stripping badges off the Jerries. Others were smoking Jerry cigars ...' The British cost of the action was forty-seven killed and 184 wounded, most of whom were hit during the approach. An attack in the night or the morning mist would have given the riflemen and their officers a better chance. There were no downcast spirits, however: the mood everywhere was of jubilance.

Regrettably, no force was available to exploit the success but Brigadier-General Bulfin can hardly be blamed for that; he had simply been told to recapture the Camerons' lost position and could not have expected such a triumph. The area of Kortekeer Cabaret offered no particular tactical advantage – it was abandoned later in the day – but its capture disturbed the German corps commander and, subsequently, the Fourth Army. The incident was reported at first as a 'breakthrough' and it is significant that there was neither a heavy bombardment of the Bixschoote-Langemark line nor a counter-attack during the remainder of the day or the night following. A few German patrols appeared, which were driven off, and it was evident that the enemy was uncertain as to what was happening. The left-hand brigade of the 45th and the whole of 46th Reserve Division had lost heavily from the Cabaret to Langemarck and its neighbour, 51st Reserve, was too heavily committed to offer assistance.

Almost unnoticed, the leading battalion of the French 17th Division arrived in St Julien at noon. The question was, where was it to go, and what

---

[15] All came from the 45th Reserve Division. Lieutenant Hyndson recorded prisoners as belonging to 205 Regiment, which seems unlikely as this Regiment belonged to 44th Res. Div., then identified at Dixmude, but see pages 87–88, which suggests a need for reinforcement at this point. He mistakenly believed, as did a number of the battalions, that the Loyals were attacking Bixschoote.

should the other eleven battalions do, marching up behind with the divisional batteries and engineers? General d'Urbal's plan had expected an advance at the beginning of the morning with a degree of co-operation at least from the British. It was now afternoon. General Dubois, IX Corps commander, had believed that his counter-attack would begin from an area of deployment on the western side of the ridge, somewhere about Zonnebeke. He learned that Zonnebeke was in enemy hands. Indeed, the whole of the ridge was in enemy possession from Zonnebeke northward through Passchendaele, giving the German observation posts points of advantage.

The two brigades of the British 2nd Division in the line had had no difficulty in holding off the enemy infantry during the day. The Germans repeatedly tried to concentrate in trenches on the forward slopes, where they were picked off at long and medium range. It was the German guns which proved fearsome. One or another sector of the 2nd Division's trenches had been under fire for the whole day, often by what the French called 'marmites' and the British 'Jack Johnsons',[16] the heavy, high explosive shells which burst with a roar, throwing out a cloud of reeking black smoke. Constant work was needed in repair of the trenches.

After some consultation, it was decided that the 17th Division should take over the entire line of the British 2nd that night. General d'Urbal proposed that he should relieve the 1st with Territorials on the 24th. These arrangements, made on the initiative of the French, promised to place under Sir John's hand the whole of Haig's Corps, a powerful reserve, and one he would presumably commit to Foch's offensive.

Or so Foch thought.

THE WEEKEND: SATURDAY, 24TH, SUNDAY, 25TH OCTOBER, 1914

It is a temptation in war to weigh often the sum of one's own difficulties and defeats but to discount those of the enemy. Foch apart, the allied commanders in Flanders sometimes yielded to it in October, and so did the Germans.

In undertaking his offensive, Falkenhayn had calculated – and accepted – two serious risks: the removal of trained formations from various sectors of the western front to the point of leaving some without any reserve: and the committal of the new corps – his only other source of manpower under arms – when they were half-trained. The prize of Calais, the necessity indeed of some such strategy to restore Germany's military position, fostered his resolve.

As planned, the attacks of Crown Prince Rupprecht's army had fallen

---

16 They were also called 'Woolly Bears' and 'Black Marias'.

upon de Maud'huy at Arras and northwards through La Bassée to Menin. The Fourth Army had swept towards the Ypres canal and the Yser. To an extent, the German armies had proved irresistible; they had gained ground at every point but the gains had been local and tactical rather than extensive and strategic. Moreover, the cost of these local successes had been dear. The daily tally of casualties was too great to be borne for any length of time; it contained a high proportion of experienced officers and men. The expenditure of shells was sustained only by rationing other sectors of the western front and the whole of the eastern theatre. The one point in the action which showed promise, which offered a prospect of *durchbruch* – a breakthrough – was the Yser crossing seized in the bend of Tervaete by von Beseler. But even this was an uncertain prospect (see map 9, p. 115). On the 23rd October, Falkenhayn warned the two army headquarters that he must shortly review their operations if they were not more successful.

This warning placed the respective army commanders under additional pressure. They were not professional soldiers, owing their appointments to their titles as rulers of Bavaria and Wurttemberg. But they had their pride and patriotic loyalties, and were anxious to succeed in what was well known to be a critical issue in the war. The pressure on their chiefs of staff was greater.

As in the other armies under the German system. Crown Prince Rupprecht's chief of staff, von Delmensingen, and Duke Albrecht's, Ilse, were in a special position. Each ran all the affairs of the army, including the broad policy of administration,[17] for the army commander as well as being his foremost adviser on operational matters. The commander was free to take up his chief of staff's proposals or to formulate his own plans and policy but, if there was serious disagreement between them, the chief of staff had the right to appeal to Supreme Headquarters for arbitration, when his own position might be upheld and his commander's rejected. Such was the power of the General Staff Corps.

Majors-General von Delmensingen and Ilse were rarely challenged by their royal chiefs. Both were respected as professional officers. The armies they served were at the focal point of the national struggle: the nature and tempo of operations was challenging in its intensity. They were favoured above all others for reinforcement and for supply. If they made a breach in the allied line and thrust through a large force to Calais – perhaps even further afield – they would not only be renowned publicly as principals in

---

[17] The French Army employed the chief of staff system but subordinated him absolutely to the commander. The British Army separated operations and associated matters and gave equal place on the staff to the chief of the administrative staff, although naturally the operations staff tended in war to shape all common policy.

the triumph but professionally as men entitled to a place in the first rank. If they failed, sector operations would sink to the routine of defence, an area of unimportance starved of men and material. The professional opportunities would pass to others. Each had therefore a personal interest in the success of the grand offensive from Arras to the sea.

At Arras, the huge mortars of the Sixth Army had ruined the city and demolished the fine remnant of its association with Spain. But they had failed to break in past the Alpine Division at Saint Laurent. At Souchez and behind Loos, the French infantry had clung doggedly to their line supported by a powerful and expert artillery. North of the La Bassée canal, the German infantry were troubled less by the guns than small arms – the British ration of shells was leaner than the French. The assaults were withered by the fire of the British rifles. It seemed, too, that the British had transformed their line into a series of fortresses.

> ...deep, covered and cunningly concealed trenches; wire, timber barriers and even carts are put out to break up our (assaulting) companies [wrote a German company commander] ... we were compelled to dig ourselves in during half the night. We had no spades. Side-arms, pocket knives and hands were requisitioned to scrape, dig, cut and tear off the clods of turf to form the ramparts behind which the men might hide. Opposed to us and right close the English were entrenching with real spades...,

ran the account of a cavalry regimental commander attacking 7th Division near Kruiseecke. The falsity of this belief would have been seen had he been able to walk forward to the nearest British trenches, torn and gaping from shellfire, filling time and again with loose sand – there were no sandbags[18] – possessing at best a covered niche into which each man might crawl when shelling intensified. The digging tools[19] brought to France and Belgium in the summer had long been destroyed or lost; the replacements issued on the Aisne and Flanders had never met the demand and numbers of these had since been smashed by fire. But these facts were not apparent to the assaulting troops; they believed that the British were in general well-concealed and saw that, despite the weight of shells and mortar bombs dropped amongst them, they were able to break up their formations and to resist much of their infiltration.

Aware of the difficulties of his regiments and impressed by the

---

[18] Thirty were issued to each cavalry regiment and infantry battalion for use with their machine-gun sections. An engineer field company carried 852. Large stocks were, however, *en route*, the first 2,000,000 arriving on 28th October, 1914 in Flanders.

[19] The infantry battalion was established for 110 shovels, seventy-six pickaxes and 937 entrenching tools.

ostensible strength of the allies, von Delmensingen proposed that the frontage of the offensive should be shortened. In view of the operations of the Fourth Army on their right, it was manifestly better to maintain those of Sixth Army on the same flank, where certain resources could be considered. A protracted discussion followed with Supreme Headquarters but the limits were finally agreed as being from the La Bassée canal to the road Menin-Ypres. As a matter of Army policy within this zone, there should be a free transfer of regiments for assault between corps, much as there was already within corps between their organic divisions. The cavalry were already in process of being reorganized, von Hollen being superseded by von der Marwitz in overall command. While Supreme Headquarters were still considering the contraction of the front of offensive operations, von Delmensingen anticipated their agreement and ordered the change.

For Major-General Ilse, the problems were different. He was not concerned with frontage or selectivity of targets for assault; at either end of Fourth Army's front, two key areas had been secured. The question was, how to exploit what they had gained? On the left, two of the new corps had established themselves on the ridge overlooking Ypres. On this ground he believed that they could break the British line and force a passage westward to seize the height of Cassel *en route* for Boulogne. On the right, von Beseler was expanding slowly his initial bridge-head across the Yser. Useful as it was. Ilse believed from beginning to end that the point at which to secure a crossing and to make a breach in the enemy line was at Dixmude.

He had the numbers still to achieve this; for although the casualties in Fourth Army numbered about one-fifth of the total – about one-third of the infantry – many of the British and Belgian units were fighting at one-third to a quarter of their infantry establishment. Amongst the numbers of German youth there was the heart and the will to carry on with the offensive, regardless of the peril. It was the quality and extent of the leadership which troubled Ilse and the staff at army, corps and divisional headquarters. They had had few enough seasoned officers and NCOs at the outset; there were now fewer still. The evidence of this state abounded: positions badly sited; attacks not exploited; units losing themselves in the night; posts abandoned due to muddles and misunderstandings; supply bottlenecks going up and medical bottlenecks coming down from the line. The reporting of movements and battle situations by units was infrequent and incomplete.

Quite apart from Falkenhayn's warning that he would review operations shortly, time was not on the side of Fourth Army because the quality of leadership amongst the regiments was going to become worse rather than better. The enemy's capability to resist was also likely to improve with time: Belgian and French prisoners had stated that large French reinforcements were *en route* for Flanders. It was known that Grossetti's Division was on the Belgian coast. Ilse decided that they should make a final intensive effort to break the enemy on the Ypres ridge and at Dixmude. The formal statement of Fourth Army's intentions was passed for information to Sixth Army at midday on the 23rd.

On the left of Sixth Army, VII Corps had endured a series of vexations throughout 23rd October. Time and ammunition had been wasted by both its divisions in shelling and assaulting positions from which the British II Corps had fallen back during the preceding night. Whilst the regiments were not unhappy to take ground without contest, they were not pleased to undergo a bout of sharp shelling when they occupied it. The Royal Artillery had registered to a nicety the abandoned line. Descending from the ridge, the Germans found, too, that the ground was full of water. It was necessary to build the defence works upwards and to work continuously at their repair.

That night, the line was quiet opposite the II Corps, the British husbanding their shells, the guns of VII Corps unusually inactive on the opposite side. Anxious not to be fooled twice in succession, the German regiments sent out patrols along the whole line between midnight and 5 am but chiefly towards Neuve Chapelle and Fauquissart. At 5 am. on the 24th, the guns opened to bombard the British line and a little later, in an unusually clear and sparkling morning, the first of a number of massed assaults approached it. The British marksmen gave their customary rebuff. Six miles to the north, nine battalions from the XIII and XIX Corps combined to attack the salient round Le Quesne. In the first rush at dawn, a number of German companies entered the eastern edge of the village and the British forward trenches towards Bois Blancs. All day the fighting continued. The howitzers of the Royal Artillery fired often and with some success on to the enemy batteries behind the ridge in front. Aircraft assisted in the afternoon to spot the German batteries.[20]

The fighting round Le Quesne persisted into the night of the 24th. At 9 pm assaults began once more against II Corps, with the same pooling of army resources. Seven German battalions, grouped from both VII and XIII Corps, attacked under command of a brigadier of the former. They struck on a narrow front the inner flanks of the British 8th and the Indian Jullundur Brigades,[21] where the 1st Gordons were at once driven from

---

[20] Artillery spotting by aircraft was slow and crude. There was one aeroplane wireless equipment in France for this work and, in October, it was broken.

their trenches. It was now raining hard and pitch dark except for the flash of weapons firing. At midnight, the 4th Middlesex counter-attacked the Gordons' original line. When dawn came on the 25th the firing died away along the line and heads were counted and ground looked over. The Middlesex had done their work well, recapturing every trench. Amongst them were numerous dead and wounded of the Gordons but all round almost 400 dead and wounded Germans from the night's assault. Friend and foe were mixed on the positions of the 15th Sikh on the left but 2nd Royal Scots on the other side had suffered little and punished heavily the night intruders. Opposite III Corps, the casualties were evenly divided and during the day the British salient was withdrawn.

The committal of all the resources of Sixth Army – eighteen battalions and approximately half its artillery – had failed to achieve more than the capture of a small salient. From the Lys, von der Marwitz reported on the evening of the 25th that, unless he had a greater proportion of infantry and an increase in heavy artillery support, his force could not hope to capture Messines ridge or assist Fourth Army on the Menin road.

Across this road, XXVII Reserve Corps had begun to attack the 7th Division early. At 4.30am, the first guns began to fire from behind Menin, extending north across the road until by 6am the forward slopes, across which most of the British trenches ran, were covered by the grey and black smoke of bursting shells and a fine mist of sandy soil blown into the air. The British line here ran in the shape of a V from Zandvoorde on the left down to Kruiseecke and back through Reutel to the western side of Zonnebeke, where it was taken up by the French. Two regiments of the 53rd Reserve Division came out from their night positions at 5 o'clock in the morning to be formed up in the darkness: 244 from Becelaere and 243 from a hamlet to the north. As soon as it was half light, they advanced, ahead of them the green spread of the conifers in Polygon Wood. Directly in front of the wood and 244 Reserve Regiment was the little village of Reutel, marked only by the shells of three cottages, one of which was on fire. Two of the three battalions of 244 were advancing together in mass on the north side of the road. A few ruined buildings and a little copse to the south west gave fragmentary cover to the left-hand battalion but the right was entirely in the open, crossing a huge field. The other assault regiment was lost to view but they could hear firing away to their right. Now the British ahead began to fire at them, but lightly, for they were still being shelled heavily by the German guns. In fact, the regiment was either too

[21] The Jullundur Brigade formed part of the Lahore Division, Indian Corps, had only just relieved Conneau's cavalry corps in the line.

early on its target or their gunners were late in stopping; the left hand battalion reached the edge of Reutel in German shellfire and began a frontal attack on the occupants, 2nd Wiltshires. The right-hand battalion went on unopposed until it came upon a set of trenches in considerable confusion. The handful of occupants, from 2nd Scots Guards, were crouched dazed amongst their dead, of whom some were half buried. Fortuitously, the German battalion had come upon a detached British company holding a gap between two brigades. It had received a series of direct hits from heavy shells. The destruction of the position permitted the right-hand battalion to begin working down behind the Wiltshires along the edge of Polygon Wood. At least one of its companies lost touch and attacked eventually a company of the 2nd Royal Scots Fusiliers from the rear. This opened the Wiltshires right flank. Suddenly they found the men of 244 everywhere – to the east and the south a battalion with another behind it, from the north two companies and from the west yet a third. The position collapsed and all those left alive fell into 244 Reserve Regiment's hands.

The dreadful news of the capture of Reutel and the total loss of the Wiltshires had by now reached the headquarters of the 7th Division. The commander, Major-General Capper, had no reserve and his line was under attack everywhere except at the extreme right-hand corner. He sent urgently back for help to the 2nd Division, resting in rear after being relieved by the French on the preceding night, and to the French Cavalry behind Zonnebeke. He ordered his staff to be ready with every clerk, orderly, signaller, batman and groom they could muster to fight until help came.

The commander of 244 Reserve Regiment was quite unaware of this stir. He placed one battalion in Reutel village and tentatively took the other two a little westward, uncertain as to what to do. Major-General Ilse could have told him. As it was, he sat about with his force, joined in time by some detachments of the linked division which had lost their way. Between 11am and 12pm, one of his battalions which had drifted north west into Polygon Wood was ejected by two of the British. When it joined him, the regimental machine-guns were turned on the pursuers, who fell back into cover. As the enemy appeared to be once more on their front, the whole regiment took up formal positions of defence.

They had no idea that, for two and a quarter hours, they had torn open the British line.

There were other attacks on 7th Division that day on and south of the Menin road but although they weakened the defending battalions yet more none of the line gave way. The net result for Fourth Army in the Ypres sector was the capture of Reutel, a success which did not compensate for the advance of the French 17th Division 1,000 yards beyond Langemarek on its left and through Zonnebeke on the right. A German counter-attack failed to retake any of the lost ground, though the French were irked to discover that the cavalry guarding their left flank had dashed away to the defence of General Capper and Polygon Wood. But the line – and relationships – were improved when, a little later, two brigades of the British 2nd Division came up to join them, adding Broodseinde to the modest prizes of the day.

Limited though it was, the event of a Franco-British advance coupled with the continuing costly repulse of the new reserve corps convinced Duke Albrecht that Fourth Army could no longer hope to break through the enemy line in front of Ypres. But reports from the northern half of the Fourth Army sector sustained hopes of a success. The German infantry across the Yser now totalled two and a half divisions. The Belgians had been pushed back to the line of the Beverdyk, 2,000 metres from the river and aeroplane reconnaissance showed that reserves were being drawn in from many directions in an attempt to contain von Beseler's bridgehead. Duke Albrecht and General Ilse had directed that a major assault was to be made that night on Dixmude. It might find the garrison without reserves. Opposite Dixmude, the gunners of Fourth Army had now aloft an aerial observation car, suspended from a sausage-shaped balloon. Combined with the use of powerful field glasses, it gave the artillery an intimate view of every target of substance in the ruined town. Throughout the afternoon of the 24th, 350 and 420mm siege guns shelled slowly but without respite the defences of the French marine brigade.

The French sailors had been under fire intermittently since 16th October; in continuous contact since the 18th. Some manned defences in the town, strong points constructed from fallen timber and broken masonry where they enjoyed a measure of protection from shell and bullet. But none were allowed to stay for more than a couple of days in these relatively sheltered surroundings.

Every other day – sometimes every half day – the companies would change, those under cover taking their turn in the shallow trenches on the perimeter. The sailors' boots were always under water in these pits. Often the water rose to their knees. Fortunately they were hardy young men; Ronarc'h had been obliged to take many of his recruits in September from boy enlistments. One, Yves Lebouc, was only just 16 years old. Commandant Delage held the north of the town; Commandant Varney the south. At the railway station of Caeskerke behind the Yser bridge,

Ronarc'h held always a battalion of Varney's as a reserve and a section of the machine gun company covered the approach to their position.

The crash, the roar, the blast and stench of the shelling continued into the night of the 24th, the majority of shots falling on the east and south of the town. At 1 am on the 25th, the line of bombardment began to move west towards the Yser bridge and the waiting seamen knew that the assaults were about to begin. But there were more than they expected. Between 1.30 and 6.30 am fifteen separate assaults came at them from the wet night and the first twilight of the morning. Trenches were captured and recaptured. Dead and wounded lying in the mud were trampled on, unseen. The Belgian supporting batteries fired faithfully, responding to every call but hindered by the rising unserviceability of their guns. At length, the commander of XXII Reserve Corps ordered the exhausted young German infantry to fall back to their positions and the action came to an end. Intact, reeking, its ruins redistributed, Dixmude fell silent for a little while. With the facts that are now known and without the anxiety of the hour to inhibit judgement, it seems astonishing that Duke Albrecht – Ilse – allotted the powerful weapon of the siege artillery to the uncertain operation against Dixmude rather than to support the rising success of vonBeseler. While the bulk of XXII Reserve Corps were hurling themselves vainly at Dixmude, the field guns of III were being hauled across the Yser into the bridge head by the engineers. In the morning, the Belgian infantry were pushed back from the Beverdyk on to the railway line around the village of Pervyse. These troops were demoralized by fear and fatigue. Their battalions and companies no longer existed as cohesive bodies; they had split up finally during the desperate defence actions of the night and remained in action because of the presence of a few leaders of exceptional fortitude. If the shells of the 350 and 420mm guns had been fired at this line, it must have broken beyond repair. Von Beseler had two and a half divisions of infantry[22] active, organized and present to exploit such a breach. Even without them, the Belgian line began to evaporate as individuals began to drift to the rear after daybreak. Some miles behind, the Belgian Army Headquarters prepared to move back from Furnes to Poperinghe, leaving only a small command post for the King and his military operations staff.

Then like a hero from Ouida, the commander of the French 42nd Division appeared with the first of his two brigades, marched from Nieuport. He attempted but did not press a counter-attack in the face of the enemy three times his strength. The motion of a riposte was enough to

---

[22] Including a brigade of XXII Reserve Corps temporarily under his command.

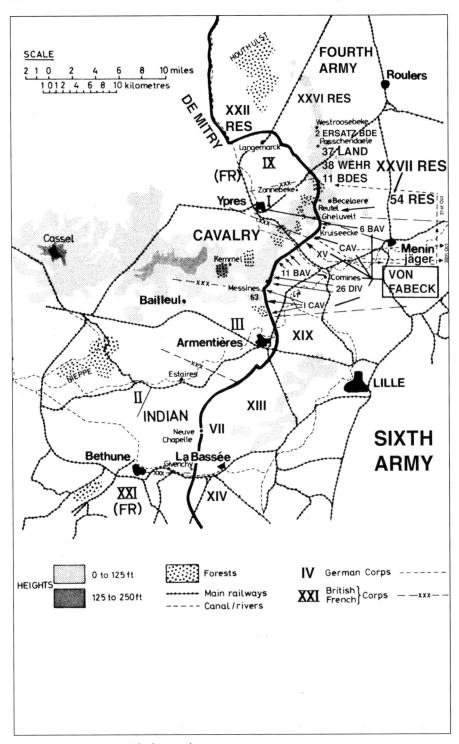

Ypres/ La Bassée: Von Fabeck's attack.

check the Germans and gave space to organize a resilient defence. Laying out his battalions on either side of Pervyse village, he had a chair brought out on to the main crossroads where all could see him. There under shellfire Grossetti exercised command through the rest of the day. 'I don't know how much will be left tomorrow of the 42nd Division', he signalled to d'Urbal, 'but so long as one man remains the Germans will not cross the railroad.'

SIGNS OF CRISIS: SUNDAY, 25TH OCTOBER TO THURSDAY, 29TH OCTOBER, 1914

Each night, Sir John French telegraphed an account of the day's events to Lord Kitchener, Secretary of State for War, in London. On the night of the 21st, restored perhaps by Joffre's pungent speech that afternoon, he ended his message with these words:

> '...In my opinion the enemy are vigorously playing their last card and I am confident they will fail.'

On the evening of the 25th, the telegram reported that the situation was growing more favourable hour by hour. '...My anxiety is over...' At the end of this Sunday of glorious weather, there were certainly reasons for being hopeful that allied fortunes in Flanders were rising. Joffre's promise of reinforcement had been honoured handsomely. Both divisions of Dubois' corps were in the line and ready to attack together on the 26th. A third division was arriving that night at the railhead and a fourth was moving to join them. A large draft of reinforcements had arrived in Flanders from the depots in the United Kingdom, including a number of experienced officers and men wounded in August but now fit and anxious to return to active service. In front of Ypres, Haig's 2nd Division strengthened the line and provided a force ready to advance with the French. The whole of his 1st Division was out of the trenches, resting in billets round the old town; a comfortable reserve. To the north, the Belgians had taken the decision to flood the coastal zone behind the Yser from Nieuport to Dixmude, a measure which should prove effective in a matter of days to safeguard the left flank. What the British Expeditionary Force needed now to take advantage of the opportunities was a continuing flow of reinforcements, an accession of new units, particularly infantry battalions and, most urgently, more shells for the guns. Sir Archibald Murray, the chief of staff, was sent back to London that night to amplify the reports of operations and to explain why men and munitions were urgently needed.

The buoyant atmosphere at GHQ was disturbed at midnight by the arrival of Sir Horace Smith-Dorrien. His anxiety deflated it. He saw Sir

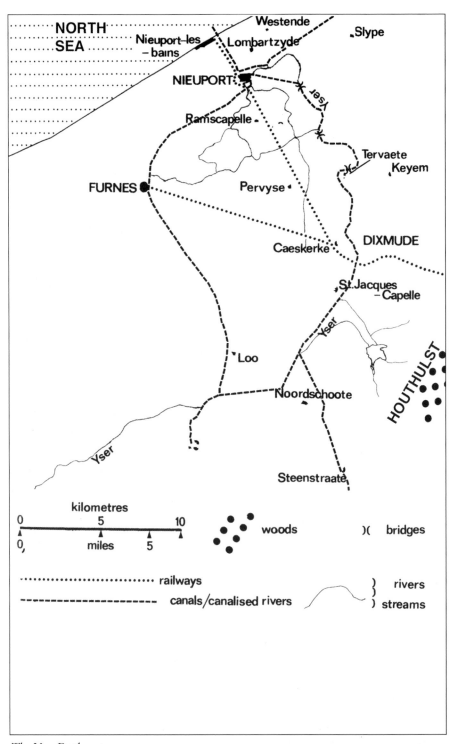

The Yser Battle

John in his private sitting room at Saint Omer and told him directly that he feared his corps line might go beyond repair during the night. 'Sir John was rather short with him,' Wilson recorded in his diary.[23] As we know, the commander-in-chief suspected Smith-Dorrien's judgement and believed him to be too easily dismayed. But whatever his feelings, he could not disregard a solemn warning of this sort from a corps commander; if his fears were realized, the consequences might be ruinous. There were more than five hours of darkness yet to run and it was raining hard. The nearest – and only – uncommitted reserve worth the title was 1st Division at Ypres, 28 miles from II Corps. Smith-Dorrien said that he had sent to de Maud'huy to ask if he could help but as yet there had been no time to obtain an answer. They discussed prospects and options restlessly for about half an hour when Sir John decided that they must hope that there would be no disastrous break that night so as to give time for more deliberate steps during the 26th. Meantime, he agreed to Wilson's suggestion that II Corps should be allotted two batteries of 4-7 inch guns at Hazebrouck which had been left out of battle because of the shortage of ammunition. He promised to release a special allocation of shells for their immediate use and to review the ration of shells permitted daily to all II Corps' artillery with the aim of increasing it.

General Smith-Dorrien drove back through the wet night to his headquarters and got to bed some time after 2am. In the morning, the skies cleared, the sun rose. From all sides came help and the swollen fears of the night drew back with the shadows.

Sir John sent from Allenby's corps the 2nd Cavalry Brigade, a battalion and a battery of guns. The ration of shells for the field guns in II Corps was raised from thirty to sixty rounds a day and, an important supplement to the corps artillery, a naval train mounting one 6-inch and two 4-7-inch guns was brought up along the canal bank behind Givenchy. These weapons were able to undertake a great deal of counter-battery fire because they had an ample supply of shells.[24] De Maud'huy offered to relieve the battalion on II Corps' right flank with one from his XXI Corps and added that.

> ...Conneau's cavalry corps is entirely at your disposal... with his nine batteries, his battalion of Chasseurs – light infantry – (greatly reduced to 300 men), his detachment of cyclists (4,500 bayonets), his battalion of dismounted cavalry (600-700 strong) in the district of La Gorge-Estaires...

[23] Wilson was acting as chief of staff in Murray's absence in London.

[24] The guns were of naval pattern and filed shells which could not be used by the army's artillery of common calibre. Their ammunition was of course supplied by the Admiralty.

1,000 British reinforcements reached II Corps on the 26th, and a second 1,000 on the 27th. Visiting Smith-Dorrien and his two divisional commanders on the morning of the 26th, Sir John reminded them that he intended still to relieve II Corps by the Indian Corps as soon as possible.

With these measures of relief in train or accomplished, there was inevitably a reaction of doubt as to their necessity. Other portions of the line might claim to be equally threatened, equally weak. The forward trenches of the 6th Division were so continuously under shellfire that Pulteney sensibly ordered the majority of the companies to be removed to the support line. The Messines ridge held by Allenby was manifestly of such importance in the sector that it must soon be the centre of a violent struggle for its possession. In front of Ypres, the trenches of the 3rd Cavalry and, still more, the 7th Divisions had received no less a battering than those in II Corps. Sir John and some of his staff at GHQ, Smith-Dorrien and his chief of staff at corps headquarters asked themselves and one another whether the warning delivered at midnight on 25th/26th had been justified.

It seems probable that those engaged in this questioning and self-questioning during and after Monday the 26th concluded that they had been overborne by the fears of their subordinates: Smith-Dorrien by his divisional commanders; Sir John by Smith-Dorrien. It is also probable that Smith-Dorrien's sensitive and affectionate nature was vulnerable to the sort of representation he had had from Morland, commander of 5th Division, and particularly from Mackenzie, commander of the 3rd, soon to be relieved due to being unfit. Sir Horace felt very deeply the burden of suffering amongst his soldiers. He did not find it difficult to believe that after 14 days of intense, unremitting action they had reached breaking point. Though he under-estimated the strength of the men he commanded, he was by no means completely wrong in his assessment of their ability to continue fighting.

There were clear signs of crisis amongst the British Expeditionary Force. In II and III Corps, during the preceding few days, some of the forward trenches had been abandoned by British battalions with little more than a token struggle. There had been similar instances along the allied line for on Sunday, 25th October, Haig wrote in his diary,

> On our left (near Pilckem) the French Territorials went into the trenches all right, but on the right towards Langemarck, they declined. Some ran back and gave as the reason 'L'ennemi a tiré w nous'...

For the 26th, this entry appears:

> ...when a report from IV Corps reaches me that the 7th Division which is holding a line from crossroads south-east of Gheluvelt to Zandvoorde is giving way, I send a staff officer to find out whether they are being attacked by infantry or whether they are merely leaving their trenches on account of shell fire. He reports several battalions in great disorder passing back through our 1st Brigade 3-4,000 yards in rear of the line). The latter sends the Black Watch towards Zandvoorde and posts two battalions between the crossroads and Poezelhoek... By 4 pm, the bulk of the 7th Division had retired from the salient about Kruisek (Kruiscecke); most units are` in disorder. One brigade came back to the vicinity of Hooge Chateau where I had my Reporting Centre. I rode out about 3 pm to see what was going on, and was astounded at the terror-stricken men coming back. Still there were some units in the Division which stuck to their trenches...

What had happened on the Menin road was that Kruiseecke, the point of the V salient, had been bombarded almost continuously for 36 hours, mostly with 210-mm shells. Captain Paynter of 2nd Scots Guards, one of the battalions holding the area, wrote of the period 25th/26th,

> Our trenches were tremendously shelled all day, some of the trenches being blown in; Drummond and Kemble, being buried in their trench, had to be dug out. A lot of cheering was heard in the distance when it became dark, and it was passed down the trenches that the French were attacking on our right. Then we noticed masses of troops advancing on our trenches. It was extremely dark and raining in torrents. Some got as far as our trenches and were shot down, others lay in front calling out 'We surrender', and 'Don't shoot; we are Allies', 'Where is Captain Paynter "G" Company?' Parties got through the line on my right and left and commenced firing at us from behind, others got into houses. We shot at and silenced all these. Fresh lots kept coming on; but, as our fire was pretty heavy, they seemed to make for places where others had got through. After about a couple of hours all was quiet.

But it was a brief respite and before dawn on the 26th the shelling began again, lasting until the middle of the morning when three dismounted regiments of German dragoons and an infantry regiment assaulted the line. At first the attack made no serious impression, though a few disorganized groups of Germans penetrated between the trenches of one or other company to the rear. Some but not all of these were captured; others hid in Kmiseecke village where they were killed or buried as their own guns haphazardly destroyed buildings. Between 10 and 11 in the morning a number of British trenches became untenable, being filled or half-filled with the sandy soil blown in by shell bursts which buried and suffocated some of the occupants, while the direct action of blast or shrapnel killed and wounded others or smashed weapons. For the survivors, the problem of keeping the working parts of their rifles and machine-guns free of grit became acute. Gradually, from every one of the four battalions, men began to fall back: fit men blown out of their trenches who were searching for the remains of their units; wounded men walking painfully to the rear; men recovering from the dreadful experience of being buried alive – the lucky ones traced and dug out by their comrades; men broken by exhaustion and the continual shock of seeing friends killed and wounded and the rising conviction that they themselves were about to die. This trickle of numbers leaving the brigade area swelled suddenly in the early afternoon. As a new assault began from the front, one of the German parties which had penetrated to the rear began to cry 'Retire! Retire!'[25] and the word was taken up. Fearful of being left isolated in their positions forward, company after company began to fall back and, seeing this, the assault forces closed upon them with a rush. Hours passed before control was restored; not because the 20th Brigade had run away in wholesale retreat but because the line had been broken up over a distance of 3 miles and scores of men by companies, platoons and smaller detachments were attempting to reorganize in rear without direction from their commanding officers – dead, wounded or captured – or battalion headquarters, most of which had been destroyed or disrupted.

Much the same sort of thing happened on the front of II Corps a little later in the afternoon of the same day. A prolonged and heavy bombardment was followed at 4 pm by a massive assault from the enemy trenches 500 yards to the east. The weakest part of the line was held by the 2nd Royal Irish Rifles which had been attacked twice in the previous day and night. There were two officers and seventeen other ranks left to hold the line and to dig out or construct afresh the trenches destroyed by shells and mortar bombs. Some men in this battalion had been buried and dug out twice; an even more horrifying experience in this sector – if one wants to be relative about these matters – because the soil was heavier and wetter than that on the Ypres ridge. These men, brought up blue in the face, some unconscious, were revived in the regimental aid post but went back to their

---

[25] On the previous night, the 25th/26th, there had been similar attempts to cause confusion by enemy from the same regiment which had penetrated in rear of 2nd Scots Guards.

places in the line at their own insistence. Is it to be wondered at that when the German assault struck the front trenches of the battalion men went back at once to the support positions when, ten days before, they might have died, rather than do so? What is remarkable is that with the exception of two individuals in the whole army during the period October-November, there were no cases of cowardice or desertion or quitting a post under fire. The military police reports from the rear, the adjutant-general's statistics and the medical returns support the evidence of the battalions and batteries and field companies, and of the brigade and divisional headquarters. There were occasions when men were taken beyond breaking point. But even those few who fell back, wild-eyed for two or three thousand yards, recovered themselves and returned shortly to join their friends at whatever point they had rallied immediately behind the lost trenches. What General Smith-Dorrien underestimated was the capacity of his soldiers to resist, whatever the extent of their losses or exhaustion or fear. And so, although the assault of the German VII Corps broke through 2nd Royal Irish Rifles to capture the village of Neuve Chapelle, it was the surviving element of this battalion that joined with companies from the units on either flank – 1st Wiltshires and 4th Royal Fusiliers – to counter-attack under Captain P S Rowan, adjutant of the Wiltshires. That evening and all next day, the struggle continued in and around Neuve Chapelle. Four British batteries were joined by seven from Conneau's corps to join the fire fight. 300 cyclists and the Chasseurs from the French Cavalry, 1st Lincolns, 2nd South Lancashire, 1st Northumberland Fusiliers, 1st Royal West Kents, 1st Duke of Cornwall's Light Infantry, 9th Bhopal Infantry, 47th Sikhs and the 20th and 21st Companies of the Indian Sappers and Miners were all drawn in completely or partly. The 14th Division of von Claer's VII Corps committed all twelve of its battalions, to which the corps commander added a jäger battalion and eleven of infantry borrowed from XIII and XIV Corps or taken from his own 13th Division. This force was supported by the divisional and corps artillery and three batteries of heavy field howitzers and three of heavy mortars. By the end of the second day, the Royal Irish Rifles, the Wiltshires and the South Lancashires were fighting collectively as a unit totalling 587, the figure including the reinforcements which had reached them on the previous day. Still in action, their presence shows that II Corps line was not in danger of breaking.

While local actions raged at Kruiseecke and Neuve Chapelle, Falkenhayn completed his review of operations in Flanders and on the 27th he came forward to Crown Prince Rupprecht's headquarters to let his conclusions be known in detail.

Sixth and Fourth Armies had failed effectively to breach the allied line, notwithstanding the free grouping of regiments for assaults south of the Menin road or the immense superiority of numbers amongst the new corps to the north of it. Indeed, not only had the line not been breached, but its occupants had turned to the offensive along the ridge north of the road, thanks to the arrival of French reinforcements. Fourth Army had been obliged to commit 2nd Ersatz, 37th and 38th *Landwehr* Brigades between XXVI and XXVII Reserve Corps to contain the French IX Corps and British 2nd Division. It was clear that neither the Sixth nor the Fourth Army had sufficient capability for decisive offensive action unless they were given substantial reinforcements.

Supreme Headquarters had been able during the preceding fortnight to appraise the needs of defence elsewhere on the western front. The French had made several withdrawals from their line to strengthen their position in Flanders. Due to these movements and certain adjustments of the defences on the ground, it had proved possible to make a complementary withdrawal of two regular German corps – II Bavarian from Peronne and XV from the Aisne. The 48th Reserve Division[26] was *en route* from Metz to Flanders to relieve the regular 26th Division in XIII Corps. 6th Bavarian Reserve was already available in Fourth Army.

This was a force of considerable offensive power: five regular divisions and one of novices, whose fresh numbers and mettle compensated for their lack of experience. Falkenbayn had no intention of offering it as a general reinforcement to the two royal army commanders. Grouped under a single chief, it should strike a concentrated blow at the centre within a renewed offensive between La Bassée and the sea.

It was a judicious concept. The concensus of intelligence was that the enemy line was weak, except perhaps along the northern approach to the Ypres ridge, where Dubois' corps was attacking. It was believed that the British were maintaining numerous local reserves behind their forward trenches. Beginning on the 30th, Sixth and Fourth Armies should attack or threaten the allied line sufficiently to compel the use of these reserves, or at least to dissuade the enemy commanders from moving them to other sectors. Simultaneously, the new force would attack and breach the enemy defences with the aim of capturing Mont Kemmel in rear, exploiting thereafter to Cassel. General von Fabeck of XIII Corps was appointed to command the operation, the force being named Army Group Fabeck,[27] It

[26] One of the divisions of XXTV Reserve Corps.

[27] He used his own Corps headquarters' staff for the direction of Group Fabeck. The responsibilities of XIII Corps were taken over by XXTV Corps headquarters, brought up from Metz.

was to form up as a new right wing of Sixth Army but Falkenhayn warned Crown Prince Rupprecht and von Delmensingen that they might not modify von Fabeck's task or withdraw his forces for use elsewhere without the permission of Supreme Headquarters. Their first duty was to provide support, including as much support in heavy artillery as the remainder of the Army could afford to supplement the additional batteries and shells provided from the Argonne and Champagne. Reserve stocks of high explosive shells were being sent forward from Germany.

It was now the common experience of both sides that while shrapnel was a deadly weapon against men in the open, high explosive was needed for those sheltering in trenches; and the greater the weight of high explosive the more lasting the effect. The British Army had never possessed large stocks of high explosive and were running out of shrapnel. The French and Germans suffered from shortages of both that autumn and winter but were benefiting by the quick adaptation of their industries to war supply. In addition to the artillery organic to Fabeck's divisions and corps, he was now allotted sixty batteries of heavy field howitzers, eight batteries of heavy mortars and one 305-mm coast defence mortar; two hundred and fifty-seven guns and mortars in all.

Intense planning ensued. II Bavarian and XV Corps arrived in their concentration areas behind the Lys; 48th Reserve Division relieved the 26th in XIII Corps line to join them. It was arranged that they should advance in darkness on the night of the 29th, relieve all von der Marwitz' troops except I Cavalry Corps on the left, and from the existing trenches advance to assault on the morning of the 30th. I Cavalry Corps, reinforced by two infantry battalions, were to remain in position to guard the left flank as the battle for Messines progressed.

The frontage of assault selected for von Fabeck's group was from Saint Yves (next to Ploegsteert Wood) to Gheluvelt. A break-in at any point on this line would offer access to Mont Kemmel along the high ground but within the sector Fabeck favoured the capture of Messines Ridge (see map 9, page 106). It was nearest to Mont Kemmel; its gain would permit him immediately to bring into enfilade extensive sections of the enemy's positions. The importance of Gheluvelt and the high point of Ypres ridge behind it was not to be underrated, however. Its possession would enhance the capture of Messines an Wytschaete and if they failed to make the capture at the first attempt, a German force behind Gheluvelt would be able to provide strong support for the second. But if the British still held Gheluvelt, their observation posts would see directly across to the rear of the assault against Messines. The early capture of Gheluvelt was therefore most desirable.

The immediate problem was access to the village. The capture of Kruiseecke on the 26th had removed one of its covering positions but the enemy still held trenches on the reverse slope and the hillock of Zandvoorde, south of the Menin road. An assault force must approach across or between these positions which commanded the ground. Because of these difficulties, von Fabeck decided to mount a preliminary operation on the 29th to capture Gheluvelt village using the cavalry and infantry currently in position immediately south of the Ypres-Menin road and two regiments of his own 6th Bavarian Reserve Division to the north of it. He asked that 54th Reserve Division should co-operate in their attack.

Fourth Army agreed and sent a signal to XXVII Reserve Corps during the morning of the 28th instructing them to postpone an attack they had planned for that day and to act in concert with the Bavarians at 5.30 a.m. on the 29th.

Unknown to the Germans, this signal was intercepted by the allies.

Unperturbed by the loss of Neuve Chapelle, Sir John French continued to look forward to the advance of his own and d'Urbal's forces on to and beyond the Ypres ridge. To tidy arrangements in this area, he passed 7th Division from Rawlinson's to Haig's command,[28] and reporting this to Kitchener that evening, 27th October, remarked that on reliable information the enemy were 'quite incapable of making any strong and sustained attack'.

Unfortunately, it was the allies who were incapable of doing so, though they did not recognize this fact. The French 31st Division had now joined Dubois' corps where their numbers would have been of value for assault or exploitation through the two divisions already in the line – the more so as each of these had shed a regiment to the left flank under Major-General Hely d'Oissel. However, such was d'Urbal's confidence that he extended the frontage of Dubois' advance and ordered him to commit 31st Division to the extension. The concept and event of the counter-offensive was a dangerous farce, winning a few hundred yards of ground for the French over the 27th and 28th at a cost of over 2,000 casualties. To their right, 1st 60th Rifles and 2nd South Staffords waited hours for the French to move and eventually pressed forward without them, across the ridge and down into the valley on the far side. They were now east of the ridge while the French were west of it but neither Haig nor Dubois made any effort jointly to exploit the tactical advantage this offered. Ahead of the two British

---

[28] 3rd Cavalry Division had been passed to the Cavalry Corps on 25th October. Rawlinson was sent back to England with his headquarters to prepare the 8th Division for active service. He returned with them later, when IV Corps was reformed with 7th and 8th Divisions.

battalions lay Keiberg, the tip of a spur running down from Passchendaele, below which they halted in the afternoon under a degree of fire from the enemy across the open, rising ground ahead. Together, it had cost them 293 casualties to get thus far and their only prospect of getting on was by a night attack. In answer to this suggestion, the usual message came back, emanating from the divisional commander visiting brigade headquarters: the hour is late (it was 3 pm); a thorough reconnaissance will be needed in daylight tomorrow prior to an attack.'

This attitude and the lack of co-operation between the two corps commanders ensured effectively that any remaining hope of upsetting the enemy by offensive action in the area was extinguished.

Nonetheless, the evidence of failure to get forward on the 26th, 27th and morning of the 28th was disregarded. Plans were in hand during the latter afternoon to continue on exactly the same lines when GHQ passed down the news that they had intercepted[29] a German wireless message from Fourth Army to XXVII Reserve Corps ordering an attack on the British line at 5.30 a.m. on the morning of the 29th. Local intelligence suggested that this would be from Kruiseecke south of the Menin road with possibly a parallel thrust immediately to the north; an estimate which placed 54th Reserve Division too far south but by luck embraced the compass of the enemy plan. It is a measure of the speed of communications in the battle zone that this warning, which reached I Corps headquarters at 3 pm on the 28th, did not get to battalion commanders, though given high precedence over other messages passing down through division and brigade headquarters, until midnight. Yet I Corps headquarters was at Hooge Chateau, only 3,000 yards behind the line. This is not a reflection of staff inefficiency – Haig had perhaps the most efficient staff in Flanders at that time under Brigadier-General John Gough – but of the problems of communications: the lack of wireless equipment forward to divisions, brigades and battalions; the difficulty of maintaining telephone cables when these were continually being cut by artillery fire; and sustaining a messenger service forward in the absence of communication trenches.

At 45 minutes past midnight on the night 28th/29th, the adjutant of 2nd Royal Scots Fusiliers sent out this message to the rifle companies.

F.23. 1. It is understood that a general attack will be made on our lines about 5.30 am today.

2. It is possible that B Company and that portion of A Company to East of it may be relieved before that time. If so, B Company will join D

---

[29] The British had a *Bellini Tosi* set in use which had been modified especially by the Marconi Company.

Company in Reserve and occupy vacant shelter. A Company if relieved will be used to strengthen its line West of track leading through its front.

3. Companies will stand to arms at 5 am.

4. Rations have been offloaded at North end of wood where battalion headquarters are and should be drawn tonight as Cooks' carts have moved off.

5. Battalion Aid Post will be at N end of wood where battalion HQ now is.

As the runners were scrambling out of the headquarters' trench to double across the open ground to the company positions, a heavy rumbling sound was heard to the east which continued until about 3 am, when the fog began to gather. A hopeful young Scot suggested that perhaps the Germans were retiring but none would accept that; the noise was in any case approaching the line.

What they heard was the rumbling of wheels on the pave as the host of heavy guns moved into their forward positions.

PART IV

A Time Of Crisis

'One must always credit the enemy with doing the right thing.'
VON MOLTKE, THE ELDER

VON FABECK'S PRELUDE:
29TH OCTOBER, 1914

Promptly at 5 am on the 29th, Haig's corps stood to arms. It was a still, dark morning and densely foggy.

Standing in their trenches, rifles in hand, the limit of visibility for the watching men was between 30 to 40 yards. Even if it had been fully light and clear many would not have had a field of view greater than 100 yards because their positions were amongst houses, gardens and orchards, particularly in the centre and on the right where the line had been pushed back from Kruiseecke.

Only two battalions of 7th Division now held trenches on a forward slope, much to Haig's relief. It is remarkable that he had failed to notice, however, that the positions he had agreed for 1st and 2nd Divisions had brought six of their units into similar positions. Whatever the ground occupied, the trenches and other defences varied a good deal in type and condition. Many of those in the 1st and 7th Divisions were in the former support trenches, dug deep and narrow for men to shelter in while they awaited the outcome of the battle in front some days before.[1] A few were in fire trenches, constructed as such with traverses and fire steps, and perhaps a small dugout or two buttressed by timbers from nearby cottages. Here and there buildings had themselves been crudely fortified by earth

---

[1] During Rawlinson's initial advance towards and retirement from Menin.

packed into wooden frames and broken furniture, the ceilings braced by fallen joists and rafters. Elsewhere, men took cover in whatever defences they could scrape with the digging tools remaining serviceable. Wherever they were, platoon trenches were the rule, though most trenches dug for a platoon 10 days before could now accommodate a company.

It was cold, waiting in the trenches before dawn. The smell of damp earth, damp clothes, damp humanity rose all around. Guns could be heard firing distantly but all noise was increasingly muffled by the fog. Companies were isolated from one another; alone in the world, awaiting an enemy to creep from the shadows with whom they would struggle in isolation.

At exactly 5.30 am the Germans appeared to the north of the Menin road.

There was no preliminary bombardment. From Becelaere (see map 9, page 106) a regiment of 54th Reserve Division appeared silently and swiftly, guided on to 1st Scots Guards precisely by the line of the road into Gheluvelt. They attacked with one battalion on either side of the road and one in rear astride it, the dense lines a little broken by the minor obstacles in their path. By luck a light wind, a temporary eddy from conflicting temperatures perhaps, had just stirred along the valley, clearing the mist and revealing the approaching foe at 80 yards. The rifles and machine-guns of the Scots Guards trained for rapid fire.

Immediately to the south – their right – was a company of Black Watch and part of 1st Coldstream Guards under Captain J E Gibbs. They were more nearly surprised because the wind did not move the curtain of fog at half past five when a battalion of Bavarians appeared and they might have been overwhelmed but for another chance. The Bavarians had no natural feature to guide them directly on to the British trenches and were led forward by files of scouts. Off line, some of these were seen by the Coldstream suddenly at few yards range and shot, and thus everyone in the trench and close by was straining to glimpse the approaching lines when they came into view. Here, too, a heavy fire was opened but not so rapidly as amongst the Scots Guards due to an exceptional circumstance. A batch of rifle ammunition had been issued the previous evening to the I Corps line in which the brass cartridge cases were slightly oversize. A sharp movement of the bolt would force the round into the breech of the Lee Enfield but the empty case could not be extracted by the flick of the right wrist. After firing each shot, it was necessary to lower the butt to the thigh and tug the bolt back. When the breech became very hot or where fragments of sand or grit became lodged in the moving parts behind it, the rifleman was forced to place the butt on the ground and kick down on the bolt lever with his boot to free the weapon. Their difficulties would have been eased if there had been rifle oil to hand but there was none – many units had been unable to obtain a supply for three days.

Two hundred yards to the south of Captain Gibbs' position, the Becelaere road crossed the main Menin road and ran on to Kruiseecke (see map 11, page 123). This cross-roads was held by two more companies of Coldstream, a platoon and machine-gun section from the 1st Gloucesters and another company of 1st Black Watch. They, too, were attacked at 5.30 out of the fog, two battalions of Bavarians coming at them in succession. The sudden appearance of the foe, their numbers, the jamming of the rifles led to a swift catastrophe for the defence. In a matter of minutes they were overwhelmed and their trenches taken. At ten minutes to six, the Bavarians had collected sufficient numbers together to send four companies northward – two along the line of trenches and two in rear.

At 6 o'clock, the Coldstream and Black Watch under Captain Gibbs had repulsed three assaults and were taking cover in their trenches from a bombardment when Gibbs was alarmed to see a number of those in the position immediately to the south leaping out to the rear. The reason for their withdrawal was plain: the trench was filling with Germans. As soon as the German bombardment stopped – about 6.30 am. – the left of the Coldstream were fired upon from the southern flank and from the rear. Gibbs organized his numbers to face these directions as well as the front, from which a fourth assault seemed imminent, and sent runners to Brigadier General FitzClarence, the brigade commander, and to 1st Scots Guards to the north to ask for support.

The Scots Guards were themselves alternately firing their rifles – they had now begun to use, to their dismay, some of the defective ammunition – and taking cover from shell fire when the German assaults were driven back. The runner sent to Brigadier-General FitzClarence was never seen again after passing into the smoke of bursting shells. But the brigadier was informed at 7 am. of the destruction of the force on the cross-roads by a wounded officer taken into his headquarters *en route* to the dressing station. At once he sent a runner to his reserve battalion, 1st Gloucesters, to occupy the crossroads and reinforce Gibbs with one company. The commanding officer of this battalion, Lieutenant-Colonel A C Lovett, had already heard the news and was despatching help on his own initiative.

D Company was immediately ready and set off for the crossroads, shortly followed by a second company. A third went to join them but came under heavy shellfire east of Gheluvelt and were scattered in the fog. The fourth company set off to find Captain Gibbs and what remained of 1st Coldstream. Though it was now daylight and the fog less dense they missed their way and, after a sharp skirmish with some Bavarians in the half light, joined 1st Scots Guards.[2]

It was now after half past seven.

South of the crossroads, 1st Grenadier Guards had waited at 5.30 for the enemy like the other battalions in the line. Behind, brought up urgently from the rear by the brigade commander to meet the expected attack, were the 2nd Scots Guards and 2nd Border, each at half strength since the battle for Kruiseecke three days before. At 6.30, none of these units knew that the Bavarians had captured the crossroads 200 yards distant, although they had heard firing and occasional shouts through the fog. Battalions had no telephone communications to one another and there was of course no wireless. By 6.45 all sounds of battle had faded to the north – where Gibbs' detachment and 1st Scots Guards were fighting – and there was no sign of an attack on 1st Grenadiers, who began, as practical soldiers, to make their breakfast. But there was no breakfast to be had for the 2nd Scots Guards and Border because they had no rations. When called forward the previous night, the cooks' carts were just arriving from the administrative echelon in rear. There had been no time to break down the bulk of tins or open even the sacks of bread. The battalions had marched off into the fog.

Brigadier-General Ruggles-Brise decided to send them back to their respective areas to eat and rest.

They had just left at 7 o'clock when a group of German infantry began to attack the left-hand company of 2nd Royal Scots Fusiliers some way to the south of 1st Grenadiers. At 7.30, the heavy guns near Menin rumbled and for 15 minutes high explosive shells fell upon the Grenadiers and a zone in rear as far back as the village of Gheluvelt. It was this fire which broke up the third company of Gloucesters and some of it fell on the two ahead of it, making for the crossroads. At 8 o'clock, four battalions of Germans appeared from the remaining mist and were seen at about 250 yards' range by the Grenadiers like '...a crowd coming on the ground after a football match'. There were more behind.

South of the Menin Road, the relatively tidy lines of defence now broke up in close and confused fighting. First the Grenadiers, then the Gordons on their right and right again 2nd Royal Scots Fusiliers were assaulted and gradually encroached upon by the numerous enemy. To add to the difficulty of oversize cartridges, the fire of one or two of the British supporting batteries fell on the Grenadiers and Scots Fusiliers. Fortunately,

---

[2] The Scots Guards Historian for this period states erroneously on page 52 that the Gloucesters had been broken through on the Menin Road, an event which had led to the opening of the British line. 1st Gloucesters were not, of course, holding the line although they were fed piecemeal to fill the gap later.

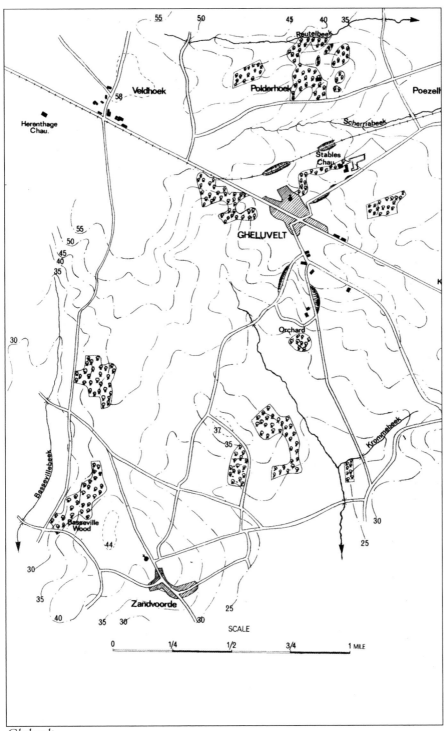

Gheluvelt

there was little of it; the field guns were rationed to 9 rounds per gun for the day because of the acute shortage and a proportion of this was reserved for striking the enemy guns. Reserves were drawn in. The Gloucesters on the crossroads were swept aside and some joined the Grenadiers and some the battalion sent up to join the struggle. Attack was met by counter-attack. Ejected from their trenches, the Grenadiers reassembled wherever they could and returned until they were spent. Four officers and 100 men were found by those who came from the rear to join them amongst the ruins of a group of houses and the brigadier then told them to withdraw.

To the north of the road, the German artillery broke gradually the little rectangle of positions which Gibbs had improvised. There had been a lull for two hours in the assaults, perhaps to arrange for the bombardment which fell at 10 am and to bring up fresh troops, who arrived at 10.30. The two remaining companies of 1st Coldstream and the company of the 1st Black Watch were then entirely killed or captured. On their left, the 1st Scots Guards hung on desperately as every reserve remaining in I Corps, regardless of brigade origin, was brought up into the line and, slowly, the trenches were won back piece by piece until, at 3 o'clock in the afternoon, the line rejoined behind the crossroads. In Gheluvelt Chateau at 4, Major-General Landon[3] met the commanding officers of the five battalions drawn in to hold the Menin-Ypres road. All that remained to be recovered were the crossroads 500 yards south east of the new line, but as they talked about the means of making this final effort of the day it became apparent that none of them thought it worth the loss of a single man.

So they dispersed to their own places; the commanding officers back to the line and a night of entrenching and putting out the barbed wire which, at last, had arrived in small quantities for the use of the infantry; the general to his headquarters. Nearby, Lieutenant-Colonel Lovett drew in his widely dispersed battalion and learnt that he had lost seven officers and 163 men during the day. What remained of the 1st Coldstream gathered under the quartermaster Lieutenant J Boyd, the only surviving officer. The 20th Brigade were taken out of the line to reorganize their numbers and re-equip with whatever ordnance supplies were to hand.

Sir Douglas Haig returned to I Corps headquarters. He had moved his staff from the Hooge Chateau during the day as an act of generosity; the commander and staff of 1st Division were living and working in a few cramped buildings close by so he gave them his own offices and quarters.[4]

[3] He had just been promoted, hence his unusual rank for the appointment he held as a brigade commander.

[4] 2nd Division headquarters were already sharing the Chateau.

I Corps moved back on the 29th about 2,000 yards to the White Chateau behind the level crossing over the railway line to Roulers. For those who may incline to put this movement down to apprehension rather than kindness, it may be said that the White Chateau stood on what became known as Hellfire Corner. It was not a safe place and Ypres was already under shellfire daily. But the move was to have consequences which Haig could not foresee.

He received that evening orders to co-operate in the French advance next day.[5] Sir John had been to see Foch and Foch had had it from d'Urbal that they were making gains steadily: Bixschoote and Kortekeer Cabaret had been recaptured by de Mitry. Knowing that Dubois had not captured a metre of ground on their common flank, Haig gave instructions that divisions should reorganize, entrench and wire during the night and reconnoitre as early as possible next day.

His expectation of a defensive action on the 30th was confirmed when his artillery commander reported that the enemy had been registering a great number of targets with heavy and super-heavy guns throughout the day.

It was true that General von Fabeck had brought his heavy guns into position early in the morning of the 29th and that his gunners had registered targets through the late morning and afternoon. In the evening, he brought in his infantry. The five regular divisions began their march to the Lys as soon as it was dark and crossed into the positions held by the cavalry. The dismounted regiments withdrew quietly, leaving I Cavalry Corps to join the newcomers; the only sign of the relief being the rumble of wheels as the infantry divisional artillery and some of the corps howitzers came into their places and the light cavalry guns went out.[6] Near the Menin road, the two regiments of 6th Bavarian Reserve Division withdrew into reserve and 11th Landwehr Brigade fell back also to march north to Becelaere. These movements were planned and executed impeccably.

An Order of the Day was issued to remind the participants of Army Group Fabeck of their purpose.

> ...The breakthrough will be of decisive importance. We must and therefore will conquer, settle for ever with the centuries-long struggle, end the war, and strike the decisive blow against our most detested enemy. We will finish the British, Indians, Canadians, Moroccans, and other trash, feeble adversaries, who surrender in great numbers if they

[5] The instruction was to continue operations as on the previous day; that is to continue attacking with the French.

[6] Only the super-heavy, heavy and some of the medium guns came forward on the night of the 29th. The field guns had to wait until, battery for battery, they relieved those of the cavalry on the night of the 30th so as to avoid detection during the day of the 29th.

are attacked with vigour...

Again, the night was quiet except for the rumbling wheels.

OFFENCE RENEWED: 30TH OCTOBER 1914

Along the Yser, the Germans were puzzled by the rapid softening of the ground and the growing nuisance of flood water. They put it down to the heavy seasonal rain. Perhaps Duke Albrecht and his chief of staff began to suspect that the Belgian engineers were operating the sluice gates in reverse, or perhaps they were merely anxious to press their sole enterprise under the new plan of operations. Whatever their motive, Fourth Army reopened the offensive a day early, attacking heavily on the afternoon of the 29th along the perimeter of the Yser bridge-head and with particular force against Ramscapelle and Pervyse. While daylight lasted, the Germans were held back by artillery fire – those at Ramscapelle being assisted by the naval gunfire from Rear-Admiral Hood's flotilla.[7] But as evening fell it was no longer possible for the ships to give close support and the Belgian infantry waited in Ramscapelle and along the railway across its front for the assaulting troops to reappear. A wind had sprung up from the sea at dusk, bringing with it heavy rain. At 9 pm, there was a short intense bombardment which stopped abruptly to allow two regiments of the 5th Reserve Division to storm across the railway embankment. Between 10 and 3 am next morning fighting continued along the railway line, around and through Ramscapelle village to the west. At 3, the Belgians fell back, their units unable to continue without reorganization and a period of inactivity followed until dawn.

The morning of the 30th found Pervyse intact in French hands but von Beseler's 6th Reserve Division had drawn close enough to the railway embankment to throw grenades across it at many places. The German platoon in these foremost positions were hard to dislodge because they were shielded by the track-way above, low as it was. After many anxious days, the defence of the Yser had reached the nadir of its fortunes; for if von Beseler held and passed across the railway any quantity of troops the whole scheme of inundation would be valueless; the allies would be forced back to defend the canal de Furnes and canal de Loo, a line three times the length of the railway. The matter was so serious that Ronarc'h sent from Dixmude two companies of his sailors to reinforce Pervyse.

Dixmude was quiet on the morning of the 30th. To the right, the canal line running south to Ypres was quiet, too. But at Bixschoote, two

---

[7] Joined that day by five French torpedo-boats.

regiments of the XXIII Reserve Corps attacked de Mitry's Territorials[8] and wrested the ruins from them once more. Langemarck was attacked at the same time but without success.

Dubois' corps had attempted obediently to capture Poelcapelle. The infantry could not do more than leave their trenches, endure a fierce fire for a few minutes and then return, their casualties honouring their obligation. They were opposed by the two divisions of XXVI Reserve Corps, a regiment of the Marine Division,[9] the 2nd Ersatz and 37th Landwehr Brigades: thirty French battalions[10] attempting to attack by frontal assault thirty-nine of the Germans with the latter on commanding ground.

Some of Dubois' troops were saved from this folly by the presence of the enemy on their own ground. The Germans bombarded the junction of Dubois' and Haig's lines from 6 to 7 am, the majority of the shells falling in the triangle Gravenstafel-Broodseinde-Zonnebeke. In the darkness – it was foggy again but the rain from the coast had not reached the ridge – there was no indication of what this fire might presage but *poilus* and Tommys stood to arms. At half past six, when the shelling switched to Polygon Wood, about seven battalions attacked from the mist; the exact number being uncertain as many remained hidden in the gloom. They did not close on the British trenches on this morning because barbed wire, received and put out only the previous night, checked them. The French battalion on the left had fewer obstacles but did not – at least for a time – receive a direct assault, the Germans striking the British positions first and then side-stepping towards them in an attempt to evade their fire and find an opening on the flank. These attacks, made with persistent bravery by Landwehr regiments, continued until 9 am and stopped only then because their numbers were too few to form more than a single line. Their dead and wounded lay strewn along the British wire and across the approach to the French trenches. We do not know what the German soldiers were told was the object of their attack. They may not have realized that the operation was a feint, its purpose to draw off reserves supporting Gheluvelt.

The gallant feint was not successful; neither the French nor British believed their positions were endangered and thus no call was made for reinforcement – though a platoon was sent forward gratuitously. But it was not the fault of the Landwehr that the attack on Gheluvelt failed. 54th Reserve Division attacked once more along the north of the main road

[8] De Mitry's command now comprised the 87th Territorial Division, the 5th and 9th Cavalry Divisions.

[9] The remainder were employed on coast defence.

[10] Six battalions had been detached to Hely d'Oissel's flank guard. Even with their presence, IX Corps had inferior numbers.

with the newcomers, 30th Division on their right. But it was not an affair of stealth, as on the previous morning. The artillery bombarded the defenders of Gheluvelt from 6.45 to 8 am and then advanced in full daylight. In sight for 500 yards, the lines of assault were destroyed or dispersed by British rifle fire before they had closed to 200. A second attempt was made an hour later, when Generals von Deimling and von Hohenbom, the divisional commanders exhorted their soldiers as they formed-up, with very much the same result. Apart from the dead and wounded, however, a number of 30th Division remained forward when the assault line scattered and small parties engaged in skirmishing with an advanced post of the 1st Queen's for some hours.

The prized ground of Gheluvelt remained, therefore, in British possession; and on the left flank of von Fabeck's sector, Ploegsteert Wood, Saint Yves, Messines and the ridge to Wytschaete would not give way. The pressure of his numbers and the weight of his artillery were too great, however, to be withheld at all points. The heavy shelling from 6.45 to 8 a.m. which fell upon the Gheluvelt defences proceeded in parallel to the south where 1st and 2nd Life Guards manned trenches with the machine-guns of the Blues below the hillock of Zandvoorde. The high explosive fell and blew and blasted amongst the squadrons, some of whose trenches were dug in echelon across the forward slopes, the remainder running west across the valley to the bank of the Ypres-Comines canal. Those on the slope of Zandvoorde hill fared worst and the 400 men, the sum of two regiments, who had stood to at dawn had been reduced to 320 by 8 o'clock. The brigade commander then saw a mass of Germans approaching – two regiments of the 39th Division and three battalions of *jäger*. He decided that his regiments must be moved back before they were overwhelmed and sent these orders to the two commanding officers. But the two squadrons on the slopes and the section of machine-guns could not get out; the enemy guns had already fired on the target of their trenches many times and the moment they were seen in the open, shrapnel was added to high explosive. They were annihilated.

The Life Guards belonged to the 7th Cavalry Brigade in 3rd Cavalry Division. Major-General Julian Byng, the divisional commander, had watched the action from a wood about 800 yards in rear and as soon as he saw the confusion, he sent an officer back to tell Haig what had happened – Haig's headquarters was the nearest – and to telephone from there the news to Allenby's headquarters in Kemmel. A galloper brought forward the 6th Cavalry Brigade to protect the withdrawal of the 7th. These actions safeguarded his front, at least for the moment, and ensured that the 7th

Division would be informed of the position. And so they were, I Corps telephoning to them by 8.40, but thereafter it took a good deal longer to pass the information to the battalions.

An hour before the warning that Zandvoorde was lost came down from brigade headquarters, they had learned it from other sources, and more strikingly. By 9 am, several German batteries had come into action on the west side of the Zandvoorde feature to fire directly into the British trenches to the east. Fortunately, they were spotted by two British field gun positions – 'we had very little ammunition but plenty of time to look for targets', one of the battery commanders said – and the crews hit the targets neatly. The German infantry were not so vulnerable, having found plenty of cover round the outskirts of Zandvoorde village and from these positions they were out of sight of the British guns but nicely placed to enfilade the British trenches to the east. 1st Royal Welch Fusiliers were the nearest unit and while they were struggling to find other positions from which to reply on equal terms, a battalion of *jäger* worked round their open flank to a ditch 30 yards from them. Another German field battery found their range with shrapnel and 20 minutes later the battalion ceased to exist. The commanding officer was killed and with him 275 others. Only fifty-four remained to be taken prisoner and none of these was unmarked by shrapnel or bullet.

The two battalions beyond were now menaced in the same way. Their only advantage was that each had seen the Germans advance and each had time to make some sort of preparation against it.

2nd Royal Scots Fusiliers were next in line and managed to place a section across their right flank. These eight rifles prevented the enemy from approaching on them from the rear but could not suppress the German artillery. It was a matter of time before the batteries of the 39th Division found positions in enfilade. At 12.45 in the afternoon, a runner arrived with a message sent directly from divisional headquarters telling them to withdraw. D Company and battalion headquarters drew back but it was too late for A, B and C. Whenever they attempted to leave their trenches, the shrapnel descended; for the ground behind, across which they had to travel, was open and rising. The three companies therefore remained where they were and prevented the German infantry from closing.

Their presence assisted the Green Howards, who did not receive the message to withdraw until 3.30 – the first runner despatched to them had been killed. In commanding positions and with a covered line of withdrawal along hedgerows and through a wood, the Yorkshire battalion coolly and skilfully slipped away unscathed but for ten of their 318 officers and men. They were followed after darkness by 130 of the Royal Scots Fusiliers.

Even with wireless communications, men tend to become absorbed with the drama of their own affairs when action abounds on the battlefield. Without radio or telephone, the Green Howards and the Royal Scots Fusiliers had no information of any kind as to the efforts set in hand to recapture Zandvoorde and restore the line around them. By nightfall, when they had rallied inside the new perimeter, they were too tired to care.

From 10 o'clock onwards, Allenby had been concerned to delay the advance of the German 39th Division and the Bavarian Corps so as to give Haig time to reinforce the sector and then counter-attack. Quite early that morning, Allenby had sensed that the attack he had expected for many days was about to break upon him and having few reserves he created one by withdrawing three regiments and a battery from Gough. With the loss of Zandvoorde, he passed this at once to Haig to strengthen the 1st South Staffords and the 2nd Battalions of Gordon Highlanders, Royal Warwicks and Bedfords. Individually, as they appeared, and later in various combinations of association the cavalry and infantry tried to push back into Zandvoorde – but all failed. Each was a pointless endeavour; they were out-numbered and forced sooner or later to come wholly into the open. As soon as this happened, the German artillery opened fire, the quick response being due to the fact that at least three field batteries lying back were firing over open sights.

It became clear in the early afternoon that the offensive was being undertaken by a very large German force indeed; far more numerous than they had expected or believed to be present in the area. Haig was then obliged to consider whether he could indefinitely resist the pressure of these numbers – many of the units he had sent forward were extremely weak; the Royal Warwicks under Captain Sydenham consisting of six officers and 150 men. Hollebeke had been lost and, after a long stand by a squadron of the Royals, Hollebeke Chateau. What other ground would be lost before the Germans, advancing slowly but steadily, were halted? On the high ground behind Zandvoorde he had placed General Bulfin[11] with Cavan's brigade and two other battalions but there were no reserves left to fill the gap between this reasonably strong position and the point at which, eventually, the left of the cavalry came to rest.

He had sent once that morning to Dubois for assistance and had received immediately a brigade of cuirassiers. At ten to three he sent again. Without any delay or enquiry as to priority of demands, Dubois released

---

[11] Also recently promoted.

his corps reserve of three infantry battalions and, later a further two and three batteries. The force was placed under command of a brigadier from 17th Division, General Moussy. From the late afternoon onwards, these troops began to assemble behind Verbranden and the gap, 2,000 yards across, held tenuously by the 18th Hussars.

When night fell the line was joined and backed at every point by some sort of reserve. Sir John, who had visited Allenby and Haig during the afternoon, was quite calm and promised to order forward the strongest of Smith-Dorrien's brigade from its rest area – though it had not been out of the line for 24 hours. Neither Allenby nor Haig had any illusions that the offensive was over; they knew it was just beginning.

Between 7 and 8 pm, there came a lull. From Bixschoote to La Bassée the night calm was only occasionally disturbed by shellfire and in a long interval of peace, the British cavalry were astonished to hear a band playing selections from light opera in the Hollebeke Chateau.

NIGHT WATCHES: 30TH – 31ST OCTOBER, 1914

Towards the end of each day – between 8pm and midnight each evening as a rule – the senior commanders and their staffs met to assess the intelligence gathered during the day and to prepare orders for the morrow. The aim was to meet late enough to permit all the essential information to come in from a wide variety of sources and early enough to have time for the order to percolate to the battalion, battery and field engineer company commanders who had to put them into effect. Because of lack of experience in all the Armies of the nations engaged, and because of the poor communications facilities, orders for operations often arrived at a battalion headquarters only an hour or so before they were due to be effected. There were numbers of occasions when orders arrived after the notified start.[12]

At Saint Omer that night of the 30th, the staff were not busy, however. In accordance with Sir John's promise, they had ordered General Smith-Dorrien to send his strongest brigade to support the Cavalry Corps and they had heard from II Corps headquarters that a composite force was being assembled as quickly as possible under Brigadier-General Shaw.[13] They expected shortly, a reinforcement of Territorial Force battalions and a yeomanry regiment, the result of Sir John's plea for men. Murray had

[12] This tendency grew worse as the war progressed due to increasing lack of professionalism to be expected as casualties mounted; and to the worsening of conditions for the telephone in trench warfare. (The pre-war Genera) Staff were eventually to rue their suspicion – and partial rejection – of the wireless.

[13] Brigadier-General F C Shaw had his own 9th Brigade headquarters and 1st Northumberland Fusiliers and 1st Lincolns, with 2nd King's Own Yorkshire Light Infantry (KOYLI) and 2nd King's Own Scottish Border (KOSB) from 13th Brigade. None of the battalions had more than 400 effectives.

reported the details of their movement and, with a gloomy satisfaction, confirmed that preparations were in hand to safeguard them in the event of a disaster in Flanders. Yet the pessimistic GHQ did not know exactly what they feared. The intelligence staff did not know what enemy formations were attacking with such vigour and power. The operations branch did not know what had transpired in front of Ypres and Kemmel since Sir John had left the area that afternoon but they feared the worst. So, too, did Captain Requin, a staff officer sent forward by Foch to obtain information. At 10 pm this officer returned to Cassel to say that there was a gap in the British line which there were no men to fill – he referred to the line behind the Hollebeke Chateau held by 18th Hussars – and does not appear to have taken into account the infantry and artillery reinforcements *en route* from General Dubois' corps. Apprehensive of a setback, Foch telephoned GHQ to ask what news they had had that evening and when he heard that there was none said that he would motor over at once to see Sir John.

At Saint Omer, he found Wilson waiting. It was half an hour after midnight and he asked him to have the British commander-in-chief wakened. Sir John was nose-diving: 'We're all in for it,' he said. 'We shall see,' Foch replied. 'In the meantime hammer away, keep on hammering, and you will get there. It's surprising the results you attain in this way.' He promised to send eight battalions of the 32nd Division[14] and three batteries to the weak area behind Hollebeke Chateau next day; as soon, indeed, as the infantry detrained at Elverdinghe and, continuing in this hopeful and helpful way, succeeded in cheering his British colleague.

When he left, the operations staff were deciphering a message sent to them at 10 p.m. by Haig. In addition to the details of the reorganized line, it gave the substance of this plan for the next day: an advance to recapture Zandvoorde, Hollebeke and Oosttaveme – all the ground lost during the 30th. At 6.30 am. on the 31st, Major-General Bulfin would advance with some portion of his force of six battalions on the left – Haig ordered him to retain a strong reserve; the 2nd and 3rd Cavalry Divisions on the right; and five battalions of French infantry in the centre. If ambitious, it was simple and straightforward and certainly, on the face of it, in every way preferable to sitting on the ridge to be shot at and attacked by German initiative. It was a viable concept but for two facts: Haig, its author, did not know the extent of the enemy's strength – he judged himself to be facing still the German cavalry reinforced by a regular corps; and he and his staff

---

[14] This division came from XVI Corps and was linked with the 31st. The Corps was selected originally by Joffre to relieve de Mitry in Flanders.

chose to ignore the immense potential, so frequently demonstrated, of the German fire support. They took comfort too easily from the modest enterprise of their own counter-bombardment plan and the direct support arrangements for the infantry and dismounted cavalry. The whole artillery effort comprised one 9-2-inch howitzer, one 6-inch gun, the second armoured train of 4-7-inch naval guns, sixteen of the old 4.7-inch guns, four 60-pounders and eight British and French field batteries. The allocation of ammunition of all calibres was 837 rounds and the disposal of such a quantity placed the reserve stocks temporarily in jeopardy.

The German guns fired this number of shells and more on to the Messines ridge in the first hour of their bombardment on the 31st.

Falkenhayn was somewhat better informed of the day's operations than Sir John French, though he was five times more distant from the Flanders front. Although he did not have the full details of the battle that evening, the 30th, he was aware that they had failed to breach the allied line at any point in the centre and that the Messines ridge and Gheluvelt were still held by the British. Sixth Army were ordered to persist in attacking these targets on the 31st to break the enemy line; a breach which was sought even more eagerly when it became known after midnight from Fourth Army that the Belgians had inundated the Yser battle ground. As a measure of encouragement to the troops, it was announced that the Emperor would come himself to see the assault of von Fabeck's group.

Von Fabeck's staff meantime had issued his orders for the 31st and were engaged in controlling the regrouping of his force. A number of medium and heavy batteries were moved forward. One regiment – 16 – was taken from 6th Bavarian Reserve Division and committed to the left flank of 54th Reserve Division north of the Menin road. It was this regiment which had co-operated with 54 in the attempt to capture Gheluvelt on the night of the 28th/29th and they were jointly to try again on the 31st. The remainder of 6th Bavarian Reserve Division was marched from Menin along the north bank of the Lys to Comines, where they turned off the main road into lanes and tracks which led to Wambeke and Oosttaverne. It was a good night for marching and undertaking reliefs. Overcast at first, the skies soon cleared and the moon shone brightly, easing the problem of those who were guiding the columns of men. Towards the end of their journey they were checked by the quiet gruff challenges of the sentries and disturbed by sporadic bursts of fire and the booming and banging of their own artillery.

They were relieving the left regiment of II Bavarian Corps and the right of 26th Division, taking over from them the responsibility for the capture of Wytschaete and permitting the 26th to concentrate on the village and environs of Messines. The concerted attack of von Fabeck's group was to begin with a mighty bombardment at 8 o'clock in the morning but, on its own initiative meantime, 26th Division were raiding the British lines throughout the night, some of their parties being disguised by turbans as they knew there were Indian troops amongst the defence. From 4 to 5 am., one brigade attempted to seize the southern end of the ridge but were driven back after a hot, confused encounter with the 2nd Inniskilling Fusiliers, the 57th Rifles of the Indian Army, whom they were in the process of relieving and the doughty cadre of the 4th Dragoon Guards reduced to a tenth of their numbers.

In the latter part of the night, the mist began to gather, though thinly, clinging only along the watercourses of the Douve, south of the ridge, the little brooks running down on either side of Wambeke and, more densely, along the Ypres-Comines canal.

At 5.30 a.m., the French and British stood to arms. The Germans dozed and waited in their trenches for the bombardment to begin.

IN THE BALANCE: 31ST OCTOBER 1914

Soon after 6 am on the 31st, the daylight spread through the thin mist. Without preliminary shelling, 16 Bavarian and 246 Regiments were launched along the road to Gheluvelt – but they had misjudged the weather and the hour. It was going to be a fine day, despite the drizzling rain which fell as they advanced, and they lacked the gloomy fog of the previous few days to screen them. Their lines were struck by the bullets of the British riflemen at medium range. Killed and wounded fell at every succeeding yard and the only portion of the assault which penetrated the British line was the extreme left, where a platoon of 2nd 60th Rifles held an orchard to supplement the numbers of 1st Queen's. By half past seven, all but these intruders had been killed or captured and the German assault had drawn back. About 150 wounded and unwounded prisoners were taken.

There was a pause, while the British soldiers ate a hasty meal of bread and bully beef. They did well to take advantage of this opportunity. At 8 the bombardment opened – 'The worst we had ever had,' in the opinion of a sergeant of 1st Queen's. 'The ground was literally shaking as if we were in the middle of an earthquake.'

At 9 o'clock, the shelling of the nearest defences stopped along the Messines ridge and the main work of von Fabeck's offensive began. It was cunningly undertaken by veterans with a distaste for the formal assault. Small groups began to double forward across the broken ground; riflemen first and then, when they had gained temporary cover, machine-gunners followed under cover of their fire. By these tactics, two of the three battalions of 119 Grenadiers infiltrated amongst the southern edge of Messines village during the forenoon, while all three of 125 Regiment worked forward in the north east through the cemetery into the first block of houses. Between 11 and 12 o'clock, a field gun was dragged up by hand to snipe at houses held by the squadrons of British cavalry.

While the struggle mounted amongst falling bricks and mortar in the ruined houses of Messines, a strong but indeterminate encounter had occurred to the north from Wyteschaete spur to Zandvoorde. Although two of the five battalions of French infantry had not arrived at 6.30, and the commander of the force. General Moussy, was still on his way forward from Haig's headquarters, the senior officer present began the counter-offensive. Within a few hundred yards, his movement was brought to a halt by the massed rifles and machine-guns of the Bavarian Corps lying on either side of the canal in readiness for their own assault at 9 am. Their field batteries had been brought forward in the night so as to be available for immediate close support of the morning's action and these shot a dense cloud of shrapnel into the ranks of the French.

This was a serious setback and meant that Cough's cavalry to the south and Bulfin's force to the north remained in their trenches; for their own advance depended on the French reaching the first objective in the centre. But their plan brought them a capital consolation prize. The variety of shells gathered by the French and British gunners for offensive action now began to descend upon the German Infantry, packed forward in the trenches; a riposte to which the Germans were unaccustomed when attacking a British line. This continued until 8 am, when a second attempt was to be made by the French battalions to advance.

At 8, however, the enemy's major bombardment fell exactly as planned and the British and French were driven back, company by company, from their forward posts to seek shelter in rear. Yet there was no immediate assault when the bombardment ceased: the first waves of the Bavarian attack had been crippled by the allied artillery fire and several hours were to elapse before the reserve battalions could be organized to take up their work. For a little while, therefore, French and British watched and waited. As an hour and more passed, casual reports from the 7th Division and northern units of Bulfin's force told of the enemy advancing from Zandvoorde in parallel with the Menin road. The sound of battle swelled, the smoke grew thicker behind them. There was no news for a time until, quite unexpectedly, a gunner observation post reported that the enemy were surging along the road into Gheluvelt, and soon a messenger came from 7th Division to say that Gheluvelt had been lost. A large body of enemy was believed to be moving swiftly down the road to Ypres.

When the bombardment began in front of Gheluvelt at 8 am, the small lodgement effected by the enemy at dawn in rear of the Queen's and 60th Rifles was still intact. The force sent immediately to eject it had proved too weak and the opening of the bombardment had delayed a company counter-attack. At 9, with the bombardment slackening on the front trenches, this company attempted to close by stealth on the enemy orchard but was driven off – not surprisingly as there were upwards of 130 Germans in the area. In an enterprising way the orchard party sniped continuously, whether under attack or not, and dug a number of temporary positions. They knew, of course, that friends were close at hand.

While they waited, the bombardment continued, the pattern changing from saturation of the Gheluvelt defence zone to selective concentrations of high explosive on the British support line and shrapnel and explosive mixed on either side of the main road.

Immediately south of the road, 2nd Welch lost in killed and wounded about fifty-six – the strongest company – by 9.30 and the commanding officer, Lieutenant-Colonel C B Morland, decided to pull back the handful remaining to his support line. Sending a runner to tell the Queen's and the 60th across the road of his withdrawal, he doubled himself to 1st South Wales Borderers on the left.

It seems probable that the runner carrying the message concerning the retirement of the Welch right flank to the Queen's and 60th ran into the German party in the orchard. He went unwittingly in that direction and was not seen again alive. These two battalions therefore faced the renewed assault to their front unaware that the positions on the main road were no longer manned, a situation made worse by the fact that the enemy in the orchard were now free to link up with the oncoming assault and to exploit directly to the rear. 1st Queen's were suffering the additional discomfort of fire; all the houses and outbuildings, barns and ricks round which their left hand company was dug in had been fired by shell bursts and the heat by 10 am was intense.

At this hour the first assault wave of the Germans was seen moving towards them: three battalions with their right on the Menin road. To the rear and left in echelon were seen another three; all, as it happened, from 30th Division. As the Queen's and 60th Rifles opened fire, this concentration seemed to be checked for a few seconds, the front rank almost stopping while the ranks behind crowded on to them. Then, as if

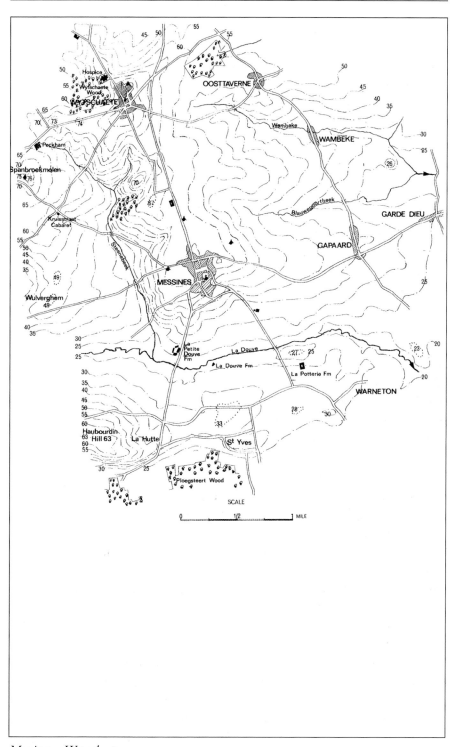

Messines – Wyteschaete.

they had been gathering tension like a spring, the compact mass of men hurled themselves forward, shouting, cheering, singing.

While the German shelling hampered and hit the British riflemen standing in their trenches, it hit too the German infantry attempting to close. The combination of fire was too much and the assault broke down when every man in the first and second ranks had been hit. Orders were shouted and those Germans remaining unwounded behind ran into cover. Their shell fire having stopped, they were obliged to stay there until fresh numbers appeared and artillery support could be renewed.

North of the road, meantime, four battalions of 54th Reserve Division – a regiment plus the divisional *jäger* – had advanced from Kruiseecke crossroads. The two remaining companies of 2nd Welch, 130 strong when left in position by Lieutenant-Colonel Morland, now totalled forty, and twenty-two of these were wounded. They held off the Germans in their area until 11.45, when thirty-seven remained to be captured. But while part of the attacking force was held also by the 1st South Wales Borderers and 1st Scots Guards to the north, two to three enemy companies had penetrated into Gheluvelt village and from positions on the southern side opened fire with rifles and four machine-guns[15] on to the rear of the 60th Rifles and the two rear companies of the Loyals.

Some time between 11.30 and noon, the British position round Gheluvelt began to collapse. The 2nd 60th Rifles lost over 400 from German shellfire and the bullets fired from all round. 1st Loyals were reduced to 160 and beyond them 2nd Royal Scots Fusiliers had already lost half of the 172 surviving from the action on the previous day. 143 Regiment, of 30th Division, had now come forward to reinforce the assault and two field batteries followed them up along the road. While the infantry were preparing their charge, the gunners and a company of infantry worked round on the northern side of the road to connect with the force in the orchard. From about 400 yards range they opened fire into the Queen's from the northern flank.

The commanding officer of the Queen's had been mortally wounded in the first morning encounter and the battalion was now under command of Major C F Watson. He perceived that to remain in his position would be suicide. Orders were quickly given to fall back into some old support trenches 300 yards in rear where he expected to be able to link up with the Welch and the 60th. But the Welch had gone and so, by this time, had what remained of the 60th. Carrying back the dying commanding officer on a stretcher,

[15] Machine-guns were organized in the German Army into companies – one to each regiment. Whilst they had no greater number than the British at this time, their organization made the control and concentration of these weapons more effective.

the Queen's attempted to fight their way out. They saw the stretcher party through but used up in this way the few remaining minutes of a chance to slip back any number. Two officers and twelve men constituted the fighting portion of the battalion that night. To add to the horrors of the day, they learned that 143 Regiment had clubbed to death and bayoneted some of the wounded and stripped all the prisoners of clothing, watches, wallets and trinkets.

Behind this scene of frenzied fighting and occasional savage reprisal,[16] the sense of confusion and an atmosphere of crisis had been rising since 9.30. The stream of wounded, walking and carried, had been growing. Men scattered by the German artillery fire and trying to find their units were wandering about asking if there was news of their battalion or company. Lieutenant-Colonel Morland of the Welch had reported to brigade headquarters that Gheluvelt was undefended, and the brigade commander, Major-General Landon, had sent forward as a temporary measure, to cover the village, D Company of 1st Gloucesters. This detachment set off for the village eighty strong but was reduced by shrapnel to thirty by the time it reached the western end and fifteen in the middle where it met two companies of 54th Reserve Division. A little to the north, Brigadier-General FitzClarence, commander of 1st (Guards) Brigade, had heard of the deteriorating situation by telephone which, luckily, remained open to 1st Scots Guards. He rode forward to find that the South Wales Borderers and the Scots Guards had combined their headquarters in the stables behind Gheluvelt Chateau and from then on he or his staff captain, Captain A F A N Thorne, continued to come forward to see how the line was holding.

When the last forward position of the Welch was taken at 11.45, the Guards and the Borderers realized that Gheluvelt must be open to capture if not already taken. Their apprehensions were confirmed when they came under a heavy fire from the village, in view on the ridge to their right, just as a storming party threw them back through the grounds of the chateau. Lieutenant-Colonel H E B Leach, commanding the Borderers, drew together every man he could call to by voice, which included a number of Scots Guards interwoven with his own men. They fixed bayonets and charged. This regained the south eastern edge of the chateau wall but with the force remaining unwounded, there was no question of counter-attacking Gheluvelt village. The prospect now was they would shortly be attacked from that flank or from the rear. Both he and the acting

[16] This was one of several incidents of inhuman treatment of British prisoners by the German Army but such behaviour was not common. 2nd Royal Scots Fusiliers were treated most honourably the same day.

commanding officer of the Scots Guards foresaw that they would in time be surrounded and destroyed. They determined to make a stand to the end.

This danger was equally clear to Brigadier-General Fitz-Clarence who had, by noon, seen the whole line from the rear of Gheluvelt to Polygon Wood. He hastened back to find his divisional commander, Major-General Lomax, established for the day 2,000 yards in rear on the highest point of ground overlooking the divisional front. FitzClarence confirmed the worst of the reports given by the wounded coming back and General Lomax agreed that the last reserve, 2nd Worcesters, must now be committed.[17] Brigadier-General FitzClarence returned to his headquarters to arrange this while General Lomax went back to Hooge Chateau to confer with his colleague, General Monro, the commander of 2nd Division.

At 1 pm, they met in Monro's office in the annexe to the main house, with the principal members of their staffs and certain Royal Artillery officers. While they were talking, at 1.15, a heavy shell fell near by, its blast shaking the annexe, and a few seconds later another landed on Monro's office. Lomax was severely wounded – he died a few months later -and almost every officer present was either killed or wounded, General Monro fortunately being only concussed. This sudden and wholly unexpected disruption of both divisional headquarters delayed inevitably the preparation of measures to hold back the Germans. The only barrier to a breakthrough ad interim was therefore 2nd Worcesters.

Brigadier-General FitzClarence, like several of his colleagues that day, was setting a superb example as a commander in battle. Returned to his headquarters, he sent a warning to the Worcesters to be ready to move forward quickly and called for an officer from the battalion to whom he could give orders. The staff captain. Captain Thorne, was sent to reconnoitre the approaches to Gheluvelt. This gave him a few minutes to consider what he should do.

The Worcesters had been placed at Polygon Wood as a force of last resort. Originally, the I Corps plan had been to keep a brigade there to be committed only if the line was actually breached to the south, when the brigade would counter-attack on to the flank of the enemy pushing through. But there was now only a battalion, under half-strength, and he could not afford to make a mistake either by extending them too widely or concentrating them at too strong an enemy point. He decided to put one company out at once to watch the western exit from Gheluvelt – towards Ypres – and to counter-attack with the remainder the chateau, where the

---

[17] 2nd Worcesters belonged to 2nd Division but had been allocated to General Lomax for his use as necessary.

Scots Guards and the South Wales Borderers still held a flank. It might then be possible to continue the offensive action into Gheluvelt from the north.

Captain B C Senhouse Clarke, adjutant of the Worcesters, returned to his commanding officer with the orders to detach a company to watch Gheluvelt and confirmed that they would be making a counter-attack with the remainder. Shortly, the commanding officer, Major E B Hankey, went off to Brigade headquarters himself to be given the detailed instructions.

By 1.45 in the afternoon, A Company of the Worcesters was lying in the light railway cutting behind Gheluvelt while B, C, and D were on the march for Gheluvelt chateau, preceded by scouts on the look out for Germans and, no less practically, barbed wire obstacles which might hinder the advance. To speed movement, the companies marched at first in file but after a march of 1,700 yards they drew towards open country. A mile ahead, with scarcely a scrap of cover between, they could see the trees on the north side of the chateau park. Shells were bursting noisily amongst them and already the German artillery was coming across the open ground which they must cross, seeking to prevent just such a counter-attack as they were about to deliver. Major Hankey marched his three companies on a few more yards into the shelter of a stream re-entrant and extended his ranks to assault.

A mile is a long distance for the approach to an assault. It is longer still when there is no fire support and the enemy has found the range with a quantity of his guns. Wisely, Major Hankey had left packs behind and the adjutant had personally seen to the lightening of loads. Everything was discarded except what was immediately needed: rifles, bayonets, cartridges, water-bottles. Thus equipped, Major Hankey took his place front and centre of his battalion, the adjutant immediately right flank rear. 'Advance at the double – advance!' Major Hankey shouted over his shoulder. They flew across the stubble to the chateau.

The shrapnel worried them more than the high explosive. The extended lines were made threadbare by the flying fragments of scorching metal. Over a hundred fell in the next mile. But now they were over the light railway and through the woods to the very edge of the open grassland in front of the chateau. Struck immediately by rifle fire as they emerged from the trees, the two leading companies of the Worcesters charged into the foe, firing rifles and stabbing in a surge of hot blood the Germans remaining in their path.

Suddenly the tide of contending fortunes was reversed.

There were close on 1,200 Germans in and around the chateau, of whom a number were looting inside the house while others attacked the

Guards and the Borderers behind. Two companies had been casually watching the western side of the park but had not crossed into the trees. Behind them were several more companies all from 16 Bavarian and 245 Reserve Regiments. The majority were in that dangerous state of relaxation to be found when inexperienced troops have taken a first objective under unseasoned leaders. Alertness declines; euphoria follows relief from fear. The bold and determined charge of the Worcesters, a fighting entity still despite their losses, thanks to the mature discipline and spirit amongst their ranks, swept into the German midst like a thunderbolt. Three batteries of 2nd Division Artillery opened fire from behind Polygon Wood a few minutes later, shelling the boundary of the park and village, and part of the sunken road along the southern side. Surprised, wounded, unbalanced, routed, the German force fled, abandoning much of their armament and equipment.

From behind the chateau, the South Wales Borderers came to help the Worcesters pursue the enemy south and east. Major Hankey and his adjutant had not expected to see lieutenant-Colonel Leach and his second-in-command[18] when they approached, believing that they had been driven back or destroyed.

'My God, fancy meeting you here!' said Major Hankey.

'Thank God, you've come,' Colonel Leach replied quietly. ' Immediately in rear of the Worcesters, Brigadier-General FitzClarence watched the three companies attack and win back the left section of the broken line. As A Company came forward in a converging operation on the village, he galloped back with the news. It was passed within ten minutes to the chief engineer of I Corps, reconnoitring a new defence line, and he hurried back to Haig at the White Chateau.

Haig was about to get into the saddle to ride forward a second time that day to the very edge of the fighting line to see for himself what was happening. He had decided to take command of the mixture of groups and brigades holding his front until the divisional headquarters were re-established but had been delayed by the arrival of Sir John.

Apprised of the loss of Gheluvelt and the extending pressure on either side of the Menin road. Sir John promised to find Foch to see what extra help he could afford. He had just left Haig when the chief engineer arrived at the White Chateau to tell them that the Worcesters had closed the gap. Haig's ADC ran after the commander-in-chief to give him this encouraging news. When he returned, his corps commander was in the

---

[18] Colonel Leach's second-in-command, Major A J Reddie, was particularly well known to the Worcesters as his brother was serving in that regiment.

saddle, trotting along the road to Menin.

Upright in a clean suit of service dress and breeches, his boots polished, a cavalryman carrying immediately behind a lance with his personal pennant fluttering below the point, Haig's face we are told by a dozen eyewitnesses remained calm. About noon he had trotted forward with some of his staff in just this way, observing without comment or apparent emotion the ragged figures of the stragglers, the painful flow of the wounded, the guns and howitzers tugged back with empty traces among the teams of horses. When the report came through that Gheluvelt had been re-entered, he showed no joy, no elation. He was a dour man. Yet of all the commanders available in the British Expeditionary Force at that time he was probably the officer most suited – perhaps the only one – to direct operations in front of Ypres. At times small-minded, given to criticizing faults in others of which he was himself guilty, he had none the less a high sense of duty, a cool head and a degree of comprehension and instinctive skill in higher tactics. Though he knew less as a cavalry man about the practical capabilities of the infantry than Smith-Dorrien, an infantry officer, he knew more than Rawlinson who, despite his infantry background, had never commanded anything in a regiment above a platoon. Haig had never shunned regimental service. He lacked Allenby's power as a commander and his boldness; but he was more calculating. He had now to calculate the extent to which he could hold the present corps line. There was an immense temptation to fall back. Haig had told his chief engineer to select a defensible line in rear towards Ypres but he knew that whilst this might appear to offer a relief for his weary soldiers, they would find it difficult to break cleanly from the Germans at all points; and they would in any case be pursued quickly to a line in which, as yet, there was not a single trench dug.

He rode forward to find Major-General Landon and Brigadier-General FitzClarence.

South of Gheluvelt, the last of 2nd 60th Rifles were being withdrawn. They were under fire from three sides and were unable to obtain any cover nearby. The commanding officer of 1st Loyals decided to stay where he was; his trenches were on either side of a spur and, although he had lost most of his two companies in the support line due to the fire from the rear, he still had 120 forward well-placed to fire at the assault just appearing, a movement which he had been expecting since the attack on the Queen's and the 60th that morning.

A Reservist recalled to the ranks. Private Bolwell of the Loyals, was on the left of the battalion front where -

We continued to fire until the Germans were on our trenches and coming through the line the King's Royal Rifles (60th) had vacated on our left... where I heard some of the conversation between the two COs. Just in front of the King's Royal Rifles trenches was a huge German officer waving his troops on. It did not seem much good for us few men to attempt to fight that dense mass of Germans, but we did...

The assault eventually reached the Loyals' trenches and broke over it, when a few, like Bolwell, managed to escape.

I had a run for my life that day. A chum of mine who was with us had a cock fowl in his valise that morning from the farm but he had not quite succeeded in killing him; and as we ran this bird began to crow. As for myself, I had no equipment; I had run having left it in the bottom of the trench...

1st Loyals were destroyed and, next to them, 2nd Royal Scots Fusiliers. The headquarters party of the latter had been killed or captured when the second assault passed through Gheluvelt to their rear. Now, with the Loyals, those forward were overwhelmed, twenty-five being men of the latest reinforcement who had come into the line only the night before.

With the removal of these battalions, the way was clear for 105 (Saxon) Regiment to advance to the Menin-Ypres road behind Gheluvelt; for the British line had apparently been breached to a width of 2,000 yards. A field battery amongst them, the Saxons pushed forward two battalions while the third remained to comb out the positions they had taken. Ahead lay Veldhoek. Fortunately for the British, Major-General Landon had insisted on leaving 1st Gloucesters as long stop in this position – although he had been obliged to detach D Company to Gheluvelt – and their demise – earlier. The small force of Gloucesters under Colonel Lovett, had gathered fragments of 2nd Welch, 2nd 60th Rifles and those few individuals who had escaped in the final rush on to the positions of the Queen's and the Loyals. At 700 yards they opened fire on the Saxon infantry, driving them to ground. To ease the approach, the German field battery deployed, one gun being placed forward on the edge of the main road. It began by shelling three cottages held by some of the composite force. Lieutenant-Colonel Morland of the Welch was killed by shrapnel and the stretcher bearers began to be busy with the wounded. For a change, however, the local strength of the artillery was in the British favour.

Though well forward amongst the whole line, the Royal Artillery had only been partially used during the 31st. For one thing, the intensity of German shell fire had quickly cut the telephones of the forward observing officers and killed or wounded many of their signallers and the battalion runners who had attempted to take instructions to the guns by hand. There was still an acute shortage of ammunition of almost every calibre – but there had been a small powerful bonus which was already being spent: limited stocks of high explosive rounds had arrived for the 18-pounder field guns. Colonel Lovett's position was backed by three batteries and they had their share of high explosive. 54 Battery detached a sniping gun from its own position under Lieutenant R Blewitt and with their second round the crew hit the German piece and destroyed it. The remainder of the guns now fired shrapnel, sprinkled with high explosive, into the Saxons sheltering behind banks and walls, and along ditches. The Saxons ran and the Gloucesters, Welch, 60th, Queen's and Loyals ran hard to catch them, taking over 100 prisoners.

The afternoon was waning. It was a quarter to four and units up and down the line had been under bouts of extremely heavy shell fire since 8am, while many had been fighting as well for hours to hold back the assaults on their positions. Left of Polygon Wood, the line was exceptionally quiet on the 2nd Division front, but south west of Veldhoek, where Bulfin's force was engaged between the skeleton of 7th Division and the French infantry, the line had thrice been at the point of breaking. Capper, commander of the 7th, and Bulfin had both been active personally immediately in rear of the trenches reorganizing groups of men whose company organizations had disappeared – every officer, warrant officer and non-commissioned officer were killed or wounded in one company by shell fire before the enemy infantry assaulted. Others came close to this plight afterwards. Regrouped, led to a place in the line, the soldiers fought on. There was, however, a limit to the casualties a unit could take while holding the same length of trenches. Bulfin's reserves – Capper had none – were committed entirely before 1 o'clock in the afternoon to resist a combined assault by Bavarians and a brigade of 39th Division. After that they could only call on unit cadres such as 1st Grenadiers and 2nd Royal Warwicks. In the middle of the afternoon. General Bulfin decided that as he could not maintain a defence he must try an attack.

It was a daunting concept. The number forward of his six battalions would not complete a single line of assault but Colonel Jeudwine of Haig's staff was with him and Bulfin asked him to find the corps commander and seek the release of the corps reserve. In case there were none, he determined to bring back 2nd Gordons whom he had sent with half the

2nd Sussex to start a new defence line in rear. When Jeudwine had gone, Bulfin called in the commanding officers of the Guards and 1st Northamptons and gave his orders. The Germans were tiring, he told them, and they knew from their own observation what casualties had been inflicted on the enemy through the day. He had sent back for reinforcements. They were to tell their soldiers that when they heard cheering behind, it meant that the reinforcements were coming through. They were to gather as much ammunition as possible and when the cheering began to open rapid fire for one minute – the old 'mad minute' practised sometimes on the ranges in peace when ammunition permitted. Then they were to get out of their trenches and advance with the reinforcements. He did not know whether they believed his statement that reinforcements were coming but it did not matter; they trusted him to do what was right and went back to their battalions.

While he waited, Bulfin tried to get messages to the 2nd Oxford and Buckinghamshire Light Infantry – the 52nd – on his right beyond the Sussex, and to headquarters 7th Division to warn the units on the left of his plan. After 40 minutes there was still no acknowledgement from either but his 'reinforcements' arrived. It was not the 200 men of 2nd Gordons he had expected: there were only eighty-four of them and these included drivers, cooks and storemen from the quartermaster's department. They were commanded by the huge figure of Captain J R E Stansfield who listened carefully to the general's orders before taking the Highlanders away under cover of the trees.

Bulfin considered waiting a little longer in the hope that Colonel Jeudwine would obtain a bigger reinforcement for him from General Haig but it was 4.15, and it would be dark in an hour and a half. Nothing could be worse than to try to hold his current line with present numbers and the initiative in German hands. He decided not to wait.

Strung out in line so that each man could only just see those on his right and left amongst the trees, the Gordons heard Captain Stansfield pass the word to cheer. The eighty-four Highlanders gave a prolonged shout, most of which consisted of the word 'Hoorah' though a number of others were thrown in on the right of the line. Northamptons' and Sussex' rifles opened a rapid fire and the Gordons ran down through the woods to join them on the front edge. All now sprang forward, cheering spontaneously. General Bulfin's batteries, redeployed, opened fire. Astonished, the Germans began to fall back, at first in small numbers but soon by platoons and companies. On the right of the Sussex, the 52nd joined in. On the left, the infantry of 7th Division caught the spirit before they had been told officially what it meant and advanced without hesitation. Sent on from Haig, the Royals and two squadrons of 6th Cavalry Brigade arrived in time to swell the assault while C Battery dragged a 13-pounder through the trees to smash a machine-gun position dug into the walls of a hunting lodge. A company of sappers, 26th Field Company, doubled to join the advancing line.

By 5.30, they had recovered most of the ground taken by the enemy during the day. It was not a cheap victory; 1,090 officers and men were killed and wounded. It was not one single glorious sweep; after the first 500 yards there were numbers of strong points, mostly in copses and farmhouses, to destroy. But it was not worthless. The ground recovered did not matter particularly – though it gave a buffer zone below the ridge – but the drubbing given to the Germans was exceptionally valuable. It secured the tired men a quiet night. It enabled them to eat without alarm the half rations brought forward and some to brew tea. It restored their morale in a way which nothing else could have done. It sealed, at least for the night, the line towards the French and cavalry.

On the Messines ridge, too, the line had stabilized. Brigadier-General Shaw's composite brigade from II Corps had arrived to reinforce Messines village and the London Scottish[19] had strengthened the ridge to Wytschaete. After a day of street fighting to secure the eastern half of Messines village, the regiments of von Fabeck's 26th Division were too tired to persist. 50 yards from their positions across the main street of the village, 1st Cavalry Brigade were relieved silently from amongst General Shaw's Brigade by the 2nd and not a man was lost.

Sir John found Foch that afternoon of the 31st by lucky chance. Driving due west from Ypres on the road to Poperinghe, he passed through the village of Vlamertinghe, where his car and flag were recognized by a French staff officer. The car was stopped and he learned that General Foch was in the mairie, talking to d'Urbal and Dubois. The British field marshal was a shaken man. He painted, Foch tells us,

> ...a particularly black picture of the state of I Corps. The troops were in full retreat towards Ypres, the heavy artillery were retiring at a trot towards the west, the roads were blocked by ammunition wagons and vehicles of every description, as well as by crowds of wounded streaming back towards Ypres. It was the beginning of a defeat.

Did Sir John really think things were as bad as this? He had heard the news

---

[19] The London Scottish was a battalion of the Territorial Force, the first to be committed to the line. It was not, however, one of those T F units promised by Kitchener as a reinforcement. It had been in France since September 1914 on line of communication defence.

that Gheluvelt was restored. It was true that the medium and heavy guns had been coming back at the trot; and the wounded were streaming in; and there had been at midday stragglers 'wild-eyed with terror' as Haig had seen before. But these men were also to be seen returning of their own accord to find their broken units. The heavier guns were moving into new positions to accommodate the withdrawal of the line. Sir John had seen streams of wounded before. Perhaps he wanted to impress Foch sufficiently to obtain the whole of the French 32nd Division to buttress his front. Whether his attitude was assumed or genuine – or a mixture of both – it was impressive. He added that if he had to continue the battle without help, 'there is nothing left for me to do but go up and be killed with I Corps'.

'You must not talk of dying but of winning,' Foch replied. He promised to send six battalions of the 32nd Division to attack with Moussy next morning while part of Dubois' corps attacked on the left. This was two battalions less than he had promised the previous evening but it was a more realistic gesture. He then sat down to write what was in effect a directive, tactfully worded to take account of his lack of authority, as much to aid in fixing my own ideas as to furnish them in definite and precise form to my interlocutor. I there and then handed this informal scrawl to Sir John French. It read as follows:

> 'It is absolutely essential *not to retreat*; therefore the men must dig in wherever they find themselves and hold on to the ground they now occupy.
>
> 'This does not preclude organizing a position further in rear which could join up at Zonnebeke with our DC Corps.
>
> 'But any movement to the rear carried out by any considerable body of troops would lead to an assault on the part of the enemy and bring certain confusion among the troops. Such an idea must be utterly rejected.
>
> 'It seems particularly necessary that the 2nd British Division maintain itself in the vicinity of Zonnebeke, keeping in touch with the French IX Corps.
>
> 'The lateness of the day makes this organization feasible. It is useless to fall back, dangerous to do so in broad daylight.'

Sir John had this translated and then added his own minute of association, to be sent to Haig.

> 'It is of the *utmost importance* to hold the ground you are on now. It is useless for me to say this, because I know you will do it if it is humanly

possible. I will see if it is possible to send you any more support myself when I reach headquarters. I will then finally arrange with Foch what our final role is to be.'

The paper was taken at once by Sir John's ADC and private secretary to I Corps headquarters.

Haig had already decided that, apart from an adjustment of the line to the west of Ghemvelt, where the trenches could be dug on a reverse slope, he would hold on where he was. At 7 pm, Brigadier-General Gough signed his orders: 'G.583. Troops will hold their positions...'

TWELVE DAYS OF NOVEMBER:
1ST-12TH NOVEMBER 1914

With November came uncertainty.

Falkenhayn was uncertain as to the potential left in the Flanders battle. Could he hope that the enemy was truly as weak as prisoners reported; or were there reserves in rear, reinforcements to hand of which they knew nothing? Should he withdraw more troops from the line to the south for Flanders, concentrate there more guns and ammunition for one more effort? Or should he cut his losses and settle to a winter of trench warfare from La Bassée to the sea? There might be other sectors on the western front more suitable for an offensive. It might be necessary to divert all his offensive resources to buttress Hindenburg's hard-pressed armies in the east.[20]

Joffre was uncertain as to the needs of the Flanders line relative to his own wish to gather forces for an offensive elsewhere. The allies had clearly missed their chance to make a turning movement in Belgium. He had sent IX Corps under Dubois to make a final attempt to break out but instead it had become involved in support of the British defence line. Grossetti's division had been similarly diverted in aid of the Belgians – by 1st November he had a complete corps[21] underpinning their line. Yet a third corps, XVI, had been drawn into the defensive battle round Ypres, its 31st and 32nd Divisions being separated. How safe was the Flanders line? Would the recent defeat of Hindenburg in the east oblige Falkenhayn to close his offensive in the west? If so, Joffre might withdraw some of his own troops from the sector to contribute to a French striking force.

Sir John French had uncertainties of other kinds. He was uncertain personally as to his position. On 1st November, Kitchener had crossed to Dunkerque for a meeting with the French president, minister for war and

[20] The German army in Poland had been in retreat since 21st October. Hindenburg assumed command of both Eighth and Ninth Armies on 1st November.

[21] XXII Corps under General Humbert, which included Grossetti's division and Ronarch's brigade.

[22] M Ribot, French finance minister, and M Cambon, ambassador in London, were also present.

Joffre.[22] Foch had been present later in the day. Foch had told Wilson that Kitchener proposed to Joffre a change in the command-in-chief of the British Expeditionary Force: Sir John French should be replaced by Sir Ian Hamilton. According to Foch, Joffre had strongly opposed the idea and had been supported by President Poincaré. Whilst this reassurance warmed Sir John it also rekindled his belief that Kitchener would work for his removal; a belief he had had since he and the secretary of state for war had clashed on 1st September, when the allied armies were in retreat.[23]

As commander-in-chief, there was no doubt that Sir John would be held responsible if the British Army in Flanders failed. Yet, as he often told the senior members of his staff and his corps commanders, they could not continue indefinitely without men and munitions. Excluding the Indian Corps, whose British and Indian casualties were mounting fast, there were eighty-four battalions of infantry in his force. Of these, on 1st November:

eighteen were at cadre strength (below 100 all ranks)
thirty-one were very weak (100 to 200)
twenty-six were weak (200 to 300)
nine were middling (300 to 450)

These figures should be considered against the war establishment of a British battalion, thirty officers and 977 other ranks, with with which most had come to France in August,[24] some being a little stronger, none being less than 966 all ranks. All had long since absorbed their first reinforcements and the figures given above include reinforcement drafts sent forward as recently as 28th October.

There were plenty of men joining the Colours in the United Kingdom – over half a million had responded to Kitchener's pointing finger on the posters by the end of September, but they were running out of trained men. In August and September, the Army had been able to swell to its full war strength and keep something in hand thanks to the recall of 138,624 reservists -men with recent service – and 61,009 special reservists – men outside the liabilities of the compulsory reserve. By October, this flood had abated to a trickle: the figures were 1,927 and 1,276; in November 625 and 1,545. By this time the former high quality of the special reservists was much debased. The first to be trained of Kitchener's new armies would not

---

[23] Sir John French protested at Kitchener's appearance in France dressed as a field-marshal and inclined to give detailed direction of operational policy when his office was currently that of a civil official, secretary of state for war. However much his visit and instructions may have been justified on this occasion, Kitchener certainly wished to assume rights and duties as a generalissimo to which his office gave him no title.

[24] In the case of 7th Division, to Belgium in September.

be ready until the spring of 1915. Meantime, there was one more regular division available to come to France, the 8th, which was about to embark, and apart from this, nothing but the Territorial Force and Yeomanry.

These last – part-time, volunteer soldiers, the brain child of Haldane shaped much by Ian Hamilton – would have done excellently had Kitchener not thrust them aside in preference to the enthusiastic but totally untrained hosts whom he summoned. About 84 per cent of the Territorials were fit and volunteered to go to France[25] and some 92 per cent of the Yeomanry. They were denied modern equipment. What stocks existed were taken for the new armies and the London Scottish came to Flanders equipped with the old Lee Metford, whose magazines were so defective that rounds had to be fed in by hand singly. Six Territorial battalions had been promised by Kitchener in October and he agreed to a further five on 1st November. But equipment policy had now to be reversed to meet their needs and the first units did not reach the line for some months, together with yeomanry regiments and field engineer companies. Fortunately, there were already four regiments of yeomanry[26] and seven battalions of Territorials on the line of communication, excluding the London Scottish, and these were freed to come forward from mid-November onwards.

Formed units were particularly valuable, even if inexperienced, because they had their complete complement of officers, warrant officers and NCOs. The British Expeditionary Force lacked most of all its experienced regimental leaders. Drafts might come and the wide potential amongst the old regular private soldiers for promotion might be taken up but this would not restore a battalion in a month, let alone a night, to its former condition of skill and balance. Many of the best formation commanders and staff officers were falling, too; those who got out amongst the regiments, battalions and batteries to exercise personal command were inevitably more vulnerable to shell or bullet. Major-General Bulfin received three wounds in quick succession at noon on 1st November. Next day, Brigadier-General Ruggles-Brise went back half dead of a dreadful wound on a stretcher and his brigade-major, now the senior officer in 20th Brigade, took command in his place. Almost all the commanding officers had long since fallen or been promoted but here the long continuity in regimental training permitted captains to take command without difficulty.

Losses amongst the Royal Engineers in the field companies and signals

[25] Their original enlistment had been for home service only. New terms of engagement were undertaken by the volunteers for foreign service.

[26] The Oxfordshire Hussars, one of these four, was serving in the line under Altanby.

[27] The Signals service was provided at that time by the Royal Engineers. Cavalry, infantry and artillery provided as now their own internal signallers.

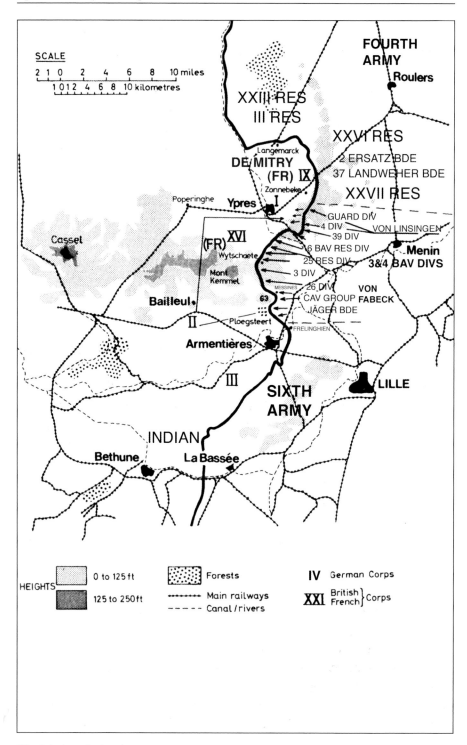

Von Linsingen's Attack

branch[27] were not severe but were as difficult to make good as in the infantry. Of all Arms, they were the most suitable to replace from the Territorial Force because many individuals in the latter originated from the profession and trades of civil engineering. There was no call for reinforcement of the Royal Artillery, however; for although they had taken their share of casualties, particularly in the field batteries, the continuing shortage of ammunition made it unnecessary to employ so many fire units in the forward area. Batteries were sent selectively in rotation to the rear to rest and re-equip until the supply improved. The effect of this temporary withdrawal was offset by the introduction of new 'groupes' of French artillery.

Somewhat grudgingly, Joffre continued to reinforce Flanders. He could not ignore the fact that the German offensive continued. After their failure on the 31st October, they attacked Messines ridge on the night of 1st November with 6th Bavarian Reserve Division,[28] the reopening of a struggle in which this ground and Wytschaete village were captured and recaptured by either side over several days, until it was held securely at last by the Germans. Messines was evacuated. The route through Gheluvelt was again used for attack and the battle was resumed sporadically for the wooded slopes held by Cavan, Bulfin's successor, and the 7th Division. Attacks continued on III Corps, holding the ring doggedly from Hill 63 along the edge of Ploegsteert Wood to Le Touquet and the outskirts of Armentières. The fighting lacked the intensity of the high days such as the first strikes of Fabeck's corps on 30th October but its continuing harsh demands sapped the remaining strength of the defence. Often shelled, often standing to fight off an assault, they had little time to do more than maintain their elementary trenches. If the French elements lodged amongst the British were to attack – and Foch stated that he wished to do so – then it was necessary for Joffre to commit all that he had promised to send in late October. But even with six divisions in front of Ypres, strengthened by the reinforced cavalry corps under General Conneau, the French could not advance more than an occasional hundred yards. As often, they were forced to withdraw. It was of satisfaction to Joffre that the commander of XVI Corps was removed by Foch on 7th November and replaced by Grossetti. On 2nd November, Falkenhayn made up his mind to continue the offensive in Flanders. For the relief of the front in the east, he sent all the recruits in the final stages of their training and two cavalry divisions. From the western front he took other divisions to reinforce Crown Prince Rupprecht: from the region of Roye, II Corps; a brigade

---

[28] Though brought into the line on the night of the 30th to attack Wytschaete on the 31st, it did not do so owing to the inability of II Bavarian Corps on the right to advance that day.

from each of the 1st and 2nd Guard Divisions in Artois; artillery from Arras. Fourth Army were already under orders to withdraw much of their strength from behind the inundation along the Yser, though not to the extent of withdrawing the force threatening Dixmude.

A difficult period followed. Falkenhayn wished both Sixth and Fourth Armies to continue attacks from Annentières to Bixschoote but insisted that they must do so without the quantity of ammunition which had supported other extended assaults. It was necessary to husband a reserve for the major thrust on either side of the salient formed by the French and British between Bixschoote and Klein Zillebeke. There was therefore some reduction in the shelling as attacks were pressed from 6th November onward; a reduction reflected in the casualty figures by comparison with those of the earlier attacks, but the losses were still high and, having regard to the low numbers in units, their effect was the more profound.

Thus, though these attacks had little success, they achieved their main purpose for Falkenhayn by eroding continually the capability of his enemy to defend the line. By the 8th November, a force was assembling in Sixth Army which he hoped would overwhelm whatever strength remained on either side of the Menin road.

The attack was to take place on 10th November. On the left, von Fabeck's Group would 'maintain its position west of the (Comines) canal, its task being to continue to press forward and at the same time to support the attack of the left wing of the Army Group Linsingen by as powerful enfilade fire as possible from its right flank batteries'. The remainder of Sixth Army to the south and the whole Fourth Army were to attack energetically so as to pin the allies to their positions and prevent them from moving reserves from one point to another. In the centre, with three divisions south of the Menin road and one to the north was the new Army Group Linsingen, named after the commander of II Corps brought up to enhance his already high reputation as a vigorous, driving general. His group comprised the XV Corps – 30th and 39th Divisions – which had failed to break-in at the end of October; and the composite corps under Plettenberg – Linsingen's own 4th Division of Pomeranians and Winckler's Guard Division. These last two were established in the line on either side of the Menin road on the night 9th/10th November.

Not surprisingly, the weather had continued to deteriorate. The rain was more frequent and turned sometimes to sleet. Away from the narrow pave of the roads, the soaked, shell-churned earth was softening to a thick film of mud. The lower ground was already beyond entrenching to any depth and all defences there were raised above the surface. The early morning fog clung now among the trees, across the open fields until noon, sometimes persisting throughout the day.

The advanced parties of Plettenberg's corps had reached Menin on the 6th November but due to the fog had been unable to complete their reconnaissances by the 9th. They therefore asked for a delay, a proposal which suited the engineers who had much work to do along roads and tracks to open routes forward for the guns. While von Linsingen supported and Crown Prince Rupprecht approved a postponement to the 11th, they either omitted to tell Fourth Army headquarters or it was decided to let Duke Albrecht's plans continue uninterrupted. For promptly on the 10th their offensive began from Langemarck to Dixmude, with little result except one which was unexpected by the allies: Dixmude fell at last. But the possession of the ruins was now valueless. The Yser bridge west of the town was demolished by Belgian engineers as Ronarc'h withdrew his veterans and the Zouave detachment which had recently reinforced him. The extreme left of Fourth Army had not joined in this offensive on the 10th; held back, perhaps, by design. Of the five divisions south of Langemarck, 54th Reserve was again to attack towards Ypres in parallel with the thrust along the Menin road. It was familiar with the ground.

Next morning, 11th November, at the official hour of dawn, Sixth and Fourth Army's guns began to fire. The stock of shells accumulated for the bombardment permitted the German artillery to deliver the heaviest concentration of the war to date. Though the British trenches were deeper, they still lacked overhead cover and were not connected with the rear. As trenches filled up with flying soil, men had to run into the open to seek less exposed positions in the support line. The only cover worth the title was found in the roughly fortified posts – timber and packed earth – constructed by British and French engineers in a connecting chain in rear at Haig's behest. Some of these were also headquarters positions.

Between 8 and 9 am, the shelling increased. Those few men who had stayed forward were now driven back. At 9, the shelling began to lift towards the rear and the infantry knew that the assault was coming. Platoons began to double forward to whatever remained of their original fire positions. But not all were quick enough. Out of the fog came line after line of German soldiers, massed, dressed, officers leading with swords ready, the soldiers carrying their rifles at the port or the secure.

They had little support on their extreme left from the Messines ridge but 30th Division managed to push back General Moussy's brigade to capture Hill 60 on the railway cutting towards Ypres. The 39th and 4th Division could not keep pace with them, the riflemen in Cavan's force and 3rd Division[29] kept them from closing on their trenches except, for a brief time, on the flank of the London Scottish. Two enemy companies threatened to exploit a gap and the commanding officer, Lieutenant-Colonel G A Malcolm, brought up his battalion headquarters to join the line. For 20 minutes, Briton and German stalked each other at a range of yards until the London Scottish worked round the intruders and opened fire steadily. The gap was closed. On the right, the 54th Reserve Division do not seem to have come out of their trenches. 'The troops are getting naturally more indisciplined,' wrote one of their number. '...the cold weather makes them more susceptible to illness'. The advance along the road was therefore left to the twelve battalions of Winckler's Guard Division alone.

The four regiments advanced through the fog in line: 4 Guard Grenadiers, 2 Guard Grenadiers, 1 Foot Guard, 3 Foot Guard; the three battalions in each regiment banked in column. Hidden from their foe, they appeared 'like grey ghosts coming down out of the clouds' to the battalions on the north of 3rd Division. 4 Guard Regiment were shot through with bullets but their formation continued to march on like automata as officers and men fell, the pace of their destruction being hastened by the shrapnel fired at the response of a Royal Artillery officer who had doubled back along his broken telephone cable to tell the battery to fire. 4 Guard reeled, halted and broke at last.

On the road, 2 Guard Grenadier found its way into a gap between 4th Royal Fusiliers and a company of 4th Zouaves. Caught by surprise as they came forward to occupy their trenches, the British were forced back behind Veldhoek followed soon by the Zouaves. Believing, correctly, that they had made a breach, the 'Fusilier battalion (leading 2 Guard Grenadier) penetrated into the wood,' says the regimental account. 'As, however, the troops on either flank were not abreast of it, it was surrounded on all sides in the thick undergrowth, and suffered heavy losses. Attempts made by the I Battalion to relieve it did not succeed...'

A counter-attack of 1st Royal Scots Fusiliers and a company of 2nd Royal Sussex took part of the Fusilier Battalion in flank and rear as they sought to push south behind the 3rd Division's trenches. This cleared, too, the remnant of 4 Guard. To the north, 2nd Duke of Wellington's killed or captured the remainder and took back the support trenches of the Zouaves

---

[29] This division of II Corps was a composite force brought into the line to relieve 7th Division on 5th November. Part of 5th Division, II Corps were holding Ploegsteert Wood.

and Royal Fusiliers. The line was re-established but they could not oust the reserve battalion of either regiment from the former British firing line. Further north, a much wider gap had been made.

Brigadier-General FitzClarence had only one unit of his brigade remaining, 1st Scots Guards; the remaining battalions had been scattered to other commands in the previous fortnight. But he had acquired two other units: 1st Cameron Highlanders and the Black Watch. On to all three, 1 Foot Guard Regiment advanced at 9 am, at a jog trot, reaching the British fire trenches when they were only partly manned.

Their assault rolled massively over this line, directed towards the gap between Veldhoek and Polygon Wood. On their right was 3 Foot Guard. Within 10 minutes, they had overwhelmed the three battalions in defence and seemed capable of marching through to Ypres.

The 3 Foot Guard had been relying on 54th Reserve Division to attack Polygon Wood and seem to have assumed that it had been neutralized. As they came closer to the southern boundary of its trees, 1st King's opened fire from their weapon pits within and continued to fire deliberately into the Prussian ranks as the regiment turned towards the wood to assault it at a distance of 50 yards.

The attention of 1 Foot Guard was distracted from this spectacle by the resistance of Lieutenant F Anderson and a company (forty men) of the Black Watch in a strong point ahead and four Scots Guardsmen in another to their left. These riflemen held the Guard regiment in check until the guns near Hooge fired into the middle of the leading battalion.

A period of confusion followed: rifles and machine-guns firing, German shells landing on Veldhoek and Polygon .Wood, British shells from Hooge, the cries of unknown men.

When it grew quieter and the smoke of the shells had drifted eastward, 1 Foot Guard had broken up and a proportion were seen running into Nonne Boschen (Nun's Copse) between Polygon Wood and the Menin Road. In the Polygon, 1st King's saw what appeared to be another wave of enemy coming forward in the uncertain light, but minutes passed and the bank of grey figures did not move. Then the fog and smoke cleared a little more; the wind was freshening from the west. They saw all at once that it was not a line of enemy advancing but a bank of enemy lying dead across their front.

3 Foot Guard had been destroyed except for stragglers and the reserve battalion in rear. 1 Foot Guard had managed to collect 900 men in Nonne Boschen, but they were almost leaderless.[30]

---

[30] II Battalion had lost all its officers, the entire headquarters and most of its senior NCOs.

The news that the Guard had broken through Brigadier-General FitzClarence's front reached Major-General Landon – now commander of 1st Division – quickly. He sent forward 2nd Royal Sussex to occupy the empty trenches of 1st Scots Guards and ordered 1st Northamptons to find General FitzClarence, who had been firing at 1st Foot Guard from his headquarters strong point. The 52nd Light Infantry were requested to clear to Nonne Boschen. The German artillery was still active and it took time to complete these moves. The 52nd were not in position before about 2 pm and they had not stopped to rest.

Extending into open order, the outline of Nonne Boschen was pointed out to the soldiers and the battalion then charged, covered by two field batteries. They plunged into the wood. Seeing them enter, a company of the Northamptons joined in from the south and 5th Field Company, Royal Engineers, from the north. The combined effort of British soldiers appearing suddenly amongst the trees after a completely silent approach unnerved the Prussians, who bolted. After them went the 52nd and the detachments of sappers and Northamptons, pursuing the Guard into the former support trenches of the Black Watch and Camerons, where the last men alive surrendered. Just as the 52nd made ready to go on, some of Dubois' guns to the north, hearing that this sector of the line was occupied by Germans, opened fire on it and forced the Light Infantry back. It was dark before they could return.

The rain hanging about all day began to pour down at dusk and the rising wind drove this into the trenches, soaking men above and below ground. At 5 pm, Brigadier-General FitzClarence reached headquarters, 5th Brigade on the north side of Polygon Wood, to suggest that they should retake the original forward line of his trenches, all that remained to the Guard from the day's fighting. He had no units left as such but offered to pool what detachments he could find. 5th Brigade commander agreed to send the 52nd and 2nd Highland Light Infantry to reoccupy the former front line.

The rain and clouds darkened the night so that they could see nothing. It was arranged by Colonel Davies of the 52nd that they should delay movement until 1 am, when the moon might give some faint light even if the clouds had not cleared. Meantime, he and the brigade-major would reconnoitre. They were soon stumbling amongst dead and wounded, helping those they could on the edge of the forward trenches. From one of the luckless men lying chilled almost to death on the sodden ground, they heard that the Germans had moved back to the east about 100 yards, where they had dug in. This was confirmed by others but although some sounds of the enemy could be heard faintly against the wind, they could not be seen.

The brigade-major returned to 5th Brigade headquarters to advise that the occupation should be cancelled: they did not know the exact line of the new enemy trenches and might pass directly in front of them in moving back to the old line. The troops were sent back.

While these events took place, Brigadier-General FitzClarence was seeking what men he could find to support 5th Brigade and found on reaching his headquarters that General Landon had sent him the 2nd Grenadier Guards and the Irish Guards. He explained their task and led them personally along the track towards 5th Brigade headquarters. At the corner of Polygon Wood he met the 52nd and Highland Light Infantry returning and heard from Colonel Davies of the decision not to go on with the reoccupation. He was very disappointed. After a few minutes discussion beside the dark torn trees, he told the quiet columns of the Guards to wait while he went forward to see for himself. He was not more than a few steps on when he was mortally wounded by rifle fire.

That ended the business of the night and, to all intents and purposes, the battle.

> O! that a man might know
> The end of this day's business ere it come;
> But it sufficeth that the day will end,
> And then the end is known.

For a little while the attacks dragged on. Attempts were made by the Germans to secure positions of advantage for the trench warfare of the gathering winter. They did not succeed. The line settled. German units began to move back from Flanders *en route* to Poland. The British handed over to the French their sector of the line between Zonnebeke and the Ypres-Comines railway. I Corps went back for a short spell of rest and refitting. The 8th Division arrived and, with the 7th, reconstituted IV Corps under Rawlinson. Soon the whole Expeditionary Force was settled in and behind the line from Ploegsteert Wood to La Bassée.

No; not the whole Expeditionary Force. It would never be whole in the original sense again. Typical of its battalions, 2nd Highland Light Infantry was relieved on 16th November by the French to set off '...marching through Ypres to Bailleul and losing an officer and four men by shellfire on the way. Out of all the officers and men mobilized at Aldershot a bare three months before, there were now scarcely thirty left.'

The tale of losses is too continuous to sustain an impact; the mind becomes saturated with figures. It is true, too, that the total number of their casualties is insignificant in comparison with those suffered on the Somme or in the attempt to clear the Ypres ridge again in 1917. But it is not for the number fallen, much as they were mourned, that they deserve to be remembered; or for their courage and patriotism – they were, after all, doing their duty as professional soldiers, holding the ring while their countrymen took up arms. What marks them is the standard they set as fighting men, holding for weeks a wide sector of attack against an enemy four to seven times their strength.

Falkenhayn might write after the war, 'That which had to be attained under any circumstances, if the war was to be carried on with any hopeful prospects, was attained' – that is, stabilization of the western front from the Alps to the sea. But that was not what he had aimed at. He had aimed to break through to Calais.

It is only fair to say that the allies too had hoped to envelop the enemy line or to break through, but the point is that while it was most desirable for them to do so it was not essential. It was essential for the Germans. Time was not on their side, notwithstanding the errors of their adversaries.

One of these errors, often remarked upon, was the retention of the Ypres salient long after all the ground of tactical significance had been captured by the Germans. The soldiers who came later could not understand the policy. Historians surmise that its retention was due to an obsession by the senior commanders for holding ground – any ground – rather than release it to the enemy gratuitously. But some at least, however misguidedly, felt that the army should hold on to what it could because they had fought for the ground; they had hallowed it with the blood and bodies of comrades with whom they had soldiered all over the world through a lifetime. The old British Army with its venial faults and marvellous quality had died there in its defence. They could never forget that. Neither should we.

BIBLIOGRAPHY

For brevity, the full titles are omitted of the four national official military histories, the British naval and air histories of 1914, the German monographs *Antwerpen* and *Ypem*, the Belgian C-in-C's report and the German and British individual regimental histories. These sources are invaluable and for the benefit of those beginning research all are obtainable in London with the exception of the German regimental histories. Enquiry for these should be made to Militargeschtliches Forschungamst, 78 Frieburg i. Br., Kaiser-Joseph *Strasse* 262. A Bibliography of Regimental Histories of the British Army has recently been published by Francis Edwards Ltd (1965). To the same end, I have not listed books or documents in more than one section, though many of those listed contribute to others. Where titles by foreign authors are shown in English, the work is the English translation.

THE PLAN

Bauer, Col. M Der, *Grosse Krteg in Feld laid Heimat* (1921)

Bemhardi, Gen. F von, *Germany and the next war* (1912)

Boetticher, F von, *Schlieffen* (1957)

Bredt, J V, *Belgian neutrality and the Schlieffen deployment plan* (summary in Army Quarterly) (Summer, 1929)

Büllow, Gen. K von, *MOB rapport surla bataille de la Marne* (French translation) (1920)

Churchill, W S, *The World Crisis, 1911-14* (1927)
Craig, G A *The Politics of the Prussian Army 1640-1945* (1955)
Crutwell, C R M F, *A History of the Great War, 1914-18* (1936)

Demeter, K, *The German Officer Corps in Society and State, 1650-1945* (1965)
Dupont, Gen. C J, *Le Haut Commandemant allemand en 1914* (1922)

Foerster, W, *Graf Schlieffen under Wellkrieg* (1925)

Godspeed, Col. D J, *Ludendorff* (1966)
Golovine, Lt-Gen. N N, *The Russian Campaign of 1914* (1933)
Görlitz, W, *The German General Staff* (1953)

Hoffman, Maj.-Gen. M, *The War of Lost Opportunities* (1924)
Howard, Professor M, *William I and the Reform of the Prussian Army* (Essays for A J P Taylor: *A Century of Conflict, 1850-1950*) (1966)

Joffre, Marshal J J C, *Memoirs* (1932)

Kluck, Gen. A von, *The march on Paris and the battle of the Marne, 1914* (1920)
Kuhl, Lt-Gen. H von, *Der Deutsche Generalstab in Vorbereitung und DurchFürung der Weltkrieg* (1920)

Moltke, Col-Gen. H von, (the younger) *Erumemngen-Briefe-Dokumente, 1877-1916* (1922)

Palat, Gen. B, *La Grande Guerre sur le front Occidentale, vols i-viii* (1920-27)

Ritter, Professor G, *The Schlieffen Plan* (1958)
Rupprecht, Crown Prince of Bavaria, *Mein Kriegstagebuch, vol i* (1929)

Stürgkh, Lt-Gen. Graf J, *Im Deutschen Grossen Hauptquartier* (1921)

Tappen, Maj. Gen. G, *Bis zu Marnesduacht* (1930)
Times, The History of the War, 1914, vols i-iv (1915)
Tyng, S, *The campaign of the Maine* (1935)

Wrisberg, Maj.-Gen. E von, *Erinnierugen an die Kriegsjahre im Königlish-Preussichen Kriegsministerium* (1927)

A DIFFICULT SITUATION

Azan, Gen. P, *Les Beiges sur l'Yser* (1929)

Deguise, Lt-Gen., *La defense de la Position fortifiée d'Anvers en 1914* (1921)

Falkenhayn, Gen. E von, *General Headquarters, 1914-16, and its critical decisions* (1921)

Galet, Gen. E J, *Albert, King of the Belgians in the Great War* (1931)

Jünger, E, *Storm of Steel* (1929)

Messimy, Gen. A, *Mes Souvenirs* (1937)

Zwehl, H von, *Erich von Falkenhayn* (see also *Army Quarterly,* April 1926) (1926)

THE GLORIOUS ENTERPRISE

Ballard, Brig-Gen. C, *Smith-Dorrien* (1931)
Bickersteth, J B, *The 6th Cavalry Brigade, 1914-19*
Binding, R, *A fatalist at war* (1929)

Callwell, Maj. Gen. Sir C E, *Field-Marshal Sir Henry Wilson* (1927)
Coleman, F, *From Mons to Ypres with French* (1916)

Essen, L van der, *The invasion and the war in Belgium from Liège to the Yser* (1917)

Foch, Marshal F, *Memoirs* (1931)
French, F M, Earl *Despatches* (1917) *1914* (1919)

Gleichen, Maj.-Gen. Count E, *The doings of the Fifteenth Infantry Brigade* (1918)

Haldane, Lt-Gen. Sir A, *A brigade of the old Army* (1920)
HM Public Record Office, *War diaries, operations and signal logs, intelligence reports and associated data of the BEF, 1914*
HMSO, *Field Service Pocket Book* (1914)
Hyndson, Capt. J G W, *From Mons to the first battle of Ypres* (1932)

James, D, *The Life of Lord Roberts* (1954)

Lewis, P, *Squadron Histories* (1959) *The British Fighter since 1912* (1965)
Liddell Hart, Sir B, *Foch, Man of Orleans* (1931) *French military ideas before the First World War* (Essays for A J P Taylor: *A Century of Conflict, 1850-1950*) (1966)

Macready, Lt-Gen. Sir N, *Annals of an active life* (1926)
Magnus, Sir P, *Kitchener, Portrait of an Imperialist* (1958)
Maurice, Maj.-Gen. Sir F, *The life of Lord Rawlinson of Trent* (1928)
Maze, P, *A Frenchman in khaki* (1934)

Norris, G, *A history of the RFC* (1965)

Poincaré, R, *Memoirs* (1926-9)
Poseck, Lt-Gen. M von, *The German Cavalry in Belgium and France, 1914* (1923)

Smith-Dorrien, Gen. Sir H, *Memories of 48 years service* (1925)

US Cavalry, *Cavalry Combats* (1937)

Vogel, Hofprediger Dr, *3,000 Kilometer mil der Garde-Kavallerie* (1922)

War Office, UK, *Reports on Conferences and staff rides, 1905-13* (War Office internal circulation) (1905-13)

War Office, USA, *Histories of two hundred and fifty divisions of the German Army which participated in the war, 1914-18* (1920)

Wilde, Capt-Comdt R de, *De Liège a l'Yser* (1918)

Young, Maj. B K, *An R E, Subaltern with the BEF, 1914* (published in the *Royal Engineers Journal*) (1933-4)

THE END OF OCTOBER

A TIME OF CRISIS

Barton, J S, *Langemarck* (article in *The Back Badge,* Journal of the Gloucestershire Regiment) (Winter 1964)

Baumann, Domprediger, *Mit der Garde im Westen* (1919)

Blake, R Ed., *The Private Papers of Douglas Haig, 1914-18* (1952)

Bolwell, F A, *With a reservist in France* (1916)

Boullaire, Maj.-Gen., *Historique du 2e. Corps de Cavalerie du 1er. octobre 1914 au 1er. janvier 1919* (1921)

Dubail, Gen. A, *Quatres années de commandemant, 1914-18* (1920)

Dubois, Gen. M, *Deux ans de commandemant sur le front de France, 1914-16* (1920)

Duff Cooper, A, (Lord Norwich) *Haig* (1935)

Haig, F-M, *Earl Private Papers* (see Blake)

Hankey, Lord, *The Supreme Command, 1914-18* (1961)

HMSO, *Statistics of the military effort of the British Empire* (1922)

Humbert, A, *La division Barbot* (1919)

Jack, Brig.-Gen. J L, *General Jack's diary, 1914-18* (Edited and introduced by John Terraine) (1964)

Merewether, Lt-Col J W B, *The Indian Corps in France* (with Sir Frederick Smith Bt.) (1919)

Ronarc'h, Vice-Adm., *Souvenirs de la Guerre (Août 1914-septembre 1915)* (1920)

Smith, Sir F Bt. See Merewether

Terraine, J, See Jack

Willcocks, Lt-Gen. Sir J, *With the Indians in France* (1920)

Index

Abbeville, 42

Aire, 81

Aisne, river, 27, 31, 32, 34, 35, 39, 41, 42, 43, 44, 45, 70, 80, 99,114

Albert, King of the Belgians, 89

Albrecht, Gen., Duke of Württemberg, 25, 39, 45, 72, 76, 98, 104, 105, 126, 155

Allenby, Lt-Gen. Sir E., 62, 67, 71, 76, 84, 109, 110, 128, 130, 131, 143

Alsace, 13, 15, 22, 39

Amiens, 42

Anderson, Lt. F., 157

Antwerp, 31, 33, 36, 38, 39, 43, 44, 70, 71, 72

Ardennes, 22, 23, 70

Ardoye, 73

Argonne, 27, 31, 70, 115

Armentières, 9, 44, 60, 61, 62, 63, 64, 65, 66, 70, 153

ARMY:
    Austro-Hungarian, 31

Belgian (see also military index), 36, 39, 44

British (for details of the Army in France and Belgium see British Expeditionary Force under military index)
    background, 45
    in colonial campaigns,45, 55, 56
    manpower, 150

French,
    defeat of (1870-1), 12
    Peoples', 12, 13
    fortress system, 15
    defeated on frontiers, 22
    Territorials, 23, 35, 41, 50, 87, 89, 96, 97, 110
    rebuked by Joffre, 26
    relieves BEF on Aisne, 43
    line extended, 43, 44
    experience of war, 55

German,
    war plans (see Schlieffen Plan)
    economy and manpower, 15-18,

38, 39
Law of 1913, 18
tactical policy and fire power, 18-20
organisation and training, 18-19, 33, 34, 56
in deployment, 21, 22, 30, 32
Supreme Headquarters 24, 28, 30, 28, 30, 31, 32, 34, 98, 100, 114, 115
recovers, 38, 39

Arras. 36, 38, 39, 77, 82, 90, 98, 99, 153
Artois, 39, 153
Aubers ridge, 66
Auchy, 48, 54
Austria-Hungary, 13, 14, 16, 21, 32

Bac St Maur, 63, 64
Bailleul, 56, 59, 60, 61, 64, 159
Bapaume, 39
Barton, T S, 90
Becelaere, 85, 90, 102, 120, 121, 125
Belgium:
    neutrality jeopardised, 15, 17
    invaded, 21-24
    occupation extended, 33-35, 39
Beseler, Gen. von, 36, 38, 39, 40, 44, 45, 66, 68, 71, 72, 80, 89, 98, 100, 104, 105, 126
Bethune, 44,46, 81
Beverdyk, 104, 105
Billy, 53
Bismarck, O von, 13, 14
Bixschoote, 87, 96, 125, 126, 131, 154
Blewitt, Lt R., 145
Bois Blanc, 101
Bois Grenier, 65
Bols, Lt-Col L J, 50, 51, 53, 54, 55
Bolwell, F A, 143, 144
Boulogne, 42, 81, 100
Bourges, 41
Boyd, Lt J, 137
Broodseinde, 104, 127
Bruges, 40, 44, 71, 80, 89
Brussels, 29, 36, 38, 63, 71

Bulfin, Maj.-Gen. E S, 94, 96, 145, 146, 151, 153
Büllow, Gen. K von, 23, 28, 29, 31
Byng, Maj.-Gen. Hon. J, 128

Caeskerke, 104
Calais, 40, 42, 70, 97, 99, 160
Cambrai, 39
Capinghem, 52, 56, 78
Capper, Maj.-Gen. T, 85, 103, 104, 145
Cassel, 22, 42, 100, 114, 132
de Castelnau, Gen. N, 35, 38, 43
Cavan, Brig. Earl, F R, 130, 153, 155
Champagne, The, 39, 70, 115
Chantilly, 28
Chapelle Saint Roch, 52
Charleville, see Mézières
Chateau de Flandres, 78
Churchill, Rt Hon. W S, 43
Claer, Lt-Gen. von, 113
Clercken, 83, 87
Coblenz, 24, 27, 30
Comines, 68, 70, 128, 133, 134
Communications (included under wireless)
Cortemarck, 73
Courtrai, 62, 68, 71, 89
Cuinchy, 51, 54

Daniell, Maj. E. H. E, 77, 78, 79
Davies, Lt-Col. H. R, 158, 159
Deimling, Maj.-Gen. von, 128
Delage, Comdt., 104
Delmensingen, Maj.-Gen. Krafft von, 98, 100, 115
Dixmude, 44, 69, 71, 72, 87, 100, 101, 104, 105, 107, 126, 154, 155
Dneister, river, 31
Douve stream, 134
Dual Alliance, The, 14
Dubois, Lt-Gen., 97, 107, 114, 116, 125, 127, 130, 132, 147, 148, 149, 158
Dunkirk (erque), 36, 82

Eiffel Tower, The, 24
Einjahrige, 18

Englos and Fort d', 78, 79
Ennetières, 78, 79, 80, 81
Erquinghem, 63, 64, 79
Escobeques, 78
d'Esperey, Lt-Gen. Franchet, 29
Estaires, 46, 50, 61, 62, 79, 84, 109

Fabeck, Lt-Gen. von, 79, 114, 115, 116, 125, 128, 133, 134, 147, 153, 154
Falkenhayn, Lt-Gen. E von, 24, 70, 71, 97, 160
    succeeds von Moltke and stabilises battle, 30-36
    orders capture of Antwerp, 38
    regroups, 39
    warns Fourth and Sixth Armies, 100
    forms Fabeck's group, 115
    uncertain as to future in Flanders, 149
    final breakthrough attempted, 153, 154
Fauquissart, 101
Fergusson, Maj.-Gen. Sir C, Bt., 52
Festubert, 51
Fismes, 39
FitzClarence, Brig.-Gen. C, 121, 140, 142, 143, 157, 158, 159
Flanders, 23, 39, 55, 68, 70, 71, 81, 82, 89, 97, 99, 101, 107, 121, 140, 142, 143, 157, 158, 159
Flêtre, 58
Fleurbaix, 62
Foch, Gen. F,
    on the Mame, 29
    agrees strategy with Sir J. French, 44, 45
    letter to Joffre, 63
    background and command problems, 68
    seeks to attack, 89, 97, 125, 153
    alarmed by reverses, 132
    agrees to assist BEF, 147-149
    Fontaine Houck, 58, 59
Fournes, 65, 77
France,

sues for peace, 1871, 13 on eve of war, 1914, 21 economy and manpower, 16, 26, 34, 35, 36, 43 attacked, 23 frontier railways cut, 26 principal enemy of Germany, 32 coast to be occupied, 39, 40
Franco-Prussian War, The, 12, 13
Frelinghien, 65
French, F M. Sir J, 89, 97, 125, 131
    leads the BEF to Mons, 23
    reluctant to join Mame offensive, 29
    withdraws BEF from the Aisne, 43, 44
    strategy with Foch in Flanders, 44, 45
    relations with Smith-Dorrien, 46
    orders II Corps forward, 46, 50, 52
    Smith-Dorrien asks for help, 60
    continues advance, 62, 63, 69
    relationship with Foch, Wilson and Rawlinson, 66, 69
    in crises, 80-82, 107-110, 116, 132
    seeks assistance for BEF from Foch, 142, 143, 147-149
    told of plan to replace him, 150
Fromelles, 65, 78
Furnes (Belgian GHQ), 82, 105, 126

Galicia, 32
Gallieni, Gen. J S, 29
Germany,
    defence problems, 12-15
    aggrandisement, 16
    Social Democratic Party, 16
    Pan-Germans, 18
    Reichstag, 18 on eve of war, 21, 22
    attacks, 22, 23
    reverses, 32-34
Gheluvelt, 111, 115, 116, 120-122, 124, 127, 128, 133, 134, 135, 136, 138, 139, 140-144
Ghent, 40, 44
Gibbs, Capt. E J, 120, 121, 122, 124
Gits, 75
Givenchy, 51, 53, 54, 60, 63, 81, 109
Gleichen, Brig.-Gen. Count E, 51, 54

Gore-Langton, Lt, 60, 61, 62

Gough, Maj.-Gen. H de la P, 85, 117, 130, 149

Grand Couronné, 27

Gravenstafel, 127

Grossetti, Maj.-Gen., 82, 89, 101, 107, 149, 153

Haig, Lt-Gen. Sir D, 80, 83, 85, 87-90, 97, 107, 110, 116, 117, 119, 124, 125, 127, 128, 130-132, 135, 142, 143, 145, 146, 148, 149, 155

Haldane, Maj.-Gen. A, 58, 59, 151

Hamilton, Maj.-Gen. H, 52

Hamilton, Gen. Sir I, 150, 151

Hankey, Maj.-Gen. E B, 141, 142

Hausen, Gen. M K von, 23, 29, 31

Hazebrouck, 44, 56, 58, 109

Hellfire corner, 125

Hentsch, Lt-Col, 28, 29, 30

Herlies, 77, 78

Hill 60, 61, 153

Hindenburg, Fld-Mshl P von, 149

Hohenbom, Maj.-Gen. von, 128

Holland, neutrality in jeopardy, 17

Hollebecke and chateau, 85, 130, 131, 132

Hollen, Lt-Gen. von, 60, 100

Hood, Rear-Adm. Hon. H I A, 126

Hooge Chateau, 111, 117, 124, 140, 157

Hooghe, 73, 75, 76

Hooghlede, 73, 75

Houplines, 65

Houthulst, forest of, 83, 87, 88

Humbert, Gen., 149 fn.

Hungary, see Austria

Hunter-Weston, Brig.-Gen. A, 64

Hyndson, Capt. J J G W, 41, 42, 95

Ilse, Maj.-Gen., 98, 100, 105

Italy and the Dual Alliance, 14 fn.

Jeudwine, Col. H S, 145, 146

Joffre, Marshall J J C,
    options for redeployment of

    forces, 25

    general character, 26

    failure of plans, 26

    warns of need for ordnance, 26, 32

    rebukes Army, 26

    recovers, 26, 28, 29, 34-36

    agrees to send help to Belgium, 38

    relieves BEF on Aisne, 43, 44

    seeks open flank, 38

    command problems, 56, 57, 68

    sees King Albert, 82

    honours promise to reinforce BEF, 107

    uncertain as to future in Flanders, 149

Kaiser, see Wilhelm II

Keiberg, 117

Kemmel, including Mont, 60, 114, 115, 128, 132

Kitchener, Lord, 46 fn., 107, 116, 147fn, 149-151, 150 fn

Klein, Zillebeke, 154

Kluck, Gen. A von, 23-25, 27-29, 31, 35

Koekuit, 90, 92

Kortekeer Cabaret, 88, 89, 90, 94, 96, 125

Kruiseecke, 99, 102, 111, 113, 116, 117, 119, 121, 122, 138

Kuhl, Maj. H von, 11

La Bassée, 44, 46, 48, 50-53, 60, 63, 65-67, 70, 88, 90, 98, 99, 100, 114, 131, 149

La Fere, 31

La Gorge, 109

Landon, Maj.-Gen. H J S, 124, 139, 143, 144, 157, 159

Landsturm, 18, 22, 33

Landwehr, 18, 22, 33, 39, 80, 114, 125, 127

Langemarck, 90, 96, 110, 127, 155

Lanrezac, Lt-Gen. C, 23

Laon, 31

Lassigny, 36

La Vallée, 79, 80, 81

Leach, Lt-Col, H E B, 139, 142

Le Bizet, 52, 56

Lebouc, Yves, 104

Lee Enfield, short magazined rifle, 78, 120

Le Gheer, 84, 85

Le Pilly, 77, 78, 79, 81, 84

Le Quesne, 101

Le Touquet, 79, 80, 153

Lichtervelde, 73

Liège, 36

Lille, 43, 46, 52, 60-63, 65-67, 70-72, 78, 84

de Lisle, Maj.-Gen. H de B., 58, 60

Lomax, Maj.-Gen. S H, 140

Lomme, 79

Loo, 126

Lorgies, 46, 50

Lorraine, 13, 15, 22, 25, 26, 39

Louvain, 36

Lovett, LL-Col. A C, 121, 124, 144, 145

Ludendorff, Maj.-Gen. E, 17

Luxembourg, 21, 24, 26, 27, 28, 30, 31

Lys, river, 61-65, 67, 70-72, 77, 79, 84, 85, 102, 115, 125, 133

Mackenzie, Maj.-Gen. C J, 110

MacEwen, Lt-Col. D L, 88

Maastricht Appendix, 17 fn

Main, river, 13, 14, 22

Malcolm, Lt-Col. G A, 156

Marne, river, 34, 80

Marwitz, Lt-Gen. von der, 100, 102, 115

Mauberge, 31

de Maud'huy, Lt-Gen., 36, 38, 43, 44

Maunoury, Lt-Gen. M-J, 26-29, 35

Menin, 61-63, 66-68, 70, 71, 72, 75, 76, 81, 85, 90, 98, 100, 102, 103, 111, 114, 117, 120, 121, 122, 124, 125, 133, 135, 136, 142, 144, 154, 155, 157

Merris, 56

Messimy, Gen. A, 26

Messines, 62, 85, 102, 110, 115, 128, 133, 134, 135, 147, 153, 155

Meteren, 58, 59, 60

Meterenbecque, 56, 58, 59

Metz, 22, 114

Meuse, river, 34, 70

Mézières-Charleville, 34

Millerand, E-A, 35, 36

Moltke (the elder), Fld-Mshl Count H von., 12-15, 22, 119

Moltke (the younger), Col.-Gen. H von, 17, 18, 21, 22, 24-32

Monro, Maj.-Gen. C C, 140

Mons, 7, 23, 44, 46, 81

Mont des Cats, 58

Mont Kemmel, 60, 114, 115

Mont Noir, 60

Moorslede, 76

Morhange, 22

Morland, Lt-Col. C B, 136, 138, 139, 144

Morland, Maj.-Gen. T L N, 110

Moussy, Brig.-Gen., 131, 135, 148, 155

Murray, Lt-Gen. Sir A, 29, 60, 62, 67, 80, 107, 131

Myslovitz, 14

Nancy, 26, 31

Navy, Royal, 81 and fn., 89 and fn.

Nieuport, 44, 72, 82, 87, 89, 90, 105, 107

Nethe, river, 38

Neuve Chapelle, 101, 113, 116

Neuve Eglise, 60, 61

Nieppe, 60, 63, 64

Nonne, Boschen, 157,158

Noyon, 39

Offizierstellvertreter, 33

Oise, river, 31, 35, 38, 39

d'Oissel, Maj.-Gen. Hely, 116

Oosttaverne, 133

Osborne-Smith, Lt-Col. G, 88

Ostend, 40, 44, 80

Ourcq, 29

Paris, 13-15, 25, 27-29, 35, 36, 39, 42
Passchendaele, 83, 85, 90, 97, 117
Paynter, Capt. G, 111
Peronne, 114
Pervyse, 105, 107, 126
Petit Morin, 29
Picardy, 36, 38, 39
Pilckem, 110
Plan XVII, 26
Ploegsteert and wood, 60, 61, 115, 128, 159
Poelcapelle, 127
Poezelhoek, 111
Poincaré, R (President of France), 150
Polygon Wood, 102, 103, 104, 127, 140, 142, 145, 157, 158, 159
Pont Fixe, 50, 51, 53, 54
Pont de Nieppe, 61, 63, 64
Poperinghe, 44, 67, 105, 147
Pradelles, 56, 58
Premesques, 66, 78
Pritchard, Maj. H L, 90
Prussia, East, defence of and war in, 24, 30, 31
Pulteney, Lt-Gen. W P, 56, 58, 60, 62, 64, 67, 65, 67, 70, 78, 80, 84, 110

Radinghem, 78
Railways, European, 8, 14, 21, 23, 25, 26, 31, 36, 38, 39, 43, 51, 58, 66, 70, 79, 104, 105, 125, 126, 141, 155, 159
Ramscapelle, 126
Rawlinson, Lt-Gen. Sir H, 44, 56, 66, 67, 72, 76, 85, 87, 90, 143, 159
Reutel, III, 102, 103, 104
Requin, Capt., 132
Rheims, 31, 39
Rhine, river, 13, 14, 22, 24
Ribot, Finance Minister, 149 fn.
Roberts, Fld.-Mshl Earl, 55, 56
Rouge de Bout, 65
Ronarc'h, Rear-Adm., 38, 44, 69, 89, 104, 126, 155
Roper, Maj. R T, 51

Roulers, 40, 63, 66, 67, 75, 81, 89, 125
Rowan, Capt. P S, 113
Rue, d'Ouvert, 52, 53
Ruggles-Brise, Brig.-Gen. H G, 122, 151
Rupprecht, Gen., Crown Prince of Bavaria, 25, 27, 31, 39, 40, 65, 70, 71, 76, 79, 98, 113, 115, 153, 155
Russia, 13-17, 21, 31, 32

Saarbourg, 22
Sailly-sur-la-Lys, 62-64
St Julien, 97
St Laurent, 99
St Omer, 58, 60, 81, 107, 131, 132
St Yves, 104, 115, 128
Sambre, river, 23
Sarrail, Lt-Gen. M, 34, 35
Schlieffen, Col-Gen. Count A von, family life, 11, 12
  working on plan, 12, 17
  chief of the general staff, 13
  anxiety concerning successors, 22
  Schlieffen Plan, The, 12-15, 21, 22, 23
  and Holland, 17
  routes for rail deployment, 21
  attempts to modify, 22
Senhouse Clarke, Capt. B C, 141
Shaw, Brig.-Gen. F C, 131 and fn, 147
Silesia, 32
Smith-Dorrien, Lt-Gen. Sir H, 45, 46, 48, 50, 52, 56, 60, 63, 65, 66, 67, 69, 70, 80, 81, 88, 107, 109, 110, 113, 131
Somme, river, 39
Stansfield, Capt. J R E, 146
Strazeele, 56
Sydenham, Capt., 130

Terband, 85
Tervaete, 98
Thorne, Capt., 139, 140
Thourout, 40, 66, 71-73, 75, 80, 89
Tirlemont, 36
Trotha, Maj.-Gen., 53, 54

Turcoing, 63
d'Urbal, Gen, 81, 87, 89, 90, 96, 97, 107,
    116, 125, 147

Vandeleur, Maj. C B, 53
Varney, Comdt, 104
Veldhoek, 161, 162, 176, 177
Verbranden, 145
Verdun, 27, 31, 34
Vermelles, 44, 46, 48, 50, 51
Vesle, river, 39
Vistula, 31
Vlamertinghe, 147
Vosges mountains, 31

Waldersee, Gen. Count von, 13 fn.
Wambeke, 133, 134
Warneton, 70, 71
Watson, Maj. C F, 138
Westroosebeke, 83
White Chateau, 125-142
Wilhelm II, Emperor, 13, 21
Wilson, Maj.-Gen. Sir H, 68, 81, 90,
    109, 132, 149
Wireless & communication systems,
24, 28, 46, 117, 122, 130
Wytschaete, 56, 60, 61, 115, 128, 133,
    147, 153

Ypres, 42, 44, 56, 66, 67, 80, 85, 87, 98,
    100, 101, 103, 104, 107, 109, 110,
    112, 114, 115, 116, 124, 125, 126,
    132, 136, 140, 143, 144, 147, 149,
    153, 155, 157, 160
Ypres – Comines Canal, 128, 134, 159
Yser, river, 44, 71, 72, 80, 81, 89, 98
    100, 104, 105, 107, 126, 133, 154, 155

Zandvoorde, 102, 111, 116, 128, 129,
    130, 132, 135
Zonnebeke, 90, 97, 102, 103, 104, 127,
    148, 159

MILITARY FORMATIONS
AND UNITS

British Expeditionary Force:
  at Mons, 23
  on the Mame, 27-29
  en route to Flanders, 42-44
  ordered to advance east, 62, 68
  early encounter with Sixth Army, 70
  defensive base at Boulogne, 81
  in need of reinforcements and
  ordnance, 107, 150-151
  reinforcements arrive, 109

Corps:
  I, 55, 80, 90, 117, 124, 125, 129, 140,
    142, 147-149, 159
  II, 43, 45, 46, 48, 50, 52, 55, 56, 60,
    62, 65, 66, 101, 109, 110, 112, 113,
    131, 147, 153, 154
  IV, 44, 60, 62, 67, 68, 72, 80, 81, 85,
    111, 159
  Cavalry, 55, 56, 58, 59, 60, 61, 62, 63,
    66, 68, 71, 76, 80, 109, 110, 115,
    125, 128, 131
  Indian, 43, 88, 101, 110, 113, 134, 150

Divisions:
  1st, 58, 83, 87, 97, 107, 109, 119
  2nd, 97, 102, 103, 104, 107, 114, 119,
    142, 145, 148, 153
  3rd, 38, 44, 46, 50, 60, 62, 65, 84, 156
  4th, 58-60, 63-65, 154, 155
  5th, 46, 50, 110, 126
  6th, 58, 59, 63, 64, 65, 81, 110
  7th, 38, 43, 44, 67, 68, 80, 85, 99, 102,
    103, 111, 116, 119, 135, 136, 145,
    146, 153, 159
  8th, 43, 159
  1st Cavalry, 56
  2nd Cavalry, 56, 147, 151
  3rd Cavalry, 35, 41, 63, 70, 74, 80,
    120, 127 f.n., 142, 147

Brigades:
  1st (Guards), 90, 139
  3rd, 90
  5th, 158
  8th, 101
  10th, 58-59

11th, 64
12th, 59
13th, 48, 50, 51-53
15th, 50, 53
18th, 64
19th, 80
20th, 112, 124, 151
Jullundur, 102
1st Cavalry, 147
2nd Cavalry, 56, 109
6th Cavalry, 128, 147
7th Cavalry, 128

Royal Artillery:
  general, 77, 82, 101, 140, 144, 153, 156
  Batteries,
    C, RHA, 147
    H, RHA, 56
    54, RFA, 145
    88, RFA, 58

Royal Engineers, Indian Sappers and Miners, Companies:
  general, 151 and f.n.
  5th, 158
  7th, 64
  12th, 64
  26th, 90, 147
  38th, 64
  20th Indian, 113
  21st Indian, 113

Regiments; cavalry:
  Dragoon Guards, 4th, 134
  Hussars, 11th, 60
  Hussars, 18th, 60, 131, 132
  Lancers, 9th, 56, 58
  Life Guards, 1st, 128
  Life Guards, 2nd, 128
  Oxfordshire Hussars (Yeomanry),
    151 and f.n
  Royal Horse Guards, 128
  Royals, 130, 146

Regiments; infantry:
  Bedfordshire & Hertfordshire, 1st, 51, 53, 54, 55, 130
  Bhopal, 9th, 113
  Black Watch, 1st, 111, 120, 121, 124, 157, 158
  Border, 2nd, 122
  Cameron Highlanders, 1st. 88, 95, 157
  Cheshire, 1st, 52, 53, 54, 55
  Coldstream Guards, 1st, 99, 120
  Dorsetshire, 1st, 50, 51, 53, 54, 55, 88
  Dublin Fusiliers, Royal, 2nd, 59
  Duke of Cornwall's Light Infantry, 1st, 84, 113
  Duke of Wellingtons, 2nd, 156
  Foresters, Sherwood, 2nd, 79, 80
  Gloucestershire, 1st, 90, 121, 122, 124, 139, 144, 145
  Gordon Highlanders, 1st, 102, 122
  Gordon Highlanders, 2nd, 130, 145, 146
  Green Howards, 2nd, 129, 130
  Grenadier Guards, 1st, 122, 124, 135, 145
  Grenadier Guards, 2nd, 124, 135, 145
  Hampshire, 1st, 63, 64
  Highland Light Infantry, 2nd, 158, 159
  Inniskillings Fusiliers, Royal, 2nd, 134
  Irish Fusiliers, Royal, 59
  Irish Guards, 1st, 159
  Irish Regiment, Royal, 2nd, 65, 77
  Irish Rifles, Royal, 2nd, 112, 113

King's (Liverpool), 1st, 157

Leinsters, 2nd, 66

Lincolns, 1st, 113

London Scottish (TF.), 147, 151, 156

Loyal North Lancashire, 1st, 41, 94, 138, 143, 144, 145

Middlesex, 4th, 102

Norfolk, 1st, 48

Northamptonshire, 1st, 88, 89, 146, 158

Oxford & Buckinghamshire Light Infantry, 2nd, 146, 158

Queen's, 1st, 94, 95, 128, 134-136, 143

Rifle Brigade, 1st, 64

Royal Fusiliers, 4th, 113, 156

Royal Northumberland Fusiliers, 1st, 113

Royal Scots Fusiliers, 1st, 156

Royal Scots Fusiliers, 2nd, 103, 117, 122, 129, 130, 138, 144

Royal Welch Fusiliers, 1st, 129

Scots Guards, 1st, 120, 121, 139, 140, 157, 158

Scots Guards, 2nd, 103, 111, 112

Scots, Royal, 2nd, 102

Sikhs, 15th, 102

Sikhs, 47th, 113

60th Rifles. KRRC, 1st, 116

60th Rifles, KRRC, 2nd, 134, 136, 143, 144

Somerset Light Infantry, 1st, 64

South Lancashire, 2nd, 113

South Staffordshire, 2nd, 94, 116

South Wales' Borderers, 1st, 136-138

Sussex, Royal, 2nd, 145-147, 156, 158

Warwickshire, Royal, 1st, 58, 59, 130, 145

Welch, 2nd, 136, 139

West Kent, Royal, 1st, 113

Wiltshire, 1st, 113

Wiltshire, 2nd, 103

Worcestershire, 2nd, 140, 141, 142

Royal Flying Corps, 62, 65, 81, 87

German Armies:

First, 23-29

Second, 23, 27-29

Third, 23, 27, 28

Fourth, 25, 27, 39, 40, 71, 72, 90, 96, 97, 100-104, 114, 126, 133, 154, 155

Fifth, 25, 27

Sixth, 25, 27-29, 39, 65, 66, 70, 77, 89, 99, 100-102, 114, 115, 133, 154, 155

Seventh, 25, 27

Eighth and Ninth, 149 f.n.

Fabeck's group, 114-116, 125, 133, 134, 147, 153, 154

Linsingen's group, 154

Corps:

II, 153, 154, 156 f.n.

III, 72, 81

II Bavarian, 114, 115, 130, 133, 135, 153

VII, 65, 67, 70, 77, 83, 84, 88, 101, 113

XIII, 65, 70, 71, 78, 101, 113, 115

XIV Reserve, 113

XV, 114, 115, 154

XIX, 65, 66, 70, 83, 84, 101

XXII Reserve, 71, 72, 81, 105

XXIII Reserve, 71, 81, 82, 127

XXIV Reserve, 71 f.n.

XXV Reserve, 71 f.n.

XXVI Reserve, 71, 75, 81, 85, 87, 114, 127

XXVII Reserve, 71, 81, 85, 87, 114,

116, 117
Plettenberg's, 154, 155
I Cavalry, 40, 50, 71, 115, 125
IV Cavalry, 40, 50, 60, 71

Divisions:
1st and 2nd Guard, 153
Winckler's Guard, 154, 156
2nd Ersatz, 114
3rd, 156
4th, 154, 155
4th Ersatz, 72
5th, 156 and f.n.
5th Reserve, 126
6th Reserve, 126
6th Bavarian Reserve, 114, 116, 25,
    133, 153, 39 f.n., 71 f.n.
14th, 113
25th Reserve, 79
26th, 79, 114, 115, 133, 134, 147
30th, 128, 136, 138, 154, 155
39th, 128, 29, 130, 145, 154, 155
45th Reserve, 73, 87, 88, 96
46th Reserve, 73, 75, 87, 96
48th Reserve, 114
51st Reserve, 75, 76, 96
52nd Reserve, 75, 76
53rd Reserve, 102
54th Reserve, 116, 117, 120, 127,
    133, 138, 139, 155, 156, 157
Marine, 127 and f.n.
Guard Cavalry, 53
Bavarian Cavalry, 56
3rd Cavalry, 60

Brigades:
2nd Ersatz, 127
11th Landwehr, 125, 127
37th Landwehr, 127
38th Landwehr, 114

Jäger (including divisional) 48, 59,
    73, 85, 138

Regiments:
1 Foot Guard, 156, 157
2 Guard Grenadier, 156, 157
3 Foot Guard, 156, 157
4 Guard Grenadier, 156
16th Bavarian Reserve, 134, 142
39th Lower Rhineland Fusiliers, 18
105 (Saxon), 144
119 Grenadiers, 135
122, 79
125, 135
143, 138, 139
243 Reserve, 102
244 Reserve, 102, 103
245 Reserve, 142
246 Reserve, 134
1 Chevaulegers, 62
Uhlans, 68

French Armies:
Second, 36
Fifth, 23, 28, 29
Sixth, 28, 29
Ninth, 29
Tenth, 63

Corps:
IX, 81, 114, 148, 149, 127 f.n.
XVI, 132 and f.n., 149, 153
XXI 48, 67, 69, 109, 82 f.n.
XXII, 71, 72, 81, 105

Conneau's Cavalry, 46, 62-3, 66, 68, 69,
81, 82, 88, 91, 119, 172
de Mitry's Cavalry (and mixed), 69,
    70. 79, 80, 88, 93, 97,140 and f.n.

Divisions:
17th, 90, 97, 104

31st, 116, 149, 132 f.n.
32nd, 132, 148, 149
42nd, 82, 105, 107
87th Territorial, 127 f.n.
5th Cavalry, 127 f.n.
7th Cavalry, 116
9th Cavalry, 127

Brigades:
33rd Brigade, 71, 81, 104
3rd Dragoons, 75
6th Cuirassiers, 130

Regiments:
16th Chasseurs, 82, 113
Zouaves (Senegalese regiment supporting Marine Brigade), 38

Belgian formations and units:
36, 38, 39, 44, 63, 66, 68, 69, 71, 72,
81, 82, 90, 100, 105, 126